365 Meditations for Teachers

Anne Marie Drew
Joan Laney
Ellamarie Parkison
Anne Wilcox

DIMENSIONS
FOR LIVING
NASHVILLE

365 MEDITATIONS FOR TEACHERS

Copyright © 1996 by Dimensions for Living

All rights reserved.

Library of Congress Cataloging-in-Publication Data

365 meditations for teachers / Anne Marie Drew ... [et al.].
   p.   cm.
   ISBN 0-687-01025-X (pbk. : alk. paper)
   1. Teachers—Prayer-books and devotions—English.   2. Devotional calendars.   3. Education (Christian theology)—Meditations.
I. Drew, Anne Marie.
BV4596.T43A19   1996
242'.68—dc20   96-8738
                                             CIP

This book is printed on recycled, acid-free paper.

96 97 98 99 00 01 02 03 04 05 — 10 9 8 7 6 5 4 3 2 1

MANUFACTURED IN THE UNITED STATES OF AMERICA

Contents

Foreword

For most teachers, teaching is not only an occupation but also a vocation—a calling to help others learn, grow, and blossom into the full persons that God has created them to be. This calling reaches beyond the classroom and the school calendar into every aspect of a teacher's life. That's why this unique devotional book for teachers has been designed to offer inspiration for *every* day of the year— from the first day of school to the last day of summer.

Beginning with the month of September, you will make your way through the school year and then through the summer months with four Christian writers who also share the life vocation of teaching. As they address common concerns and challenges of a teacher's daily life, they draw upon a rich variety of experiences and perspectives, from both inside and outside the classroom, to offer practical and spiritual encouragement and insights for your own faith journey. Whether you teach kindergarten, fourth grade, tenth-grade algebra, or Sunday school; whether your classroom is in a school or a church; whether you are a full-time, part-time, or substitute teacher, you will gain new appreciation for the ways in which teaching children has affected your sense of God's presence in your life, your understanding of God's plan for your life, your relationships with others, your attitudes toward God's world, and much more.

About the Writers

ANNE MARIE DREW (March–May) has taught English at both the junior and senior high levels. Currently she teaches at the United States Naval Academy in Annapolis, Maryland, where she is the director of Masqueraders, a student theater group. She is the author of several books, including

Empty Nest, Full Life, The Innkeeper's Wife: And Four Other Dramatic Readings for Christmas, and *Rainbows in the Twelfth Row*, a novel for young readers. She has three grown children.

JOAN LANEY (December–February) has been a high school English teacher, a university composition instructor, and a Sunday school teacher and youth group leader. In addition to the demanding job of full-time mother to four young children, she tutors special needs students in her home part-time, volunteers at her children's school, and works with her pastor husband in various ministries of an inner-city church in Memphis, Tennessee. She is also a contributor to *365 Meditations for Mothers of Young Children*.

ELLAMARIE PARKISON (June–August) currently teaches reading, math, and language via computer to students in grades 3–6 at Park Avenue Elementary School in Nashville, Tennessee. In twenty-five years of teaching, she has worked with students in kindergarten through seventh grade. She also has written Sunday school curriculum for various age groups. She is the wife of a minister, mother to four grown children, and grandmother to five, ranging in age from two months to seven years.

ANNE WILCOX (September–November) teaches literature, history, science, and language arts courses to elementary school students. She is former Bible study columnist for *Today's Christian Woman*, the author of two books, and a contributor to *365 Meditations for Mothers of Young Children* and *365 More Meditations for Women*. She lives with her husband and teenage daughter in Seattle, Washington.

September
Lessons to Teach and Learn
Anne Wilcox

SEPTEMBER 1   **Read Proverbs 1:7.**

his empty, quiet classroom will soon be transformed. Therefore, on this solitary day, I must take time to breathe deeply, feeling both the anticipation and the anxiety of teaching! On the one hand, I feel so ready; on the other hand, who can possibly be prepared for each individual student's unique needs? The configuration of this year's group might be a magic mix—or a mix that will take all my vigilance. I won't know until the doors open and the students begin that fascinating dance that signals the beginning of school.

As I sit here labeling everything—files, books, coat hooks—I wonder about my job. What is teaching, really? The communication of knowledge? The guidance toward wisdom that enables *my students* to acquire knowledge?

Proverbs 1:7 must influence my look at wisdom and knowledge on this one—and probably only—quiet day of the education process. The way we respond to God begins the possibility of acquiring wisdom, according to Proverbs.

Therefore, alongside my lesson plans, I must also view knowledge as relational. My students are not just rational creatures. Interpersonal and intrapersonal needs will determine their successful launch toward a year of acquiring knowledge and wisdom.

Lord, may I begin this year with worship and obedience—the true beginnings of wisdom. Then may I balance the relational and rational needs of my students to give them a whole education.

✎ **SEPTEMBER 2**   **Read Psalm 133.**

"Everyone knows we can't work together!" she wailed dramatically.

With the excitement of the new school year running high in my veins, I had eagerly arranged my fourth graders for one of those marvelous, cooperative group experiences—and one team was falling apart at the seams. The other teams were diving into their community tasks with all the energy of academically strong nine-year-olds.

But this team of two was headed for disaster. They were as alike as can be in a multicultural city such as ours. They belonged to the same ethnic group, religion, and socioeconomic group. They were different genders, but you would have thought they were from warring tribes with generational hatred. So much for pluralism being our primary hurdle to cooperative coexistence!

"How about if we change what 'everyone knows' and see if you can create a new pattern?" I asked. "You're both so creative. I'm certain you can tackle the challenge of working together on one project," I suggested, while ignoring the tears called on to further influence me.

The one student who was often difficult to work with took the challenge—I could see it in his eyes. He wanted things to work. With maturity beyond his years, he quietly handed his weeping literature partner their packet of work to let her sort out the papers. Then he gently offered a suggestion. It was rudely rebuffed, but he patiently replied, "How would you like to try this fun part while I watch?"

The tears stopped; the pouting continued but with less drama. Graciously and patiently, without losing all ground, the one student kept building partnership. Finally, both students became lost in the work and began creating a satisfactory project.

I know this is only the first of many "lessons" in how to get along and work together that will need to be learned in our classroom this year, but it is full of hope and promise. Teaching our students to cooperate *is* hard work, but it's also one of our greatest opportunities.

Lord, keep me hopeful about unity and cooperation throughout the year—long after the excitement of September has worn thin.

✎ **SEPTEMBER 3**   **Read Proverbs 12:1.**

Just a few days into the school year and already my enthusiasm is waning! Today I spent half the day correcting misbehavior and the other half telling students what *not* to do. Will there ever be days when discipline finds its roots in discipling—coming alongside *before* the problems arise?

How can I learn—with all these needs—to see past the immediate disciplinary needs to the discipling needs? This student would flourish and quit gouging his chair with his pencil, if I could just find a minute to assess his subtleties of learning style and design projects to excite him. This student would stop rocking in her chair and gazing toward another galaxy, if only I could keep her high capabilities stimulated while giving the others time to assimilate what she grasps after one introduction. This student would stop showing off, if I could take a few minutes to fill his very empty emotional cup with undivided, interested attention.

Where is the time to disciple? I think I get it. It is supposed to be done one-on-one. How on earth does it get accomplished one-on-thirty or even one-on-sixteen?

Lord, how do I get "double vision"—the ability to see corporately and individually? Classroom management becomes more complex each year as students come with compounded needs. In the midst of it all, help me not to forget the discipling side of discipline.

SEPTEMBER 4   Read Proverbs 12:25.

The kind words came from behind me. They were spoken so softly, I almost didn't hear them.

It had been a very busy first week of school. The students were restless from summer. They had been able to eat, jump, run, and talk whenever they felt like it. Now they were once again regulated and needed to consider community needs as well as their own impulses.

Most were making genuine attempts at transition into a new school year; some, of course, were resisting it with every ounce of their frisky young bodies. I was operating in overdrive to set the standards for behavior, study skills, and cooperative skills while building firm, yet kind, rapport with each little personality.

The first few efforts to create a civilized classroom after summer can create anxiety in even the most optimistic educators. However, that day during a wild first attempt at room cleanup, I heard amazingly thoughtful words. I had climbed to the top of a table to launch a big storage box toward a top shelf when the voice softly spoke behind me.

"Here, I thought it looked like you needed help."

In the midst of the chaos, one student had come up quietly behind me with another box. He had maturely sized up the room situation and decided that this box, too, should probably go on the top shelf.

That's all it took. Those few words gave me the energy to face the second week of school!

Lord, thank you for reminders of the importance of kind words this year—especially in the heat of cleanup time!

SEPTEMBER 5   Read Proverbs 26:2.

He was certain he had been mortally wounded. The kick in the shins at the recess soccer game was going to be fatal—according to his report. This student was filled with pain and anger. And there certainly appeared to be the beginnings of a significant bruise. However, his vehement accusations didn't fit.

10

The student who supposedly delivered the purposeful blow usually conducted himself with honorable sportsmanship. In fact, on the last report card I had included a comment praising his noble decisions for teamwork in sporting situations. But today, an injured student defied that assessment. If the bruised player was correct, our team player had violated every rule in the game and had deliberately injured a student to gain a tactical advantage.

As the wails and incriminations continued, I knew the other side must be heard. Once the accused had a moment to speak, amazing things happened. Graciously, and with kind apologies, the defendant explained his innocence regarding any deliberate kick. He also showed infinite concern for the well-being of his classmate. The false accusations and undeserved curses darted away like a swallow. The accuser was pacified and adversaries became friends—ready to play soccer again another day.

Lord, when wrongly accused may I learn to respond with even half the graciousness of this ten-year-old.

✎ SEPTEMBER 6   **Read I Timothy 6:18-19.**

"They keep stealing our stuff," he reported self-righteously.

I responded by saying that all the "stuff" in the public park where they were playing was *public*.

"But we had the stick first," he wailed.

I repeated the sticks-are-not-something-we-play-with rule. Then I added, if we were going to get technical, the stick really belonged to a tree!

"But, everything we try to build gets broken down by them!"

It was a typical fourth-grade boys vs. third-grade boys conflict. They loved to draw boundaries, to claim ownership, to build something that could be called theirs. Part of that was good; part of it was deadly.

In a class meeting, two students suggested grand ideas for compromise. "What about pooling your resources and making a really neat fort together?" Response: It would never work. "How about one day letting the fourth graders play fort and the next day letting the third graders play fort?" Response: Nope, it would never work.

What will happen if reasonable, workable compromises are simply dismissed as impossible at such a young age? I wonder what will happen when they learn that possessiveness destroys the possessor?

And that's exactly what happened. Those fighting over the stick were banned by the principal from playing fort because they could not reach a compromise. I guess sometimes the best we can do is let experience be the teacher.

Lord, grant me a spirit of generosity that can somehow infect little fort architects. Help me to encourage them, even at this young age, at least to try ideas for compromise. And when they refuse, may experience be their teacher.

✎ SEPTEMBER 7   **Read II Samuel 14:8-9.**

"But he . . ."

"What did *you* do?"

"But he . . ."

"Excuse me. I'm asking what your part in this is. What is *your* responsibility?"

"But he . . ."

Sound familiar? What is this inability to accept responsibility? It pops up every day in the classroom. It is always the other guy's fault. Always *his* issue. Never mind. If only the other person would change. If only the other person had not been that way. If only she hadn't pushed first. If only his foot hadn't been in the way. If only you had given me a test on another day. If only my parents hadn't been busy, I could have handed my homework in on time.

The excuses and the blaming go on and on. When does it stop and the growing and maturing begin? I worry less and less these days about the students who are struggling academically and more and more about the ones who find it impossible to take personal responsibility. Even at age ten you see the instinct to blame.

I wonder how many times I have traveled home from work thinking, *If only the kids had been better behaved today. If only they had listened, and if only they would come to school ready to learn.* But what about *me*? What can I be doing in the complex arena of teaching these days?

Lord, help me not to blame the difficult days on some external scapegoat. Let me look carefully at my responsibilities as I'm training students to look at theirs.

✎ SEPTEMBER 8   Read Psalm 19:12.

I corrected him with all the vengeance of a teacher who had seen it all. How could he, after repeated warnings, continue this inappropriate behavior? He was kicked out of the classroom, and that was that. I had even forgotten to give choices this time. The choice was mine, and I had had it!

The funny thing was he seemed angrier than usual. His usual reaction was the proverbial cat-who-swallowed-the-canary look. Pry open the jaws and sure enough, there was the canary. He was *always* guilty. Sometimes he would even confess to the entire infraction. This time something strange was happening.

In my intensity to keep the class functioning despite the disruption, I decided to investigate later. How could I be anything other than dead right? But something was amiss.

After the class was working again, I went out to hear his side of the fray. He had been set up. Those little angels working diligently on the literature project had loved the intrigue of seeing how much trouble they could get the troublemaker in. And I had fallen for it—perfectly.

I guess sometimes we need to be reminded that children are too creative to fit neatly into our categories and labels.

Lord, keep me from using labels and making assumptions. Remind me that fairness does not reside in unsubstantiated conclusions. As the psalmist asks for personal discernment, may I also ask for classroom discernment.

Chrissie was as wise a colleague as one could hope to work with—and she seemed to know how to inspire the best ideals in all her students.

However, one new student on her volleyball team was completely unaware of my colleague's abilities. If this young girl had known half of what she was up against, she would never have attempted a test of wills.

At the first practice, Chrissie energetically started the training with tough drills. One student, however, decided she didn't have to go along with all this hard work. When Chrissie called her to join the others, she taunted, "You can't intimidate me!"

Chrissie skillfully replied, "Of course I can't. Nor would I want to. This isn't about intimidation. This is about respect. The other athletes are showing respect for themselves and the team by diligently practicing the skills that will give us a good team. We'd love to have you join us in doing the same."

The young volleyball player looked dumbfounded. She thought everything revolved around power and control. Once she recovered from shock, she tentatively liked this "new idea" of—what had her coach called it?—respect. Somehow defiance didn't seem important. Respect began looking like the best route to belonging—and a much better option for winning tournaments.

Lord, make us peacemakers who see past defiance to the real needs of our students.

She was sobbing so hard, she was unintelligible. Both knees were bleeding and so was an elbow. As I began the first aid procedures, an older student ran up saying the injured student had been playing tag on the climber.

Tag games on this piece of equipment were strictly forbidden. The ground was too far away for students to be running uncontrollably across the play structure. At this piece of information, the wounded student escalated her sobbing.

Gently, the older student said, "I wasn't telling on you. I just wanted the teacher to know how you got hurt. Maybe when you get Band-Aids on, I can show you a new game that will be safer."

The sobbing abated for a short time as I tried to stay out of this fascinating interchange. Then the guilt and pain became too much and the sobs started up again.

The older student rolled her eyes impatiently this time and said, "Oh, for goodness sake. We all make mistakes. I forgot about not playing Climber Tag about three times when I was in first grade. Finally, after all the wounds, I started remembering."

Then in a conspiratorial tone she added, "I'll bet you're smarter than I was. It will probably take you only once. Come on. Let's get you cleaned up so we can play some more."

I decided we needed to offer this student a staff position.

Lord, thanks for those who remember what it feels like to be young and needy. Help us as adults to remember, too.

✎ SEPTEMBER 11   Read Mark 6:30-31.

Both students were highly capable and highly nervous. You could tell it in the way they held themselves and by the way they handled eye contact. They were very careful to hand in homework and equally careful at completing it meticulously. They liked to know what was happening so they could be prepared.

My classroom has *some* predictability to it; but it also creates spaces for risking. Combining spontaneity and certainty is always a challenge, but both are extremely important in education. My task then is to create an atmosphere where these little perfectionists can dare to feel okay about not always knowing.

"I am thrilled when you finally feel comfortable enough to do some risking in this classroom," I began one morning.

"By that I mean you feel comfortable offering ideas and guesses even when you are not sure of the correct answer. We will be discussing many things that require opinions and new thinking—not just memorized answers. . . ."

As my lecture went on, I couldn't help noticing my little perfectionists. The tight shoulders of one unknotted along with a very long sigh. The other one met my eye—only for a moment—but long enough to say, "I think I'll like this!"

Lord, help me, a recovering perfectionist, give these students a way to feel excited rather than panicked when there are new places to go in their learning. After all their responsible "doing" may I learn how to invite them to rest a while.

✎ SEPTEMBER 12   Read James 1:4.

She moaned so effectively, I thought she was dying. Fortunately she had simply forgotten her glasses that morning. However, according to this student, forgotten glasses meant she would be unable to take the test.

While subbing in a junior high once, I thought I had heard it all—but this time the dramatic element was ingenious. Actually, her *mother* had forgotten the glasses, she said, and nothing, especially not a test, could be expected of this dear, helpless student.

"Hmm," I commented, "seems like you need to take the responsibility for *your* glasses since your mom is having trouble handling it. You seem like the type that could be creative about limitations. I'll leave it up to you to figure out how best to take this fifteen-minute test today."

Angry sobs were the next line of fire. By this time I realized I had a tantrum on my hands—and a classroom of wide-eyed kids deciding whether or not to try other methods of getting out of the test!

I had to think fast. *Lord, give me the perseverance to hold my ground,* I prayed silently. Then I said, loudly enough for all to hear, "We all have difficult days. For that reason, we must creatively persevere to perform our responsibilities despite those difficulties. Please take a seat and begin the test."

Lord, help me be like a coach to these students—one who insists on perseverance even when it's hard. When is it ever easy? Help me deal patiently and firmly with manipulation, knowing that the real race is yet to come.

✎ SEPTEMBER 13   **Read Proverbs 20:6.**

Volumes could be written about homework excuses. So many claims and promises of completion are never fulfilled. It's hard to find faithfulness in word *and deed*. Because of the creativity of the excuses, I usually pull out the homework lecture at the first of the year, demonstrate clearly that I've heard it all, and simply expect homework in on time—*the end!*

I go on and on about promises versus substance and indicate that good intentions simply won't do. Hard, cold evidence of work completed is what I expect. On and on I lecture, ending with the catchphrase that "the dog ate it" will simply not work in this classroom.

Little did I dream that one student was listening intently—*and remembering!* I assume the students will catch one or two points and only *really* hear me when I climb up on one of the desks and "preach" my main point about homework later in the year. (Believe me, I've done it!)

Naturally I was quite surprised today to be approached by a sly smile on homework due day. Each student had carefully pulled his or her work from a notebook and was waiting for the "job well done" response—except one student. He hid his behind his back. When I asked for it, he brought forth a soggy mass of paper.

"Well," he said and smiled, "the dog didn't eat it, but my baby sister tried to. I don't have 'cold, hard' evidence of work finished, but here's 'cold, soggy' evidence!"

Here's a faithful man true to his word—even to the extent of digging it out of a baby's mouth. I should be grateful!

Lord, thank you for students who show they are worthy of trust. Help me to laugh at their sometimes playful measures.

17

✎ **SEPTEMBER 14**   Read Psalm 103:13-14.

This mother was always smartly dressed and confident. It seemed that objectivity was second nature to her. Every contact with her, before this one, had revealed a self-assured, professional woman. She seemed like one who could rule the world dispassionately if only given the opportunity!

So, why was she having trouble finding her voice in our parent-teacher conference? Why was she blinking back tears? Her child was strong academically and a delight to have in class, so the emotion was not worry. She simply seemed moved that someone cared deeply for her child. I had seen emotional and academic growth in her son, and the insights had prompted her to express her own recent joys and concerns regarding this special student. Her dispassionate exterior simply protected a compassionate mother.

After the conference, she headed toward the door—and then stopped. She wanted me to know how important it was to her to have someone else watching her child grow and succeed—someone who also cheered him on at each new stage. I reminded her that my job is made so much easier by parents who consistently give support to their children day after day. Unfortunately, many children do not have that support at home. And though we may do all we can to nurture a child, no one, not even the most gifted teacher in the world, can fully compensate for what a child needs from a parent.

Lord, thank you for the opportunity to be in partnership with concerned, supportive parents—and for the opportunity to provide at least some love and encouragement for those children who do not come from supportive homes.

✎ **SEPTEMBER 15**   Read John 1:1-5, 14.

It was the usual busy afternoon of social studies. Our topic was state history. Names and dates were flying everywhere. The noise level was high, and young historians were grappling with the correct chronology of events leading to statehood.

In the midst of it all, a group of students came across an event titled the Whitman Massacre. They were confused and wanted to know the details. As I began telling them about the Protestant mission set up in Walla Walla, Washington, in 1836, the room grew quiet. The details of white settlers bringing medicine to the Native American population intrigued them. *What a great idea,* I could feel them saying nonverbally.

Their young minds were unprepared for the next part of the story. The "great idea" became a nightmare. White settlers following the Whitmans brought with them diseases that were fatal to the Indians. Marcus Whitman would treat white settlers for measles and they would recover. He would treat Native Americans and they would die. It appeared that Dr. Whitman was killing the local tribes.

Desperate to preserve their own people, the Native Americans retaliated. The Whitmans and all who worked at the mission were killed.

Not one sound was heard in the classroom.

Finally, one student blurted, "Why couldn't they explain it to them—just tell them about the immune system and everything would be okay?"

"First, they didn't have information about the immune system like we have today," I explained, "but more important, words are inadequate when people are dying. Clear communication between different peoples and cultures has always been difficult. The potential for misunderstanding and harm is great. In our global society, you must go slowly and cautiously."

Lord, you entered our world, our human culture, and most of us misunderstood. Death resulted—but you are the Lord of resurrection. Help us to go slowly and cautiously as we interact with those who are different from us, and redeem our misunderstandings.

✎ SEPTEMBER 16   Read Psalm 32:8-9.

"If you can't settle down to work, you'll stay in from lunch recess with me. I'm providing time for you to work now and

19

if you choose not to use it, you can use your recess time to finish this work."

The brakes that I had tried to help this student remove all morning suddenly were released. The threat of a lost recess meant more than all the other educational psychology I had employed. The work was done—in five minutes—and it was done neatly and accurately.

Why did an accomplished objective leave me so empty then? After all, he had finished, and he seemed to have a mastery of the subject matter. But, when would the larger objective be achieved—the objective of self-control rather than teacher control?

Holding a big enough "stick" over him had worked—but only for this one time. Next time what would he choose—to wait until my stick was even larger? Sadly, I think that's what he was after.

My task is to motivate in some ways—but the greater task is to help the student grow in self-motivation. Lost recess will never accomplish internal control.

Lord, help me balance delicately between teacher control and student self-control. Only those without understanding need a bit and bridle (or a lost recess threat)! Help me help my students to graduate from such "motivations."

✎ **SEPTEMBER 17**   **Read Proverbs 8:33-34.**

We definitely parted company philosophically on this one. In fact, it seemed impossible to achieve a compromise of any sort that could solve the differences in teaching styles.

But a wise administrator schooled in the art of listening modeled an invaluable lesson to me. She *listened* to my frustration before offering a solution. She not only listened, she asked questions. Before I was ready for any solution, I needed to be heard. Apparently, she had anticipated that need.

Slowly, with years of handling differences behind her, she drew me out and suggested possibilities that opened new options to my mind. Maybe the differences were not so radical after all. Maybe the impossibility of compromise was merely newness disguised. We could work out a solution for covering the material needed for the administrative standards and still teach it in a way that I felt was adequate for the age level.

How facinating to feel the guard drop when your position is heard. How interesting to feel supported by someone schooled in the art of listening.

In Proverbs, we are called to listen to gain wisdom. Maybe the reverse is just as true—when we are skilled in listening, we are wise.

Lord, listening seems the only route to compromise with colleagues. Sometimes we are given the gift—may we not forget to also give it as we work.

✎ SEPTEMBER 18   Read Proverbs 24:5.

The canoe rocked dangerously and finally overturned. Seven students were scrambling to find a way to stay afloat. Fortunately, they had on life jackets and were participating in a monitored simulated accident in a YMCA pool. The personal flotation devices popped them efficiently up to the surface. They soon were even joining hands across the overturned canoe to help one another stay together.

At the correct signal the students released their hold on the boat and grouped themselves in the H.E.L.P. position, which, in a real emergency, could be used to preserve as much body heat as possible in cold water. Then, at the instructor's command, they formed huddles in the water that were designed to achieve the same result for a smaller group. They ended by going under water and coming up inside the canoe to discover the secret stash of air and protection under an overturned canoe.

I stood on the side watching and thinking about how hard I would work today to build into them reading skills, writing fluency, and map skills. But this knowledge beyond the books was paramount. I had almost canceled this extra outing because the classroom curriculum was so important. I soon became convinced that practical knowledge such as safety skills must never be preempted.

Lord, help me remember that my students need the strength common sense can provide. May I be diligent to acquaint them with "secret stashes" of practical knowledge.

✎ SEPTEMBER 19   **Read Zephaniah 3:17.**

Someone has quipped that teachers are simply frustrated CEOs. The reason they teach is because they get to initiate, create, organize, and direct a whole roomful of people.

These first weeks of school are especially a time of diligent initiating. I must self-start the day. Its tone will, in many ways, be shaped by me. I initiate excitement about new skills. I initiate the format taken to communicate new ideas. I initiate moment by moment the atmosphere of discipline, fun, excitement, control—or I balance the atmospheres between control and exploration, guidance and self-discovery, discipline and humor. The students then learn to be initiators as well while beginning to take responsibility for their education.

In this quiet moment of a prep period, I find myself wanting to have Someone initiating energy and life on *my* behalf. How exhilarating it would be to step back, just for a moment, and feel that Someone has gone before me to make my way one of inspiration and learning.

Lord, this yearning is for you. You are consistently and spontaneously initiating on my behalf—even at this very moment. What delight there is in knowing you are with me—taking great delight in your child, quieting me with your love, and rejoicing over me with singing.

✎ SEPTEMBER 20   **Read Matthew 18:2-5.**

Quietly she came out of the tangled mass of children in the hallway. Gently, but with an urgency that grabbed my attention, she said, "Please change my seat in the classroom." She was masterful at adjusting to any situation. She had the grace and patience of Job. Rarely did she ask for anything, so I had to pay attention.

I had used her mature disposition to create space between two other students who were not as capable in their ability to work independently. I had positioned her to create peacefulness, and it was working beautifully—except for her. Little did I know how often she had been "used" for the same purpose in other classrooms. In my adult ignorance, I assumed she would be thrilled with her role of helper and peacemaker. In her fourth-grade wisdom, she indicated that she liked to help, but just once she'd like to be seated where it was fun—rather than difficult.

She stopped me dead in my tracks. I realized how much we teachers often depend on those students who behave more maturely to aid our classroom control. I also realized it was time I solved my classroom difficulty in another way.

I assured her that her seating would be changed. And I applauded this "helper" for knowing that she, too, needed to be allowed to be a child!

Lord, help me strike a balance between giving responsibility and allowing childlikeness—especially in the reliable, mature children.

✎ SEPTEMBER 21   Read Isaiah 44:3, 4.

In *The Abolition of Man,* C. S. Lewis said, "The task of the modern educator is not to cut down jungles but to irrigate deserts." Of course, in Lewis's time, the modern educator was the teacher of the forties and fifties. However, his metaphor is useful even today.

The metaphor of irrigation brings back many vivid childhood memories for me—and it is perfect for the task of the teacher. Growing up in southern Idaho, I became well acquainted with a hot desert sun. Our small farming community spent much of its efforts fighting the barrenness of the desert. Irrigation ditches had to be burned each spring. Irrigation siphons had to be checked many times a day. Water rights were jealously guarded and reservoirs were anxiously watched throughout the year. Pipes were moved constantly, creating sunburned faces, sore muscles, and exhaustion. The work was never done.

But the moments of greatest effort were when the plants were young and fragile. They required the greatest, unyielding diligence I have ever watched and participated in.

So it is with teaching. The diligence can never let up. The "crops" are young and require constant watering.

Lord, this metaphor of water in the desert is appropriate. Help me to keep watering, consistently. One hundred and eighty days is a long growing season—and these plants are very young.

✎ SEPTEMBER 22   Read I Samuel 3:1-11.

I couldn't figure out why they couldn't get it! This was a highly capable class, and the concepts of possessive nouns should have been one of the simpler things we would tackle that week. I was bewildered. Constant confusion resulted from every method of assessment I tried. I had explained it with multisensory trappings. I had invented a game to practice its basic rules. I had designed study groups to peer-check the information—and the same strange thing kept happening.

The students were bent on looking to capitalization for their clues to spot possessive nouns—not apostrophes and s's. Finally, I looked at my fourth-grade language arts genius and said, "Nick, would you help me go over this? Here's the overhead pen—see what you can do."

I sat in his chair and began to see it through the eyes of a fourth grader. *Proper* and *possessive*—the two words I had used to teach about nouns—sounded very much alike when meeting them for the first time. I'd forgotten about first meetings. After all, I had been studying those terms for twenty-plus years! But Nick effectively showed his classmates the difference and quickly got everyone straightened out.

C. S. Lewis was right when he said that the student can be of more help than the teacher because the student knows less and has recently encountered just the difficulty we want him or her to explain.

Lord, may I never forget the resource of peer-teaching. May I never be hesitant to sit quietly in the pupil's chair as Eli did with Samuel—even, maybe especially, after years of teaching.

✎ SEPTEMBER 23   Read Proverbs 1:10-19.

They could hardly walk down the hall without creating a bottleneck. They bunched together so closely that navigating past their little group became almost impossible. The leader stood a head above the rest, and all eyes were constantly on him. They waited for him to laugh before they would laugh. They waited for him to move before they moved. They had become such a tight-knit group that some of us were convinced the others even waited to breathe based on his cue!

We teachers know how alarming it is to watch students become incapable of thinking for themselves. When they are taking their cues for behavior from a young, impulsive classmate, things disintegrate quickly.

With an attitude of indifference and disrespect, they waltzed into my area of lunchtime duty today. I sensed immediately that a "right of passage" for this group included blatant disrespect for anyone in charge. As they began their disrespectful antics for my benefit, I couldn't help noticing another of their classmates in the corner.

Quietly he watched. His face registered a sadness and a keen frustration. He made one attempt to stop the group, but realized he was completely outnumbered. So, he pulled apart from them and turned his back on their repeated invitations to join their disrespect.

I couldn't help but acknowledge his wisdom later. He had every opportunity to join with the powerful, energized crowd of peers—but he refused. In so many words he told me that he hoped he would never join such disrespectful antics.

Standing apart from the popular "in-your-face" attitudes of this generation is a courageous act. As a matter of fact, "standing apart," period, is a courageous act—at any age. I hope that when I know it's right to "stand apart" from my own peers, I will have as much courage as my young student.

Lord, it's not easy going against the crowd, even when I know that's what you would have me do. Give me wisdom, and give me the courage to act on that wisdom.

✎ SEPTEMBER 24   Read James 3:1.

How did I get all this homework? I thought the students were the ones with that part of the bargain. But it seems to take hours out of the classroom for one half hour of effectiveness in the classroom.

Besides researching the content, I have to plan how to present the material—which has become increasingly complex in light of new knowledge of learning styles, disabilities, multiple IQs, and available technological support. All of it makes teaching so stimulating—and so exhausting at times. Today, I'm simply overwhelmed by the arenas in which I must be an expert; they seem to be multiplying exponentially.

Somehow, I must continue learning without losing the joy of education. The complexities must exist simultaneously with the simplicity of delight in this process of training and coaching in foundational skills.

In *God in the Docks*, C. S. Lewis writes that "[No teacher] can give to another what he does not possess himself," and "As the teachers are, so they will teach." Challenging words for a challenging profession!

Lord, this mound of information and these complex issues—may I attack them all with joy today. Delight in learning must be communicated at all costs and despite all complexities.

✎ SEPTEMBER 25   Read Proverbs 10:4.

I needed the recess for last minute social studies preparation. I had things to copy and enlarge, plus a simulation game to organize. It looked like a great afternoon of learning, but someone changed my best laid plans.

He was bright—astonishingly bright. If we needed the latest scientific data on a particular point in cosmology or archaeology, we simply asked this student and *then* checked the encyclopedia!

However, he began resting in that intelligence, and laziness plus sloppiness came creeping into his work. The erosion was subtle at first. Then like the results of a flash flood, the entire hillside collapsed. The simplest task was done with great boredom and inaccuracy. Basic language skills were simply brushed off as insignificant. I knew someday he'd be writing research reports—in fact, his dream was to be a research scientist. So, I let it cost me precious prep time.

He stayed with me for recess. I would rather have been working on the offensive building instead of defensive remediation—especially for one so capable. But enough was enough. Erosion had to be stopped. He sat the entire recess redoing three language arts projects until they were correct—and legible! Over and over he practiced until the skills were in place.

I explained to him that no matter how bright one may be, a lack of diligence is always costly.

Lord, make me willing to give up important things for teaching life skills to even the most capable students.

✎ **SEPTEMBER 26**   **Read Proverbs 28:18.**

Playgrounds are microcosms of kingdoms. The hierarchy of power and servitude plays itself out with great drama. The big kids versus the little kids or the athletic versus the not-so-athletic find ways of jousting to determine social stratification. It seems crucial to discover one's place—and to make sure that place is unchallenged.

Today's recess began as an exception. Some of the gracious older students, who were secure enough not to need jousting, invited younger students to join them in a game of 4-square. I marveled at the delight these students had laughing and playing together. The older ones helped the younger ones with new ball skills. They gave second chances and cheered the younger ones' emerging abilities. The game became a time to encourage, not to conquer. The laughter was happy—never taunting. The eye contact between kids communicated safety and admiration. *What an idyllic microcosm,* I couldn't help but think to myself.

Then along came the ones who would be kings. A small group bent on power rather than community swaggered their way toward the game. Innocent and eager to include all, the 4-square players invited the new group to join them. Things changed rapidly. Laughter turned to taunts. Young ones either cried or slowly walked away to find another game.

There is great elation for all of us when those who welcome and encourage are in power. Much sadness and hiding result when those needing power dominate unkindly.

Lord, guide me in dealing with young, insecure despots. May we move them during these playground microcosms closer to the delight of righteousness.

✎ SEPTEMBER 27   Read Proverbs 14:13.

Whispered jokes and uncomfortable laughter were his specialty. He worked his way through the lunchroom creating waves of "Yuck!" and "That's gross!" After repeated incidents, I began investigating.

I assumed the great ten-year-old experiment with lavatory jokes was on. Each year it happens, and each set of students thinks they are the first and the most clever ones ever to experiment with such things. Fortunately, the fervor soon wears thin, and classroom humor moves on to a more appropriate plane.

But for this student, the experimenting didn't stop. In fact, his whole identity seemed to be wrapped around being the grossest joker in the classroom. All interventions to regain a sense of appropriateness failed.

Then, all this spilled over into his work. No longer was it whispered beyond my earshot. He had decided to use his "talents" during creative writing!

My first impulse was to say, "Excuse me, but this is simply unacceptable. Clean it up." However, at our paper conference, I told him I realized making people laugh was important to him—but had he really thought through the kind of laughter he had hoped to create? He shared that he wanted to be funny, but it wasn't working very well. He wanted wholesome laughter, but didn't know how to go about it. He even confided that he was sad about the embarrassed laughter he was causing.

We spent the rest of the paper conference experimenting with different ways to create humor in writing. Interestingly enough, he's now experimenting with more wholesome private jokes as well. Who knows? Maybe he'll have the last laugh after all!

Lord, humor is so important in a healthy classroom. Help us introduce our students to the delights of appropriate laughter.

✎ SEPTEMBER 28   Read Philippians 2:4.

Every other week the class bulletin board features a different child. With great care and excitement each student prepares a group of pictures showing the key elements of their lives. I'm not sure who looks forward to the presentations more—the students or me! I have discovered more about each student through these times than through any other project.

What I watch more than anything else is how the children talk about themselves and their world. Each time they present the part about what they want to be when they grow up, I listen carefully. I want to begin being a part of investing in that dream.

One extremely bright student was having particular difficulties in his ability to use punctuation skills. I couldn't convince this gifted mind that such details were of any importance—until I discovered he wanted to be a research scientist.

We talked about the importance of attention to details for that profession and how crucial it would be to begin habits that would contribute to his ability to write up his research findings. The light went on. Every time I correct the details or send him back to his seat to self-correct, I smile and say, "Why am I demanding that you get this right? Why am I being so hard on you? Do you remember?"

He grins and says, "Because you think I can be a great scientist someday."

Lord, help me listen carefully to students' dreams in order to invest in these young but noble aspirations.

✎ SEPTEMBER 29   Read Proverbs 26:17.

I leaned down to give what I assumed was a gentle, golden retriever an affectionate scratch. Having grown up around this breed of dog, I was well aware of their kind nature. What I didn't know in this case was that the dog was half wolf. Not until I grabbed his head did I see the savage look in his eyes. His owner lunged forward to grab him, and I froze. Never again will I make assumptions about dogs!

And never again will one boy in my class dive into a quarrel that is not his own. In the name of loyalty to a friend, he decided to meddle in another's conflict. One student had pushed the other in line, hoping to be first—which seems of paramount importance in all ten-year-old minds. The line happened to be the drinking fountain line, and the pushing started escalating. By the end, the two who had started the pushing resolved to take turns and the student who had chosen to play judge and jury for them was left with a bloody lip and a chipped tooth.

He had assumed his help would be invaluable in what he had judged to be a crucial affair of justice. However, the two tussling had a lesser agenda and were willing to spar a minute and then be finished. Since the judge escalated the entire affair, he was the one who left bloodied.

The writer of Proverbs was right. Reaching for a passing dog's ears isn't very different from intervening in another's quarrel!

Lord, help me teach these young ones that passing dogs' ears and others' quarrels should be left quite alone.

Someone has said postmodernism means never having to say you're wrong. I'm convinced the entire concept is becoming an epidemic. Most of my disciplinary interventions in the classroom include the words, "Excuse me. We're not talking at this moment about *them;* we're talking about *you.*" It is always followed by, "But they . . ." Then I start all over again with, "Excuse me. We're not talking about them; we're talking about *you.*" Around and around we go.

Today's mediation again forced its way into the curriculum as I parted two spatting students. As we went round and round, my peripheral vision picked up sheepishness on the face of another student. She quietly, hesitantly stepped toward the fray and gently pulled at my sleeve.

"Umm, I think I'm responsible for this," she whispered.

I called everything to a halt and asked her to explain. While the two warring parties stood there dumbfounded, she explained her twisting of the truth that had caused the conflict. She was able to say she was feeling lonely and felt the only way to "break into" the crowd was to cause a rift in the clique.

All of us were sobered. We quietly talked about the hurt of loneliness and the constructive ways to solve the problem. I told this student that her final honesty proved she could provide many people with an invaluable friendship.

Lord, thanks for those students who haven't bought into the postmodernism slogan. Give us all the courage to follow their example.

☆October

Growing in Wisdom

Anne Wilcox

OCTOBER 1   **Read Ecclesiastes 7:9.**

I have decided gymnasiums provide the best character classroom in all of education. Throw a ball into the midst of children and suddenly you have new insight into every student.

There are those who fudge on every rule; those who follow the rules to the letter and police the entire class to ensure conformity; those who compete with every inch of their bodies; and those who duck every time the terrifying ball comes near them. So many contrasts of personality and character are dramatically played out in front of the teacher by the innocent catalysts of a ball and a few rules.

However, the ones who let anger dominate them worry me. When they're called out of the game, they lose all control. They scream at the referee. Slam down the ball. Push a classmate into the wall and stomp off the court. The example is always before them in professional sports these days. The tightrope I have to walk is teaching them to care about playing at their peak skillwise, but having a wiser perspective on mistakes or penalties. Intensity in sports is appropriate; playing to kill is not.

So, we've decided that skill in sportsmanship is as vital—if not more vital—than the physical skills of the game. Learning to control anger becomes the chief educational objective in this "must win at all costs" culture.

Lord, I need creative ways to help them—and me—to not be easily provoked, for you have said that hot-temperedness resides in the lap of fools.

✎ OCTOBER 2   Read Ecclesiastes 10:1.

The enrichment literature class was filled with academic achievers. Each morning they came ready to conquer whatever literary task was put before them. When the homework was described for the week, cheers—rather than groans—filled the "stadium." Their imaginations never stopped and their abilities with words were astonishing for eight- and nine-year-olds. I truly thought I was dreaming.

Until one day. Intellectually, he could run circles around his peers. In fact, I sometimes wondered if he could do the same with me. His sense of humor provided a perfect balance for his book prowess. Whenever we were slogging through ideas, he could ski across the top and pull the entire class along with him. His contributions became invaluable—until he changed strategies.

I'm not sure who gave him permission to turn smarty. Maybe I had given him too much rein in class. But one day he decided to be silly—instead of appropriately homorous. Suddenly, despite his abilities and age, he played an obnoxious four-year-old baby—voice and all. I thought it would be a passing phase. Instead it became an infection. By the time the week was up several students were mimicking the disease.

The last class hour of the week was a lecture about behavior titled, "Goofiness vs. Humor." I had had it. And these usually hard workers felt the heat of my frustration.

One little capable student had dropped a fly in the ointment—and almost ruined the entire aura of this gifted class.

Lord, how true that a little folly outweighs wisdom. Help me and the class restore the freshness of the perfume.

Today was one of those tired days—no, exhausted days. Everything I did seemed meaningless. The only question that seemed to make any sense was "Why am I working so hard at this? No one cares." The students were swirling in another galaxy where spelling and pronouns and state history were insignificant. I had to ask how important they were myself for this generation of automatic spell checkers, grammar software, and controversy over slanted historical records.

I can usually pull it together, but today the students convinced me. *Really, this all may be meaningless,* I thought.

Then I turned to the preacher in Ecclesiastes. He tried it all—every bit of creativity, every project possible under the sun—and he had a day like today. Meaningless, meaningless—until chapter two. Then he decided that work satisfaction was the key to the relentless cycles of life. Our work and our ability to gain strength to work come from God. God has given us much to do during these cycles of life.

I turned to my class and said, "If the electricity goes off, John, what will happen to your spell check and your grammar check option?"

"Mary, what will people be saying about your life someday—does that matter to you? Yes? Then let's dig into this history and keep trying to piece it together."

Somehow, there were all sorts of new reasons for going on under the sun. Meaningless was transformed to meaningful—what I'm doing is crucial.

Lord, you have given us just enough perception of meaninglessness to ask crucial questions and just enough meaningfulness to continue working and walking through today.

OCTOBER 4   Read Ecclesiastes 3:1.

Every time I turned around the low singing was jamming the airwaves. Again and again, I had to firmly stop it. It was using too much auditory energy.

Every time I started giving instructions for the next task, he started up his humorous comments. Again and again, I had to stop to tell him to stop.

Every time I tried to give homework, her hand shot up. Before I could speak two sentences, she was ready with a thousand questions punctuated by a gasping, frantic waving of the hand. "Put your hand down until I'm finished with the instructions, please," I would say again and again.

I had to get back my sense of humor, so I began using Ecclesiastes. With playfulness, I began correcting and reminding students by acknowledging that there is a time for everything and a season for every activity. To the singer, I complimented his musical ability and reminded him that the time for singing was during choir. I encouraged the humorist to keep developing that wit—silently during the writing exercises. I complimented the questioner for her curiosity, which would be satisfied in the proper season.

For everything there is a season—including a teacher's sense of humor!

Lord, may my humor in training and reminding return. Thank you for the fact that what they are doing is not inappropriate always—timing is the real issue. May that restore a bit of the emotional drain caused by the day-after-day reminders.

✎ **OCTOBER 5**   **Read Proverbs 29:22-23.**

Cross words had passed between these two boys all morning. I was a bit delighted to see them chosen for the same soccer team at recess. Maybe a little working together would form a more supportive bond.

One student was the goalie and the other stayed within verbal range to continue passing insults. Fortunately, the goalie became focused on the game. Save after brilliant save was the goalie's reward for concentration.

All I heard from the other student was, "Man, you need glasses! I coulda done twice that good!" I decided it was time to pull someone from the game for a little chat.

"Wow," I said, "you're really feeling bad about yourself today. What's up?"

"It's not me; it's him! He . . ."

"Whoa, wait a minute. I see him concentrating on the game. I see you trying to cut him down on every play. Is he better than you? I mean, you don't need to cut someone down that isn't a threat."

He swallowed hard and said, "He . . ."

"We're not talking about someone who's having a great game. We're talking about his teammate who keeps shooting him down with words. Why is he a threat to you?"

He adamantly stated that *no one* was a threat to him. So I encouraged him to prove it by being a supportive team player.

Lord, these little ones love to stir up anger. Help us help them to see their own value so they can have the emotional resources to be encouraging to another teammate.

✎ OCTOBER 6   Read Ecclesiastes 4:9-12.

Individual learning has been working so well in my classroom. The variety of learning styles and abilities seems to be responding well in an individually paced track. One child is working at a sixth-grade spelling level while another needs third-grade review. One student is soaring toward seventh-grade reading texts while another is still working hard at fourth-grade word attack skills. Each student seems to be progressing nicely.

Yet there is no sense of learning *together*. The accelerated reader needs the struggling reader's artistic abilities. The random explorer needs the finishing power of the sequential learner. Often in group times, I see them competing with one another or rolling their eyes because they have no appreciation for the others' strengths.

So this week I decided to use a little wisdom from Ecclesiastes. I brought some thread and some twine to class. I asked a student to help me demonstrate. He easily broke the thread but struggled unsuccessfully with the twine. Then we launched into a discussion about the strength of community.

Based on what we've discovered, we designed a community-filled week. Literature groups have been eager and successful, rather than competitive. Study groups have been formed to help master the state history material for a coming test. Interestingly enough, those individuals have learned three times as much—and enjoyed it more.

In the classroom—and in all of life—two really are better than one.

Lord, help me see how dependent I am on those who have different abilities and aptitudes from my own.

✎ OCTOBER 7   Read Ecclesiastes 5:3.

It was a graduate class for educators. The lecture had been long and, frankly, boring. Words had been many, but content had been slight. Each point was meticulously elaborated upon; unfortunately, the points were trite, so the elaboration was a waste of time. How thrilled I was to see that a panel discussion with the opportunity for audience questions was scheduled next. Maybe we could really address the needs we teachers were experiencing in the trenches.

Unfortunately, each panel member was used to talking. More and more words were expressed, but again the substance was lacking. Finally, one of the panel members, who had graciously allowed her colleagues to express themselves, said, "We educators love to talk, don't we? However, I wonder if we are pinpointing the needs of these class members. Let's take questions to see if we can address their specific needs."

The class members brought up topics of myriad needs that were so appropriate. The comments and exchanges between professionals were invaluable. I went away learning more from those few moments of interaction than from several nonstop lectures.

I wonder how often I do that to my students—give information that could best be explored through discussion and interaction?

Lord, thank you for this example of the wisdom of fewer words.

 **OCTOBER 8**   Read Ecclesiastes 5:10-12.

I slammed my fist against the OFF button. I simply could not endure another news report about negotiating contracts for professional sports players. How could they possibly want more money for their profession? How could they even ask for more? I'd like to give them one semester in the classroom and then see if our two disparagingly different incomes are appropriate!

That's it. I am resentful. My unpaid mortgage is on the table while their villa in Europe needs remodeling. They are playing a game for our entertainment; I am teaching children the fundamentals of life—without which they cannot survive adulthod! I am shaping the hearts and minds of children; they are troubled about averages that record the number of times a wooden thing hits a round thing.

But the resentment is real. The desire to be rated valuable by the digits in my income is real. But how do you ever rate a profession that is infinitely valuable and fulfilling?

It probably is true that our incomes are ridiculously different because our culture's values are also skewed. But for today I need to remember a few wise words about money. I need to remember that "whoever loves wealth is never satisfied with his income" (Ecclesiastes 5:10 NIV). I must also remember that "the sleep of a laborer is sweet, . . . but the abundance of a rich man permits him no sleep" (Ecclesiastes 5:12 NIV).

Lord, it might be very appropriate to reevaluate the wages of teachers. But until our earnings match professional sports players, let me enjoy sleeping soundly.

 **OCTOBER 9**   Read Ecclesiastes 5:18-20.

He kept watching the clock. He must have looked up five times in five minutes. He simply couldn't stand the tension of the complex skills project in front of him coupled with his learning disabilities. He was dreaming of being somewhere else—and, of course, clock-watching was preventing his achievement of anything significant.

I decided a halt was in store. I took the entire class to the auditorium for an active state geography review on a blanket map. We ran, skipped, hopped, and crawled to the geographic areas on the blanket that bore the state boundaries. My clock-watcher had lost track of time.

Finally, we lined up at the door to return to the classroom. I informed them of the minutes left until lunchtime. I also suggested that the tasks we would return to, if attacked diligently, would make it seem as if the clock moved faster. My clock-watcher made his way through the crowd and said, "I thought time flew only when you were having fun."

I replied that time also flies when you're giving everything—your mind and your heart and your diligence—to a difficult task. Working hard is a great clock mover! He was very silent all the way back to the classroom.

This time he took one look at the clock, gave a deep sigh, and decided to see if he could get lunchtime to arrive earlier by hard work.

Often I'm like this young clock-watcher, restlessly waiting for the difficult days of my life to pass. Yet the writer of Ecclesiastes reminds me that when I am able to work diligently and find enjoyment in that work, God will keep me occupied with the joy of my heart.

Lord, remind me when I am clock-watching during the difficult times in my life that being happy in my work is one way you occupy my heart with gladness.

✎ OCTOBER 10   Read Ecclesiastes 7:10.

We both sighed. Life used to be so uncomplicated. We spent most of our teaching time *teaching.* Now we've got to figure out how to pry students' hands off the computer keyboard to learn to work in groups. They are as information fed as one could ever hope, but they are hardly capable of working on a group project.

They seem to want all the control—or should I say exclusive access to the control *buttons!* Sharing a bit of space or tolerating the brainstorming process is an indulgence that is declining. One push of the button and they get multimedia answers to their questions!

Interaction was the key to enhancing learning; now it seems to be technology. But how ridiculous could my colleague and I be? Yearning for the old days wastes valuable time and energy. It doesn't mean we can't learn from the past—but wishing that the techniques of one generation would stay the same for the other makes us miss the exciting opportunities of the present!

So, present generation, watch out! I am about to plan a people interactive project related to your interactive CD-ROM. And I think we can use the multimedia option to create a *multistudent* exploration.

Lord, stop my yearning for the "good ol' days." Keep me celebrating both the "old" interpersonal skills and these intriguing new avenues of access to information and communication.

✎ OCTOBER 11   Read Ecclesiastes 7:11-12.

All month we have been talking about shelters. Our Native American unit has introduced us to the unique log houses of the Pacific coastal tribes. Beautiful ovoid and U-form art have sheltered the stories of the people housed in these cedar dwellings. In language arts we have discussed the protection that uniform spelling provides for a language—much to the groans of those who find spelling difficult. In science we have looked carefully at the important sheltering work that natural habitat provides to certain species. We have even played a simulation game to experience the fragile balances needed for wildfowl survival. Sheltering has even found its way into health class through a unit exploring the protective human immune system.

We all need a variety of shelters for our survival. But one shelter seems to provide protection above all the rest. The teacher in Ecclesiastes speaks of this stronghold as *wisdom.* We teachers also know the value of wisdom. Besides protecting, it also *preserves* life. All the other shelters might be in place, but this one must be present for life to continue. Today I'm grateful for the shelter of wisdom.

Lord, your Word says, "The fear of the LORD is the beginning of knowledge; fools despise wisdom and instruction" (Proverbs 1:7). May I infuse my teaching with knowledge. May I somehow grow in communicating wisdom so my students may see how richly it can shelter and sustain their lives.

✎ OCTOBER 12   Read Ecclesiastes 10:18.

Writing morning had arrived and before us stretched two hours of uninterrupted opportunity for creativity. The other students had gained a mature independence with the writing process, so I was free to focus on one student who could never quite get started.

He whined pitifully that there was "nothing to write about." I used my standard response, "Well, then, let's not write. Let's just talk. While we do, I'll jot down a few notes."

The "chat" took off quickly. We hit on one particular sport his family participates in that receives national coverage each year. He went on and on about all the details he knew and all the fascinating anecdotes that had occurred as he had watched competitions firsthand.

I kept jotting notes while he talked. When we were finished, I handed him an idea web. "Look, in the center is the sport. Extending from that topic are all the main ideas and supporting details you expressed about the topic. You've got a great nonfiction report here. I think it will be fascinating to your classmates. It certainly held me spellbound."

He smiled and grabbed a pencil.

"Success!" I prematurely celebrated.

After checking progress on all the other students, I headed back to this student's desk. A half hour had gone by and I couldn't wait to see what he had accomplished.

Nothing! It was his turn to work and he found doodling on the desk much easier. Last month I attributed his laziness to the new school year. Some students find it more difficult to leave behind the lazy days of summer. This month, however, I see a pattern of practiced dependency. Looks like this student is headed for sagging rafters and leaky roofs. I'd better get to work before winter sets in!

Lord, it seems that every year I find myself making "house repairs" caused by laziness or overdependence. Help me know how to teach my students to keep their own houses repaired.

✎ OCTOBER 13   Read Acts 4:13.

He blanched completely. How could he have been chosen for one of the narrators? He had always struggled with language—reading and spelling had taken all the tenacity he possessed. And now he was supposed to stand in front of the whole school and help narrate the fourth-grade drama production.

Since the play revolved around the Revolutionary War, he would have to master words like *colonization* and *revolution.* My colleague wisely smiled at him and said, "I chose this part for you because I thought you'd be very good at it."

"But," he said to me later, "I get stage fright—really bad."

As the play practice progressed, we saw one frightened fourth grader turn into a most courageous person. With poise and courage, he loudly spoke his narration. We knew he was afraid, but he moved through that fear to do what needed to be done.

A few days after the play, we honored the virtues shown by each student during the work and performance of the play. Some were honored for enthusiasm and diligence. Some were honored for creativity and unity. Each child was given a certificate for the character qualities we had seen during this community effort. As we presented one of the actors with a certificate for purposefulness and courage, the narrator jumped up and said, "I'm going to get one for courage—I just know it!"

And of course he was right.

Lord, courage always amazes and inspires us—just as it did the people in Acts. When it comes from those who work particularly hard for it, we are especially moved by its expression. Help us always to recognize our students for their courageous efforts.

✎ OCTOBER 14   Read Deuteronomy 31:6, 8.

He had been horrified by the basic reading homework for fourth graders at the start of the year. Four nights a week, he would be required to read aloud to a parent or guardian. His eyes had registered absolute terror. Reading had been his waterloo, and he was convinced it always would be.

But in our history discussions those first few weeks, I saw a child incredibly competent with words—able to discuss and question with great intelligence.

Fortunately, we found some time for the two of us—just teacher and student—to go to the library to pick out the first books he'd use to read aloud at home. Easy readers had some great sports stories that appealed to this incredibly skilled athlete. He left school that afternoon a little less fearful.

I discovered later that the first week was very difficult for him, filled with tears and frustration. Reading aloud is so vulnerable. The mistakes are so obvious—out there for all to hear. But I didn't change his requirements. I simply suggested to his mom that they read together in a quiet place away from other family members—a place where mistakes were okay and trying was lauded continually.

Today, weeks later, we had indoor recess. I caught him in the corner reading a short historical fiction novel. The terrified reader "couldn't put it down—it was so exciting." Could he read during recess? Would it be all right—just this once?

I couldn't believe my ears. To have him choose reading over recess is a miracle indeed! His courage reminds me how important it is not only to believe in our students but also to help them believe in themselves.

O Lord, who goes before us and with us, what seems like a reasonable expectation to us often strikes terror in our young students. May we recognize their fear and then help them to overcome it.

43

Read Proverbs 3:11-12.

Even before the leaves in many parts of the country began to change color and fall from the trees, one of my brightest students decided there was nothing more in this world he really needed to learn. He is an incredible student. However, at age ten, that is a rather dangerous conclusion to draw!

His decision spread negative attitudes through the entire class. At each introduction of new material, his yawn could be felt in every corner of the classroom. I finally decided to give him a little dose of reality.

I began giving instructions for a pop quiz. He lazily followed the directions, while his classmates were panicking for fear they weren't prepared. He, of course, would ace the silly thing.

However, while he had been yawning and spreading his disease of superiority, the remaining teachable students had learned some invaluable language arts skills. We completed the quiz and I used the lunchtime to quickly correct it. The results were as I had hoped. Maybe they would encourage this ten-year-old Einstein to keep a teachable heart for a little longer.

After recess, I informed the class that those who had mastered the material from the quiz could enjoy various projects, but those who could use a reteaching of the material would meet with me. As I read the list of those meeting with me, the student's mouth dropped.

Fortunately, now I can say his little foray into intellectual superiority was short-lived. He truly is a wise young intellectual, for he received the dose of reality with soberness—realizing there might still be a few things to learn.

Lord, help me be as willing and as sober to learn when I need reteaching.

Read Proverbs 3:21-22.

My fourth graders seem to be preoccupied with jewelry and hair. These days it is no longer gender specific. Even the boys are having to decide which earring to wear.

Today one student dashed up to me right before class and began showing me every charm on her new bracelet. The miniature skis were carefully placed beside a soccer ball. She smiled and said her soccer coach would like her to give up skiing so she can remain injury free. She had also placed a piano beside the soccer ball and skis. Her piano teacher wishes she would give up both so she'd have time for practicing. I smiled and said it looked to me as if she were very well rounded.

I couldn't help but think of another ornamentation that was spoken of in Proverbs. If these qualities are possessed, Solomon wrote, they will be like an ornament to grace your neck. The qualities are *sound judgment* and *discernment*. We were about to start a class meeting, so I thought I'd start like this: "Some of you took great care in choosing the right item to grace your wrists, your ears, your necks, and even your ankles today. Our topic is about a different kind of ornamentation—some qualities that add ornamentation to who you are. . . ."

Lord, somehow help these students spend as much time adorning themselves with discernment as they do choosing just the right accessory.

✎ OCTOBER 17   Read Proverbs 6:30-31.

The trade simulation game was progressing noisily. Students had been assigned different identities for the Oregon Trail unit. Some were fur traders assigned to a fort. Some were Native Americans and some were pioneers. Each student had five items to trade and was lacking five items. Needless to say, the shouting and bartering were intense.

Finally, the open-air market sounds reached a tolerable level and students began to be seated, clinging triumphantly to the things they needed to survive another month in the Wild West!

After the last few students invented double and triple trades to finish acquiring their needs, we began to discuss the process. Many students expressed how much easier it is

45

to use currency in our age of variety and choice. The bartering/trading was fun—but would be very time consuming. Many explained the various steps they had taken to gain their desired items. The energetic discussion continued until one student raised his hand.

"I needed dried meat and saw some lying on the table—so I just stole it!"

The room of hardworking citizens became icy silent.

"Well," he stammered, "I sorta thought if people were really hungry they probably stole things back then, too."

We carefully discussed how poverty and hunger might make stealing a much larger temptation—and how feeding a starving family might throw deep questions at a well-packaged ethics framework. But we were also able to let him feel how others who had worked diligently felt about this process. It was a lesson about the effects of stealing, but it was also a lesson about integrity under difficult circumstances.

In many ways, our classrooms are like the Wild West. Our little pioneers have so much to learn in so many new frontiers—including the frontiers of morals and values. May we be dependable guides.

Lord, help me to use teachable moments to show my students the importance of values such as honesty and integrity.

 **OCTOBER 18**   **Read Proverbs 4:23, 24.**

It sounded like a locker room or a pirate ship more than a classroom, based on the vocabulary I was hearing. I stopped for a minute at the door where I could hear clearly without being seen. I waited, hoping naively that the students would realize how deeply words injure and would self-correct their behavior.

But it went on, and there were few left without wounds by the time I decided enough was enough. Genders had been disrespected. Sizes and shapes of bodies had been insensitively discussed—and valuable friendships were in precarious places at the moment.

I wanted to scream, "This will not happen in *my* classroom! These words will never be used again. The end—no discussion." However, something made me choose against my dictatorial mode of righting wrongs. I decided to come in as healer rather than as blaster—enough blasting had already taken place.

I started in a very soft tone: "Every one of you has something priceless that is the deepest part of you. We often call it the heart. It deserves to be well guarded. Some have said from it flow the springs of life. I guard your heart by respecting you—and in doing that I guard my own heart as well.

"Many of you let down your guard a few minutes ago. There are a lot of wounded hearts in this room—wounded deeply by words. In our classroom, before you speak, you must decide if the words will add refreshing water to someone's life—or if they will draw blood. Only one kind of words will be spoken here."

Teaching our students how to "keep [their] heart[s] with all vigilance" may be as important as any other curriculum we may teach.

Lord, perverse words wound. May we be your instruments in restoring our students and their friendships when they go sour.

✎ OCTOBER 19   Read Proverbs 10:23.

He had deliberately attempted to destroy several things. First it was something in the classroom. Then it was part of the playground equipment. The latest foray: public property at the local university. All of this was, of course, disturbing and deeply alarming. I would usually consider all of it a desperate cry for help from a student. But this one thinks it is "cool."

In fact, I am beginining to realize that many of the students in recent years at least have *appeared* to take great pride and pleasure in destructive pranks. It seems to have become quite desirable to get in trouble. The coolheaded plotting of destructive acts and the chilling pleasure found at their completion are becoming more common than any display of remorse or disturbed motive.

Pleasure in evil conduct is becoming quite the popular pastime.

The impulsiveness of youth without respect for others has become a dangerous ingredient in this student's life and in the lives of his peers. Even though Proverbs reassures us that these attitudes have been around a very long while, it is still disturbing to see them so well honed before age twelve.

But what can I do? Actually, I can do a lot. I can pray.

Lord, how can I help turn this one from destructiveness and winsomely present wisdom's constructive alternatives?

✎ OCTOBER 20   Read Proverbs 11:25.

Every classroom has "clock" students. They remind us of the time—constantly. They remind our students of every move they are to make—the second they are supposed to move. They make sure a truly engaging discussion is derailed by drawing attention to the time. Surely they will invent the next generation of precision timepieces, but in the meantime we all must bear patiently with them.

One afternoon a colleague overheard our special time-keeper reminding a fellow student about their shared extracurricular event that day. The nagging precision of timekeepers can be truly annoying. My colleague said she waited for the typical exasperated response of, "I know! I know! I *know* we have chorus!" It seemed the only response from one so constantly reminded about the precise second of this particular activity.

But, the timekeeper had encountered the refresher of the class. And the refresher had a surprise for Mr. Precision. He smiled graciously and almost conspiratorily whispered, "I know—and guess what? I brought an extra big snack. I'll share it with you before chorus."

Lord, we need both timekeepers and refreshers. But thanks especially for the refreshers, who turn potential irritation into an opportunity for kindness.

I think another Anne of Green Gables has emerged! She is definitely as winsome and outgoing. The hair is wrong, however—carrottop would never fit this dark-haired student. Yet she can be accused, as Anne was, of being able to "talk the hind leg off a mule."

The talk is always engaging. In fact, she often holds the entire class spellbound—until, of course, the story begins to spill over into lunchtime. No one—however engaging—can hold fourth graders' attention one minute into lunchtime.

At first I gave her high assessment marks in verbal fluency—jotting a note that verbal condensing would be our target rather than the usual encouragement of expression. Then I began to see another interesting side to the words. It became apparent that many of her academic skills have taken great effort to achieve—and will take great effort to maintain and improve.

During spelling drills, I catch her talking. During language art work, she is talking. During silent sustained reading, she finds a way to talk. And as engaging as her stories are, she has been using them to avoid the hard work of tackling new skills.

So now I'm trying to show her that this amazing verbal fluency can be a gift or a disability. If she applies that fluency to other uses of language—such as grammar, writing, and spelling—she can soar. But if she uses it to avoid hard work, her own tongue will trip her. I hope I will be able to give her the confidence to work hard and talk *later.*

Lord, help me to teach all of my students the value of words used wisely.

Suddenly the backfield erupted with angry gestures. I couldn't hear the words from where I was playing referee, but the nonverbal cues signaled serious conflict.

The play had not gone the way one competitive player

had hoped, and he was determined to pin his disappointment on a less aggressive player. He successfully destroyed any attempts his teammate might have made to improve her playing. She sulked away into a corner. Meanwhile, the "defense attorney" for the entire world jumped into the fray. She was not about to allow such harsh words to demoralize a teammate.

"You pervert!" she screamed indignantly at the unkind accuser. His retort was equally degrading. Soon they were into it farther than either of these usually gracious students would ever have gone.

I finally pulled them out of the game. As we tried to unravel the maze of derogatory comments and get to the point of the conflict, I realized the entire issue had become lost in the barrage of disparaging words.

After some separate moments to let the tempers cool, both students began to see that even one kind word at the beginning of all the problems would have prevented incredible hurt. If the competitive student could have encouraged his less aggressive teammate, she might have rallied to work hard with him toward their common goal of the game. And if the "defense attorney" had held her tongue, or had used it to turn away anger rather than stir it up, P.E. might have actually been fun.

Lord, our first response to disappointment is often unkind words. Help me teach—and model—that a soft answer turns away wrath.

 **OCTOBER 23**   **Read Proverbs 15:4.**

As the weeks of fall pass, the curriculum is getting harder and harder for my young students. They are at the pivotal age between being fed foundational skills and learning how to self-nourish. More self-discipline and more confidence are needed to ensure academic success. Daily, I concentrate on praise for their attempts—and many are responding to the extra encouragement.

However, three students continue to find excuses for

unfinished homework and incomplete tasks. They are master artists at "the-dog-ate-it" syndrome. I wonder what will make them face the realities of their own self-deception.

They are becoming so astute at excuses that today, I finally informed one student he would be at the top of the class if he would spend as much creativity on his daily tasks as he spends inventing excuses. He stopped dead in his tracks. "Yes," I continued, "you have shown an incredible amount of creativity and diligence with these excuses. How about employing those wonderful gifts in the learning process? I guarantee you will go far!"

He slowly turned away and headed back to his desk where he would have to quickly invent another excuse or really work hard to finish his task before recess. He slumped for a moment, realizing I had seen through his various shams. He is incredibly capable; this white-lying to himself and to me is beginning to cost him.

Fortunately, he sat taller and turned toward his project, choosing—at least today—to stop the self-deceit and employ his amazing talents to complete his project.

When I'm tempted to speak a harsh word to a student, I try to remind myself that "a gentle tongue is a tree of life, but perverseness in it breaks the spirit" (Proverbs 15:4). Today I think I see the promise of new growth.

Lord, help me speak healing words to these students—especially when self-deception begins to be a habit.

✎ OCTOBER 24   Read Proverbs 15:13.

I study faces the first few minutes of class every day. I put up a basic task that can be completed without questions. Then while the students are diligently working, I study their faces. I can usually tell which ones have had overnights, baseball tournaments, or a long weekend with the parent that is not the full-time caregiver. I can also tell which ones are rested physically—and emotionally. It all shows on their faces. Those expressions warn me about the coming day—and help govern my expectations.

So today during "face inspection," I was very surprised to see tears coming from one student who always wears a glowing, peaceful countenance. She does not have an easy life, but she always seems to be rested and ready to learn. *If she is having a hard day,* I thought, *we might all need a slower pace.*

The day would need to be gentle. The tasks would have to be redesigned to capture a quieter atmosphere. Slowly, I began the day using a quiet voice. We bumped the wild parts-of-speech game to tomorrow's agenda and kept a routine that allowed predictability. Today was not the day to throw the chicks out of the nest to see if they could fly; we had some gentle feeding to accomplish. Maybe tomorrow I can push again.

Lord, I look to your countenance for wisdom to discern the faces of these young learners. Grant me flexibility and wisdom to tailor curriculum to their hearts as well as to their minds.

✎ OCTOBER 25   Read Proverbs 15:15.

He simply has no reason to be so happy. He has severe learning disabilities. He is hopelessly behind in reading. Spelling is impossible for him, and math facts leave his memory as soon as he learns them. But despite all of that, he approaches each task with diligence and eagerness. He seems determined to master whatever material is placed in front of him, no matter how long it takes. And the most surprising part of it all is that he does it all cheerfully!

Meanwhile his highly capable counterpart approaches things quite differently. They are similar in height and build. Their birthdays are close and they are often seen playing together at recess. But in the classroom, no two could be so opposite. While one struggles, the other soars. While one takes all class hour to complete the simplest task, the other keeps me running ragged for enrichment projects.

And yet, the most conspicuous contrast between the two is expressed in attitudes. The highly capable student meets every task with a groan. Each enrichment project is "too hard," "too easy," "not colorful enough," "too colorful," or simply "not his style!" Meanwhile, the highly struggling student meets each task with a diligent, adventurous spirit.

As I watch them today, I am reminded that I'm both teacher and student in this classroom. Today's lesson: No matter what we have or don't have, the heart determines feast or famine.

Lord, give me a cheerful heart today and every day.

✎ OCTOBER 26   Read Proverbs 16:16.

We had launched into a discussion of birthdays. If any ten-year-old needs verbal language practice, the birthday topic will do it! Fifteen fourth graders took off with it and, of course, hardly gave one another a chance to speak. *Oh, well,* I thought to myself, *the lesson objective is verbal skills instead of listening skills!*

The topic was filled with memories of trips to water parks, overnights at cabins, and rented ice-skating rinks. It didn't take long to circle around to the gift subtopic. Birthday wants were prolific—horses, Nike Airs, CD-ROM games, and tame monkeys. The dreaming seemed to get more and more outrageous (with increased sticker shock) as the discussion continued.

One student, however, sat quietly back. She had offered several memories but the gift topic had silenced her. She was an incredible student—always eager for more information and always puzzling about wise ways to use her knowledge. I finally found a second of silence in which to ask her about her birthday desires.

She look around sheepishly at her peers. "You obviously want something vastly different from what has been mentioned," I quietly suggested.

She nodded shyly and then quietly but passionately said, "If I could have anything in the world, it would be the new set of *Oxford* encyclopedias we just got for school. I love those and I want to know everything in them!"

What a rare and precious gift it is when we discover such

an appetite for information in the classroom! Our challenge is to feed the appetite without completely satisfying the hunger.

Lord, thank you for those students who hunger for knowledge. Help us to both feed them and whet their appetites for even more knowledge and wisdom.

✎ OCTOBER 27 Read Isaiah 65:17-19.

Cheers erupted after the explanation of a homework assignment. Quite a strange phenomenon, to say the least. But, on the other hand, it shouldn't have been surprising. The assignment was to create a world.

We had been studying C. S. Lewis's fantasy series, *The Chronicles of Narnia,* and along our journey through these books, we had enjoyed Lewis's early childhood creations. Long before the Narnia series was written, Lewis experimented with the land of Boxen. He had drawn a picture of one of his characters, Lord Big of Boxen. The creature looked like a frog in a waistcoat—which charmed my students completely. He had also sketched an imaginary world titled "Animal Land." The students were fascinated that someone who had written about something as wonderful as Narnia began experimenting with fantasy worlds and characters at their age.

When given the task to create their imaginary world, these image-bearers embraced the task immediately. We were created to create—and although our medium is from something to something else while God's is from nothing to something—still we yearn to mimic him.

The worlds were as varied and delightful as the children themselves. Some were uniquely shaped; some had unearthly creatures to inhabit them; some employed all the landform elements from social studies into an imaginary island. All were fascinating.

Lord, thank you for this yearning to create—in order to mimic the One whose image we all bear.

The ambitious study groups were poring over the resources with eagerness. They all seemed determined to make an artistic and accurate contribution to the wall map of C. S. Lewis's land of Narnia. They studied original illustrations of Narnia created by Pauline Baynes; they skimmed books to discern events and places. All seemed imaginatively engaged—all except one.

At first I didn't notice him. He had cleverly hidden behind the most ambitious student in his group. He was watching the intense work with one eye and watching me with the other. I wandered purposefully from group to group keeping records of individual contributions and group dynamics. Carefully he was judging the amount of time he had left before I discovered his inactivity.

Unfortunately, I changed my route and descended on his group swiftly. Caught too early, he bawled pitifully that he had nothing to do. I simply responded: "That's very interesting. I wonder if your group would agree with that."

His group had had it with his lack of participation and exposed him completely. Apparently, they had graciously offered him a multitude of tasks—all of which he had either refused or not completed. With great insight, the leader of the group blurted, "We are all working hard but you. You're going to ruin it all."

I knew this student would never directly destroy anything or anyone, but indirectly he was doing just that. I hoped my intervention would serve as a "wake-up" call before he and his entire group would have to suffer the consequences of his laziness. Either way, it would be an important lesson to learn.

Lord, help us to teach our students that laziness can be destructive not only to ourselves but also to others.

In a small classroom, issues of personal space can be crucial. All morning long, the most crowded corner was erupting in territorial disputes. Finally, we rearranged the room to allow more individual space. It was appropriate to create some personal territory and yet, some students were creating fences out of tape and paper. Respecting the need for space had disintegrated into the poverty of keeping one another out.

However, in the midst of these disputes, two students modeled a different attitude. They were finished with their morning work and wanted to create more details for our wall map of Narnia.

Both students wanted to create the White Witch's castle. *Hmm,* I thought to myself, *I wonder how this idea territory will be worked out.* I decided, fortunately, to watch rather than intervene with peace treaty ideas. Sure enough, they did it!

One student graciously acknowledged the other's artistic ability and suggested she draw the castle. Then the artist relinquished her castle to the other student to color in since he was "so good at that part." Quietly and happily, they divided up the repsonsibilities using one another's strengths. They had figured out a way to live together, feeling the abundance of joint ownership and avoiding the poverty of stinginess.

Lord, help us learn from our students who are wise enough to choose teamwork rather than territorialism.

 **OCTOBER 30**   **Read Proverbs 20:4.**

The big history test loomed over their heads. Several students were pulling out notes and diligently reviewing. Some had formed impromptu study groups around the room and were asking review questions of one another. I was feeling quite satisfied. These young students showed great energy in developing study strategies for traditional testing situations. I even heard some students setting up "what-if" situations that could be answered by synthesizing the factual information into usable principles.

However, one student, who had been absent several days in a row, looked bewildered. I wandered over to her and asked how her review work for the test was coming. "I don't know any of this," she complained. I affirmed that she had been absent frequently, which made it all the more imperative to develop an efficient review strategy. I suggested she join one of the study groups and dive in. After thirty minutes of review time, she still sat bewildered.

The next two days of review, she used the same technique of doing nothing. Despite strong encouragement from me and her peers, she was immobile.

On test day, I watched her looking frantically around. All papers were covered; all notes were out of view. She had nothing to draw from despite repeated in-class opportunities to master material.

The importance of "plow[ing] in season" is an appropriate lesson for this harvest season. She had remained idle during plowing season. Now when harvest was essential, nothing came up in her fields. Perhaps after feeling the full effect of empty "fields," next plowing season she'll be ready to work with energized diligence.

Lord, this is my "plowing season." Help me to sow seeds of diligence in my young students.

✏ OCTOBER 31   Read Proverbs 24:13-14.

The party was a great success. Industrious parents spent hours creating special treats for the students. We had spent art time cutting out pumpkins and other decorations for the classroom.

With such capable parent help, I could stand back and reflect. The scene was one of excitement and activity as the children talked and enjoyed the delicious treats prepared for them. They tasted and tasted until I was surprised that children could tolerate so much sugar without exploding out of the building. The energy level was certainly kicking in, and I could tell it was almost time for one reflective teacher to reenter the arena with a few behavior reminders.

I couldn't help but think of one passage from Proverbs. The writer says, "Eat honey, my son, for it is good; honey from the comb is sweet to your taste." He uses our human delight in sweets to go on to teach a profound lesson: "Know also that wisdom is sweet to your soul; if you find it, there is a future hope for you, and your hope will not be cut off" (Proverbs 24:13-14 NIV).

Lord, help me package wisdom as enticingly as party treats this year.

November

Striving to be Faithful

Anne Wilcox

NOVEMBER 1   Read Romans 8:18-27.

am so restless today. Even the students are mirroring it. They can hardly settle in to the basic tasks and I, frankly, am discontent with the basics. The newness of the school year has worn off and the holidays are fast approaching. That's partly it; but there's more. Maybe I need to be teaching a different age group. Maybe I need to go back to school. Maybe I should have prepared differently. Maybe I should change professions. Maybe I should move out of the city into the country.

Maybe today is simply a day to feel intensely that all of us are, as C. S. Lewis puts it in *The Weight of Glory,* "on the outside of the world, the wrong side of the door." This restlessness is a yearning for completion. It may signal a need for some changes in the above arenas, but primarily it lies much deeper. I want to be inside. I want to be face-to-face with the One who made and loved me. Enough of this "through a glass, darkly" (I Corinthians 13:12 KJV)! I want to *know* fully as I am known— and no amount of changes on an earthly level can get at this ache. Lewis says, "And to be at last summoned inside would be

59

both glory and honour beyond all our merits and also the healing of that old ache."

Next time you find yourself particularly restless, ask yourself if your restlessness may be an outward sign of an inward longing.

Praise be to you, Lord, for the hope of someday being summoned inside. Meanwhile, please walk me through this restless yearning so I can get this classroom back on track.

✎ NOVEMBER 2   Read Proverbs 25:13.

Harvest takes everything out of those working the land. Once when I visited a farm in northern Idaho, I couldn't help noticing how exhausted the workers were in the wheat and lentil fields. They were hot, thirsty, and tired, but the crops were ready. No luxury of sleep or cool refreshment could be allowed if the crops were to be harvested on time.

What refreshment a gentle snow would create in the heat of harvest. But snow rarely comes so early. The writer of Proverbs 25:13 must have been dreaming.

And yet, I have in my class someone as refreshing as snow might be at harvest. She is a quiet, retiring student—one for whom initiative is difficult. She often hesitates before participating in any project or discussion. Her timidity doesn't correspond to her skill level or her amazing creative abilities. Recently I decided to begin giving her responsibilities beyond the usual required in class. I was curious to see whether she would rise to the occasion or whether she would need more training with taking initiative.

Day after day I give her errands to run and tasks to perform. Never once has she failed to complete the duties entrusted to her. Efficiently and conscientiously, she has performed each task until now I know I have a trustworthy messenger and worker. I know I will only have to give instructions once.

How quickly she began refreshing the spirit of this teacher!

Lord, faithfulness is rare. Help me show those hesitant students what an incredible gift they have to contribute.

✎ NOVEMBER 3   Read Proverbs 25:16.

"Can we have another one? Why not three instead of two?" "Let's do it again. One time just isn't enough." If it brings pleasure or delight, surely it should be repeated again and again and again.

At least that seems to be the philosophy of my students. After hearing this philosophy expressed in a variety of ways, I've decided to try a little experiment. One of their favorite tasks is a wild, loud, timed spelling exercise. Until recently it has been cheered. Now, however, after weeks and weeks of repetition, it is beginning to receive a few groans. Too much of a good thing has begun to sour.

Another task gaining rave reviews and requests for "Again! Again!" is a trade simulation game. The first time through was thrilling. The second time through was fun. The third time through enthusiasm waned—and I was tempted to have them do it a fourth and a fifth time just to feel the futile attempts to grasp pleasure and excitement. Sooner or later, the thrill will be over, and often too much can choke you. Sooner or later, it's a lesson we all must learn.

Lord, help me to create learning environments and experiences that keep my students wanting more—and, at the same time, help me to encourage gratitude and contentment. Choking on too much of a good thing is not good.

✎ NOVEMBER 4   Read Proverbs 25:19.

Every time I turn around, I am having to redo their tasks. Getting their attention is even worse. My helpers for the week are cruising through a different port, I've decided. This "helper" idea, which is supposed to increase efficiency, is certainly not working with these two!

Today, after struggling to gain their attention, I turned

them loose to "help" while I taught. One minute into my introduction, I realized *turned loose* perfectly described what was happening.

Instead of quietly passing out the supplies for the next project, they had turned the papers into magic carpets that they flew onto each desk. Instead of handing each student a pen, the pens were dive-bombing onto—and off of—each desk! Although I usually welcome creativity, this was not working. Stopping everything, I firmly repeated the first instructions. Finally, their task was completed responsibly, and I had worked overtime to restore classroom order. How does one compete with magic carpets and bombs?

At the end of the day, I again employed my "helpers" to collect papers and projects. Since dismissal depended on their efficiency, they were done in a flash. However, after the dust cleared, I realized the piles were in shambles! They had not bothered to follow my instructions for gathering the various pieces of the day's work. Sorting through the stack would take me another half hour. The metaphors of a bad tooth and a lame foot are perfect for reliance on the unfaithful.

Lord, I'm not so different from my young students. How often do I disappoint you, refusing to follow your instructions? Help me also to move toward faithfulness as your wisdom enables me to guide them.

 **NOVEMBER 5**   **Read Proverbs 25:20.**

There has been a rash of pet accidents among my students. First one student's cat had surgery, leaving it with a dragging front leg. Then another student's cat, who had been a part of the family for longer than the child's age, died. After that a frog and a hamster met their doom. As each incident has been reported, I've watched the students' responses closely.

For some, the immediate attempt to comfort is expressed by trying to "cheer up" the one bereft of a pet. Words like, "Well, at least it isn't suffering anymore," or "Frogs aren't really supposed to live very long, you know," are said in an attempt to help. Another strategy is the come-play-with-me-at-recess-and-maybe-you'll-forget-it approach. Through all of it, I can see ten-year-olds trying to help—trying to ease loss and sometimes making it worse.

As the wisdom writer says in Proverbs, singing songs to a heavy heart or trying to distract a heavy heart is like taking away a garment on a cold day or like pouring vinegar on soda.

Finally, someone has tried a new approach. The student whose cat will forever drag his front leg and the student whose cat died have found each other. Together they have written about their losses and together they shared memories. Heavy hearts have been listened to—not brushed off. A new sense of camaraderie between classmates has begun.

I'm grateful for these ten-year-olds' example of dealing wisely with heavy hearts.

Lord, may my students—and their teacher—remember the best way to help those experiencing loss.

✎ NOVEMBER 6   Read I Peter 2:17.

I'd had it! My every attempt to teach had been sabotaged by cute remarks. Obviously, the students' agenda for the afternoon was not state history, but a contest for who's the cleverest in the land. Smart-mouthing the teacher seemed hotter than video games this week—and my patience was gone!

I scrapped all learning activities and put them to work individually. No talking; no creativity—just fill in the blank! Fortunately time rescues all teachers; there is at the end of every day a final bell. However, I have a hard time letting students leave with tension between us. So I tried my five-minutes-before-the-bell lecture. After one minute of lecture, a student raised her hand.

"I think I know what the problem was this afternoon," she said quietly.

"What do you think was going on?" I dared to ask.

"I think we weren't showing you any respect," she answered.

Several nonverbal agreements were expressed.

"Maybe that's why I was so angry," I answered. "Did I do something to give you permission to treat me that way today?"

Fortunately her answer was no, so I asked her what respect would look like in this classroom.

"Well, first of all we would give you our attention. Then, in order to respect each other's need to learn, we wouldn't show off; we'd help each other learn."

Respect—the First Letter of Peter refers to it as honor. It's important not only in the classroom, but also in every area of life.

Lord, give us more children who not only have heard the word respect *but also can define it. May I also find ways to respect my students—even the most difficult ones—under the most difficult circumstances.*

✎ NOVEMBER 7   Read Proverbs 26:4.

I stopped the entire class and began lecturing furiously about the inattentive chatter of one student. How dare she disrupt the rest of the student body with her inability to control her tongue. On and on I went about the importance of listening attentively when directions are being given and of giving others a chance to speak during group projects.

Earlier in the day her verbosity had dominated her literature circle, giving no one else in her group a chance to offer opinions or insights. Then during grammar review, she blurted out every answer, making it impossible for others to have thinking time. Later, as I read aloud from the class book, she had a comment or question for every paragraph. Now, as I was giving homework instructions, she simply could not wait for me to finish even one sentence before her barrage of questions surfaced.

I had had it! So what did I do? I dominated the situation

with a mountain of words. I disrupted the entire class, holding them hostage to words only one student needed to hear. I was doing exactly what my student had done.

Next time she starts, I will simply say, "You may leave the classroom for a control time. I will trust you to know when your listening skills are back under control, so that you may join us again."

Lord, thanks for this mirror of folly. May my words be few when correcting too many words!

✎ **NOVEMBER 8**   **Read Proverbs 27:1.**

Efficiency has always been a welcome partner of mine, and I have always taken my lesson planning seriously. The hours I spend designing units that meet my students' needs are as crucial as the hours I spend in the classroom.

Or so I used to think. Fortunately, after yesterday, I'm not so proud. Nor do I view my lesson plans as sacredly as I once did. Yesterday changed all of that.

I had worked so hard at designing a state history unit that met various learning styles. I had diligently researched the content of the unit; I had even traveled to places unfamiliar to me in the state in order to teach "firsthand." I had designed a map blanket so the kinetic learners could run to geographic locations rather than simply look at a map. I had also reviewed Gardner's Multiple Intelligences to make sure the unit included ways to interact with the material through each of those intelligences.

Then yesterday hit. Our state had an earthquake. Suddenly, even the best lesson plans in the world were irrelevant. What was important was one topic—earthquakes. Sending students to every resource available, they discovered what they wanted to know that day. Every learning style and every intelligence merged into one goal. No behavior management was needed; no reminding of diligence was required. The unexpected created real curiosity, and all the possible educational objectives were achieved—without my diligent plans.

Lord, though I won't throw out my lesson plans entirely, help me see that on some days true education comes through the unexpected.

✎ NOVEMBER 9 Read Proverbs 27:7.

Several years ago I was working in a remedial writing lab. College students from every background were appearing in the lab in various states of panic. Somehow their strategies for writing in high school didn't fulfill collegiate demands for well-reasoned prose. By the time they reached me, they were usually destitute enough to work heartily.

One student was more diligent than all the rest. He had emigrated from Cambodia and was desperate to succeed at the college level. His English, though astonishingly good for his short time in the United States, was often difficult to decipher. His prose was filled with the expected grammatical errors. As we worked together, I began suspecting he was humiliated when I had to ask him to repeat himself.

One day I pulled him aside and spoke of his discomfort. I praised him for his recent paper and for being willing to repeat himself when I didn't understand him. I asked if there could be a more comfortable way for us to communicate.

"You don't understand," he replied. "In my religion, it is a shame to reincarnate as a woman. For me to depend on you for my college success is a deeper shame."

"Then why do you stay?" I asked.

"Because I am hungry to learn—and," he said as he lowered his eyes and tried to hide a faint smile, "because you have much to teach me."

I realized how bitter the experience must be from his worldview—yet I knew I had the opportunity to turn the bitter to honey now that he was eating.

Lord, when we're hungry enough, even the bitter is sweet. Keep me hungry for your Word and your way, Lord, so that I may taste the sweetness in even the bitter experiences of life.

        Read Proverbs 26:18-19.

The phrase "only kidding" was spreading like a disease through the classroom. Who began the infection or why it was so contagious has not been resolved. However, the banning of these words seemed like the only solution.

At first they were used to mask a lack of tact. One student remarked, "Those pants are too tight on you, aren't they? You must be getting fat—just kidding." Then the phrase began to infiltrate relational issues. One day I overheard one little girl say, "I don't like you anymore—just kidding." Finally, I heard lies being sanctioned by this unique little phrase. "I'll invite you to my birthday party," one student promised. Her new classmate's eyes lit up. "Just kidding," she taunted.

It was time to intervene. We had talked previously about the words that were appropriate and inappropriate for school use. Most of our discussions had centered around "bad" words. Now it was time to have a discussion about supposedly innocent words that had become very inappropriate. "Just kidding" was providing opportunities to forget tact, to destroy friendships, and to deeply hurt feelings. So today we explored honest, yet tactful ways of communicating and decided that "just kidding" will join the list of inappropriate words for school usage.

The wisdom writer was correct. A person who deceives a [classmate] and says, "I was only joking!" is like a madman shooting deadly firebrands or arrows.

Lord, give us all wisdom—teacher and students—to use honesty graced by tact.

        Read Proverbs 26:20.

I listened long enough to wonder whether I had been transported to England and was witnessing the feud between the Montagues and the Capulets. Then I wondered if the Appalachian feud between the McCoys and the Hatfields might be a closer analogy.

Two students were insisting on a feud. There was no hope of resolution. If put anywhere in the same location, they were convinced the feuding would begin again. When I finally pulled the warring sides apart and asked for a truce, fascinating information was revealed. The conflict had started in kindergarten over—well, they couldn't remember what—but it had started then. And they could remember several of the battles. However, the initial beginning of the conflict was long forgotten.

Now they had rallied sides, and others were being drawn into the pranks of revenge they had designed for one another. Both justified their actions based on the other's previous attack. Gossip about the other's attitudes and actions were fueling all sorts of continued skirmishes.

Finally, I assigned them a new task, since they were investing so much energy and creativity into these skirmishes. I chose a metaphor that should hit home so soon after a devastating forest fire in our state. They were to see the feud as a fire. At the end of each week, they were to report to me the ways they had doused the fire. They could not add wood to the fire; they had to douse it before the entire forest—or classroom—was destroyed.

Lord, my students are so young to sustain an elaborate feud. Give them new ways to resolve conflict!

✎ **NOVEMBER 12**   **Read Proverbs 27:9, 17.**

Things weren't quite right with the teaching staff. I was picking up comments that indicated others felt I could do a bit of changing. I wondered what others who worked closely with me might be thinking. Then I wondered if I really wanted to know. After all, it's much more comfortable to simply stay the same.

Finally, I decided to initiate conversation with two of my colleagues in particular. I was right; they had some suggestions I needed to hear. Coming from many more years of teaching than I had experienced, they had greater insight into the value of curricular flexibility. Since flexibility is not a strong virtue of mine, I had the opportunity to ask how I might maintain my content standards and still move closer to a balance between content and flexibility.

They also had observations about my inevitable burnout if I continued operating at such a high level of workload and expectation. As a new teacher, I simply thought that was how the job worked. Carefully and graciously, they made suggestions for my attitudes of invincibility and godlike influence on my students. Instead of changing the world, I might think of a more manageable goal—like moving one student a little closer to writing fluency.

On and on we talked, and I could not help but think that earnest counsel from friends is like perfume, and one person sharpens another like iron sharpens iron.

Lord, thank you for the perfume and the iron. One is pleasant; one is painful. But both are necessary for friendship and growth.

✎ NOVEMBER 13   Read Proverbs 27:21.

Recently when my students needed to master the eight parts of speech, I administered pop quizzes and games. Again and again throughout the unit, they were required to list those eight demons of grammar and play a modified bingo game called "Gramo." They loved the game, and I could quickly tell whether or not they were gaining appropriate skills.

In all of this skill and information mastery, I never once thought of praise as an assessment tool. In my mind, praise is a way to encourage. However, the Proverbs suggest that people are not only encouraged but also *tested* by the praise they receive. So I've decided to try it on my students.

This morning I began by praising the diligence and creativity they have shown so far this year. I also praised them for accomplishing many things with enthusiasm. The resulting work-time was fascinating. Some students dived into their tasks to fill the shoes of the praise, so to speak. Others, however, decided they'd done enough. If they had been so great so far—why push it? How about a break?

Lord, the Proverbs are right. Much is revealed about students in the aftermath of praise. Help me to make the best use of my observations.

✎ **NOVEMBER 14**   **Read Proverbs 28:1.**

A guilty run is always a dead giveaway. He decided to slam-dunk his unfinished beverage in the trash can. I was turned the other way, intent on conversation with a colleague. The slam dunk was miraculously silent, but the unfinished beverage still responded to the Michael Jordan–like forces. Spraying heavenward, the sticky-sweet pop created a new art form on the meticulously decorated bulletin board. Hours of student work had been invested to create phonetics-related calendars in this classroom. Now the calendar was only fitting for a New Year's confetti scene. Too bad it is only November.

The students who were appropriately disposing of their lunches when the slam dunk hit, turned white. I turned just in time to see the crowd move out. No one wanted to be associated with the action. If the guilty student had merely moved aside, I would have simply thought it was an accident and would have helped the students clean up the mess and restore their beautiful calendar as much as possible.

However, his dead run and sheepish backward glance assisted my decision to take another course of action.

"Your actions have just informed me that you think you did something inappropriate," I said after stopping the culprit. He admitted to knowing exactly what he was up to, and I gave him the entire cleanup job.

I'm grateful that he still feels guilty and acts guilty when he has knowingly violated appropriate conduct.

Lord, help me to encourage honesty and a sense of accountability in my students while also disciplining them appropriately.

✎ **NOVEMBER 15**   **Read Psalm 32:1-5; Proverbs 28:13.**

I pulled her away from the lunchroom hubbub to get to the bottom of things. All student and parent reports confirmed her guilt. In previous years under these circumstances, I would simply tell the student I had the information that implicated him or her. Then together we would design an appropriate project of restitution. But I've begun to see the value of confession. Waiting for the student to come forward takes much longer, but feeling the weight of wrongdoing and then experiencing the re-creating process of confession are worth the wait.

Quietly, I told this student what I had heard and asked if she wanted to tell me anything more about it. She swore she knew nothing. I excused her with these words, "If something you've forgotten comes to mind, would you please call me aside so we can talk further about this?" She nodded and bolted back to lunch.

In the following days, I watched her nonverbal signs. She rarely met my eye. She frantically chewed her nails whenever the topic arose. Her information during class discussions regarding the issue continued to be contradictory. Slowly, it began to eclipse her abilities to function academically and socially.

Finally, one day she stood near me looking tentative. I greeted her and said it looked to me like she had some more information to tell me. Sure enough, a tearful confession began. Forgiveness and praise for truthfulness came first. Then we proceeded with a clear plan for changed behavior and restitution.

Lord, may mercy and prosperity follow such an honest confession.

✎ **NOVEMBER 16**   **Read Proverbs 28:19.**

He had worked diligently all his early school years. Despite learning disabilities—or maybe because of them— we could always count on him to be faithful. Many times he was held up as the example for consistency—until fourth grade.

For some reason he had decided it was time to try laziness. After all, he was cool, and who needed to do all this extra work? His younger winsomeness evaporated into resistance, and he began escaping reading club, which was designed to give under-grade-level students a boost with word attack skills. Usually he hung out with friends a few minutes after the bell rang. On reading club days, he mysteriously disappeared before any of us could catch him.

Then in the classroom, he began to show the same attitudes toward work. Slipping and sliding through unfinished assignments became the norm. One day I "invited" him to join me during lunch recess.

"Since you have decided to have recess during class, you'll be working during recess. If you decide to begin working again during class—recess will again be yours."

He was furious. Stomping into my class he growled, "When you're grown up and go to work, they don't make you stay in for lunch if you don't finish something!"

"You're absolutely right," I told him. As I paused he looked bewildered that I would agree with him just when he was trying to pick a good fight. "You are correct," I reassured him. "They don't keep you in for lunch. They *fire* you! Please take a seat and get busy."

Lord, help me, with firmness and humor, to keep them from chasing fantasies.

✏ NOVEMBER 17   Read Proverbs 28:20.

The get-rich-quick mentality shows up very early in life. Unfortunately, long before gamblers hit the racetrack or long lines form for the latest lottery ticket, teachers are watching the impulse.

Instead of putting in the tough work of math facts drills, students write "cheat" charts in the back of their three-ring binders. Someday, they reason, the facts will miraculously be theirs. Why put in the effort now?

The workbook "rushers" dash toward the page goal for the day, not pausing to notice if the work is done accurately. They want to finish first; gaining skills along the way is not the issue—for them.

Legible writing also seems to carry an aura of mystery.

Daily effort is ignored in hopes that neatness will arrive on its own—out of the blue.

Mastery of information is assumed to happen without study and review. Somehow, when the test hits, the information will magically be drawn from an empty hat.

Fortunately, the need for mathematical thinking arises when the three-ring binder is out of reach. Luckily, the time to do workbook corrections can be taken painfully out of a recess break. Illegible papers can be refused with instructions to rewrite—and creative testing can reveal who has and has not truly mastered the material.

The resulting "poverty" from shortcuts can be felt quickly in the classroom, and encouragement to return to faithful hard work can be daily enforced.

Lord, give me creative ways for my students to feel the poverty of shortcuts and the abundant yield of faithfulness.

✎ **NOVEMBER 18**   **Read Proverbs 18:18.**

Every educational training program should include a course on settling disputes. If there was ever an age of justice, it is the age of ten-year-olds. They are forever testing equality and fairness. They don't sleep until every slight violation is addressed. Taking turns can never be orchestrated with enough equity. No matter how careful one is about objectivity and impartiality, they will find an infraction. For them, each case is crucial enough to be tried before the Supreme Court.

However, today in class, the highest justices of the land were absent. Although my class was convinced they should have appeared on their behalf, I reassured them that maybe we could find a solution without intervention from the federal courts. The dispute centered around which students could be my two class helpers for the week. I made the mistake of not keeping meticulous records and frankly, I could not remember who had missed their turn.

As the dispute raged, several stories emerged. Some were sure they had never had the esteemed privilege. Others were convinced they had been forever passed over and should certainly be picked this time. Finally, after some interventions about settling disputes, we resorted to "casting lots." I chose a number and the two closest to my choice were class helpers.

Proverbs seems to think this keeps the peace—and it did that day in class. I wonder, though, *What would the Supreme Court think?*

Lord, give me ways to deal justly—especially with my young students.

 **NOVEMBER 19**   **Read Proverbs 29:6.**

Every time a new task was introduced, his response was a groan. It happens to be cool this year to be negative—or so he thought. When siblings were talked about, he hated his. When spelling assignments were given, you'd think I had planned his death. Even if a new game was introduced in P.E., he was certain to sabotage its excitement.

So I began mentioning the attitude of gratitude. Then I focused our November history lessons to include the gratitude shown by past generations. However, nothing worked. He never had a light moment of singing—never a glad countenance.

In speaking with his parents, I discovered no major reasons for this attitude. I suspect it had simply become a bad habit. However, because it had begun to infect the entire class, I decided this little guy needed to be snared by his own game.

Carefully, I chose a project on a topic that was his passion. Sure enough, as I introduced it he said, "Oh, yuck!" Quickly and decisively I snapped the trap shut.

"I'm only inviting those students who are grateful for this project to participate. I guess you'll need to head to the principal for other work. Thank you for leaving now so we can enjoy this project."

Fortunately, it only took one time in the trap for him to lose the bad attitude habit!

Lord, may this student have new times of singing and gladness. When he slips back into the negative habit, may he remember the trap.

I had never seen this fourth grader happier! "What are you up to this time, my friend?" I asked.

"Well," she began, "I've just been talking to a kindergartner."

I knew this was significant since the fourth and fifth graders had gone to camp and the other grades had written about school life without the "big kids." Some of the stories expressed relief from teasing. Some mentioned inappropriate behavior they had seen which they would *never* mimic. Some, fortunately, were positive, but the whispered frustrations caused by the negative reports were circulating wildly among the two upper grades. So I was eager to hear the details from this happy diplomat.

"First, I asked her what it was like to be in kindergarten," she began. "She seemed a little wide-eyed at first, but I gently put my hand on her shoulder so she'd know I was friendly. Then I said, 'Wow, you'll be a big first grader next year. Won't that be neat!' Then guess what she said to me. . . ."

I couldn't imagine.

"She said, 'Wow! And you'll be a big fifth grader.' Then I gave her a little hug and said, 'Maybe we can play a game together on the playground next year.' You should have seen her smile. I think I've made a new friend—who won't be as afraid of the big kids next year."

I was proud of this little diplomat who learned firsthand about the rewards of kindness.

Lord, thank you for the privilege of observing such a mature and brilliant stroke of kindness.

The activity ahead smelled of disaster. Its innovation required kids in control, but the students were anything but ready for self-control. The Thanksgiving holiday break was fast approaching, and they were restless. The activity involved moving to the auditorium. Shoes needed to be removed for a physically active geography lesson.

I began realizing that my timing was less than ideal, and the activity should be for one or two students—not an entire classroom! But teachers are idealistic—to their own fault many times! And I was convinced the students could handle it all if given some pre-activity coaching.

I touted my standard line, "In order to learn from this activity, what will you need to contribute to our time?" The responses were so immediate, I realized the students had also developed a standard response.

"Self-control," they all parroted apathetically while one student yanked the other's pencil and another student sent an eraser flying across the room.

Obviously, they had missed the point. Quietly, I called them all to the floor circle. We talked in soft tones about words that mean nothing. The proof of their ability to handle a "different" geography project would be in their actions, I instructed.

In the auditorium, it was quickly clear which ones knew what self-control looks like—and which ones simply used the word.

Lord, conduct is a truer gauge than words. May conduct and words come closer and closer together—even during potentially explosive activities.

 **NOVEMBER 22**   **Read Proverbs 29:11.**

All day long I had been at the edge of anger. After all this work, how could these children be so squirrelly? After this *brilliant* lesson plan, how could they be so restless?

I finally had to excuse *myself* for a control time. The Thanksgiving holiday was coming, and I had worked double time to make the last days before the break meaningfully academic. Today I looked like I hadn't slept in a week. Finally I realized I had taken *all* the responsibility for the students' learning and behavior. No wonder I was ready to lose it!

Slowly, taking deep breaths, I headed back—not to my classroom, but to *our* classroom. Carefully, I transferred the responsibility for behavior back to the students. I employed quick, decisive control times. I gave the ones out of control time away to restore themselves and invited them to return when they could manage working with a group. The lesson plan was opened up to several avenues of student interest that could also accommodate the skill needs. Suddenly, self-direction created excitement and interest.

I no longer felt the anger rising. Instead, I saw students working hard to be responsible for their learning and their behavior.

Lord, full vent of my anger will not result in the maturity my students need. Though initially it may give me relief, remind me that another way to regain control will work for both teacher and student.

✎ **NOVEMBER 23**   **Read Proverbs 30:8-9.**

We had a pencil crisis on our hands. One day we started out with newly purchased, newly sharpened tools for everyone. The next day they were all gone.

At first we made jokes about the pencil thief. Then we tried several strategies. First, we taped everyone's initials to the pencils so one student was responsible for one pencil. Then we tried a pencil jar. The number of students determined the number of pencils in the jar. After each activity the pencils were collected and counted. Of course, this constant monitoring became ridiculous in the fast-paced classroom.

Then today, as we were hunting for pencils, one student quietly suggested that another student had quite a stash in his supply box. When I went to this student to ask about the possibility of truth in this accusation, he sheepishly grinned and opened his box. There were dozens of well-marked pencils neatly hoarded in his box.

When invited to pass them out to the class, he hesitated. He wanted to preserve his treasures to make sure he would always have enough. It took some fancy diplomacy to encourage him to find a moderate solution of keeping enough for himself and sharing his abundance. But what better time could there be for a lesson in contentment and sharing than the season of Thanksgiving?

Lord, if we don't have enough, we begin to find inappropriate ways of acquiring. If we have too much, we forget your intimate involvement in our lives. Grant me a personal sense of moderation and contentment. May this classroom also reflect that attitude.

✎ NOVEMBER 24   Read Proverbs 27:23-27.

Many commentators attribute this pastoral portion of the Proverbs to Solomon's authorship. I can't help but wonder if his insights into rural wisdom might also inform my needs in this city classroom.

First he says to pay close attention to the condition of the flocks. I must continually be attentive to the condition of my students. Their needs, their skill mastery, their learning styles, and the variety of their intelligences must constantly be considered. I must daily take the initiative to know the condition of my "flock."

However, just as "riches do not last forever," so I will also have successful years and years that are difficult. Working on the condition of my flock provides some insurance toward success, but it does not guarantee success. Diligence often yields rewards, but it sometimes must also be pursued for its own sake.

While I'm taking all this initiative, I must also realize my dependency. Though I gather the hay, Someone beyond me is causing new growth to appear. Each year this is so apparent after the Christmas and spring breaks. My students come back different children, who have grown and matured profoundly. Reading levels have changed. Writing skills have blossomed—all rather miraculously.

I am continually becoming aware that abundance in the classroom is the harvest of both initiative and dependence.

Lord, how gracious of you to invite my partnership into this flock. How comforting to know my dependence is on you.

✎ **NOVEMBER 25**   **Read Proverbs 28:11.**

The greatest intelligence in the accelerated class I taught one year often came from a student whose gift was discernment. Many of the students scored higher on traditional tests, but she always aced anything to do with interpersonal or intrapersonal perceptions. Discussions were often guided and always enhanced because she could see through all of us!

One day near the end of school, we had begun to talk about responsibility. Previous work-times had disintegrated because of tired students with "holiday fever." Bedtimes were getting later and family schedules were becoming more hectic. I was having to stand on my head longer and entertain more extravagantly than ever before. It soon became apparent that the teacher was doing all the work.

Responsibility for education had become one-sided. Therefore, I decided it was time for responsibility "ladders." Each student would evaluate their initiative and diligence by placing their initials on the rung of a ladder. The top rung represented very responsible behavior. The bottom rung was irresponsibility. All would have been very task oriented if my A+ discernment student hadn't stretched our thinking.

She put her initials high on the ladder and said she had expressed responsibility that day by having patience. She noted that being patient when your needs can't be met right away is a crucial way of expressing responsibility.

Leave it to her to move us from a "doing" perspective to a wise "being" perspective.

Lord, thank you for those students adept at discernment. They have a wealth far greater than any other riches.

✎ **NOVEMBER 26**   **Read Proverbs 25:28.**

The wisdom writer in Proverbs likened broken city walls to the person who lacks self-control. How vulnerable and how unprepared is the city whose walls have been left to crumble. When the day of attack comes, there is no time to build walls. Likewise, when the day projects and reports are due, there is no time to start building—as one of my students recently discovered.

As I gave the final reminder that reports were due tomorrow, I noticed many affirmative nods from my students. They had been working and researching for several days. Their groups seemed to have a game plan for their presentations, and all seemed well—until one student quietly came up to me during recess. She had done all the work on the project; her partner had done nothing to her knowledge. I pulled her partner aside during an individual work moment and checked on the story.

Excuses were rampant. I finally stopped him and said, "It's interesting to me that each student in this classroom seems very aware of and prepared for tomorrow's deadline—except you. I have to conclude that you are at fault for misunderstanding the deadline."

Then, instead of a lecture, I asked him what he would do about this dilemma. He, of course, listed all the things he had to do after school which prevented his completion of the project. I simply stated he would need to spend the rest of class looking at options to prevent his well-prepared partner from failing this assignment. I would not think of them for him. Since his lack of planning had created the dilemma, *his* planning must solve the problem.

Fortunately he came up with several options that cost him dearly timewise and energywise. He may get no sleep tonight, but those depending on him will not be let down.

Lord, help me teach students to diligently keep their "walls" prepared with self-management.

 **NOVEMBER 27**   **Read Proverbs 29:20.**

Before he had a chance to tell his parents about the situation, I was speaking of it to his mother after school. Firmly, in front of him, I was talking of his laziness in class and of his failure to come through with his half of the report. I continued on in the same vein I had used with him—a lecture tone about responsibility and following through with commitment to other team members.

Quietly, the mother listened and the son held his head lower and lower. Because she wasn't responding verbally, I assumed I should proceed with more information and more moralizing. Finally, I stopped, and fortunately, she was gracious.

"You know," she said slowly and a bit painfully, "we've had two family emergencies this week. It's been very difficult for all of us to follow through with anything. We'll see what we can do tonight to make sure his partner on this project isn't disappointed."

She reached for her son and hugged him. I apologized profusely and wished I had asked questions instead of jumping to conclusions. Next time, when a student's performance is lacking, I will begin with questions and save the lectures for the truly lazy.

Lord, keep me from assumptions that put more weight on broken hearts. Keep me from hasty words. Instead may listening enable me to support my students.

✎ NOVEMBER 28   Read Colossians 3:13.

I was informed that they simply weren't speaking to one another. One young girl had heard from another girl that another girl had said such and such about her favorite interest. This information was all given to me on lunch duty. I could feel the tension at the tables, and out of the corner of my eye I had watched the maneuvering of a future codependent running back and forth carrying messages between the warring parties.

First, I caught the message carrier and suggested that she pull out of the conflict. Then I called the two nonspeakers to me and said, "Let's talk a little and see if maybe we can reach a compromise here—after all, with the afternoon activities coming up, it would be helpful to get this settled."

They both stood with classic poses—back-to-back with arms folded, scowling to punctuate the anger.

However, a strange thing happened as they began unfolding the misunderstanding. They started to say things like, "Oh, well, that's not what so-and-so told me you said." Finally, they got to the bottom of the actual words spoken by each other and realized that they really had nothing to be angry about.

Apologies and hugs were enthusiastically exchanged. Ah, the simplicity of forgiveness in children. How much we have to learn from them!

Lord, give me the childlikeness that forgives enthusiastically.

✎ NOVEMBER 29   Read Isaiah 40:22, 27-31.

Today I forgot that I am remembered. I know the presence of God is certain, yet sometimes it seems intermittent. But Abraham Heschel's writings remind me that the ones beloved by God "move under the unseen canopy of remembrance." Never am I alone—actually teachers never get a moment to themselves—but this aloneness is different. It can happen in the busiest classroom. Being surrounded by students is one busy cure for aloneness; but being sustained by the Lord himself is a different cure to a different aloneness.

According to Heschel, the devout person needs no miraculous communication to make him or her aware of God's presence. Nor is a crisis necessary to awaken the person to the meaning and appeal of God's presence.

We simply reside in the company of One who, according to Isaiah 40:22 (NIV), "stretches out the heavens like a canopy" to protect and provide for us physically. But God doesn't stop there. Our way is also never hidden from God (v. 27). I may complain like people in Isaiah's day—that my way feels hidden from the Lord. But have I not heard and do I not know all the rest of this prophet's words? The Lord renews my strength so I may soar—under the canopy of remembrance—in this classroom, even today.

Lord, help me never forget that I am always remembered and gathered under your remembrance and attention.

The wisdom writer of Proverbs 30 spotted four small-but-wise creatures from the natural world. First he targeted ants, who have little strength but store up their food in the summer. Then the rock badger or marmot, who appears as soft and vulnerable as a rabbit yet has the wisdom to retreat to solid rock homes. Next, the wisdom writer highlighted the wonder of the locusts, who fly in formation as they devastate entire crops. Last, the Proverbs teacher noted the ability of the lizard to gain entrance into even the most prestigious places.

As we approach the midyear point, I think about how I, too, am in charge of ones who are small but need wisdom. I begin to look at these small creatures in Proverbs and analyze the traits of wisdom that I might pass on to those among the human family who are young and small, but need much wisdom in these days.

First, the wisdom from the ants related to provision. I have decided I must respond to the request "Teacher, I need . . ." with "How do you think you can solve your difficulty?" or "What might you do to provide for that need?" These young ones must be weaned toward self-provision and foresight.

The marmot shows us that learning to provide sanctuary for oneself in a stronger place is crucial. So I invited the police officer from our neighborhood to come to class to talk about protection. We also learned when it is appropriate to seek adult help with physical or emotional needs.

Next, the locust gives us ideas for the strength of order and community. Experiencing the value of groups and learning the skills to organize oneself within that group began to permeate our learning activities.

Last, we learned that sometimes, even though you are small, taking initiative to give input and be heard is also wise. Students learned how to write editorials and call congressmen with their concerns and issues even as children.

Look around you. What lessons in wisdom are waiting to be taught?

Lord, your world teaches us daily. Show us the characteristics of wisdom, so that we may model and teach them in the classroom.

December

Joy, Love, and Hope

Joan Laney

DECEMBER 1   **Read Romans 12:2.**

dvent is here—the season of preparation for celebrating the birth of our Lord and Savior Jesus Christ. Yet I cannot think about the Christmas story without also thinking about the Easter story.

I teach a Sunday school class of ten- to fifteen-year-olds, a very lively group. They often teach me more about God than I could possibly teach them. Last spring I was trying to think of a way to involve them in the Easter story. Most of the children in the class were struggling with questions about growing up, with conflicts at school or at home, with faith issues. I wanted them to feel that the Easter story was not simply historical but actually related to their own lives.

After talking it over with some friends, I decided to try having the children act out a part of Holy Week in the form of a mime. I figured that maybe, without having to learn a script, they could do some motions to music without too much difficulty.

The class decided to do the Last Supper where Jesus washes the feet of his disciples. We assigned parts. The boys playing

84

Judas and Peter were a little rambunctious, but I figured that if they learned something from the mime, it would be a success no matter what people said.

Every rehearsal was a disaster. The girls paid attention and did their parts with care. The boys did somersaults and flips, talked during the mime, made fun of what we were doing. We tried to slow down and refine the motions so that the mime kept the pace of the music, but I soon realized that not much short of a miracle was going to harness the energy of those two boys.

Then came the night of the mime. When we put on the greasepaint and the black clothing, all the children were shocked—at their appearance and at the reality that this was serious stuff. Right before the mime I whispered to them, "Remember, this is worship. We are making an offering to God."

For a few minutes while Pachelbel's Canon played and we broke imaginary bread and washed one another's feet, we actually felt the story: Jesus' pain and anguish, the bewilderment of the disciples, Judas's angry betrayal, Peter's impetuousness. It was all there in the story, in our story.

It was a miracle, one that I pray will touch the lives of those ten children long after they leave Sunday school.

As teachers, we have the opportunity to witness many miraculous moments—moments that lead to transformation in the lives of the children we teach. In this season of expectation, let us *expect miracles.*

Lord, teach us to expect miraculous transformation—in the lives of those we teach as well as in our own lives.

❄ **DECEMBER 2**   **Read Colossians 3:17.**

My aunt's favorite expression is "Learn to abound!" She'll walk into my house with an armload of gifts and when I protest at her lavishness, she'll respond merrily, "Learn to abound, honey, just learn to abound."

I confess: Something in me makes it difficult for me to abound. Sometimes it is guilt. I don't feel as though I deserve such blessings. I can't enjoy the good because I'm so busy waiting for the inevitable, deserved bad to come along.

Sometimes it's a different kind of guilt: Why am I so blessed when others suffer? It's not uncommon for a teacher to ask this question, for children who need so much are placed in our care. *Life is not fair,* we say to ourselves. Are we afraid to enjoy what others don't have?

Throughout the Old and New Testaments one thing is utterly clear: "God is passionately in love with *all* of creation. God wants us to abound, just as we teachers yearn for our children to abound—in love, in trust, in joy, in wholeness.

With a God like that, why are we fearful or reluctant or guilty about being joyful? Paul, throughout his hardships from shipwreck to snakebite to prison, repeats in his letters the command, "Rejoice!"

A community in north Georgia that works with refugees from all over the world sends their newsletter to our church. They have told stories of refugees from El Salvador, Guatemala, Thailand, Vietnam, and Bosnia—gut-wrenching, tragic stories. Yet they insist on celebrating life and hope in the darkness. Their favorite song is "The Celebration Song," which includes these lines:

For the sun and for the rain,
Through the joy and through the pain—we celebrate.

May we learn to abound—and perhaps the children in our care will learn from our example!

Lord, teach us to abound, for your reign is breaking into our darkness, even now.

❄ **DECEMBER 3**   **Read Romans 15:13.**

Mr. and Mrs. Kittrell were members of our church years ago. At the time my pastor husband, Billy, first came to the church, they were shut-ins, and it was only a year or so before they moved into a nursing home together.

Not long after they were settled in the nursing home, Mrs.

Kittrell died, leaving Mr. Kittrell, in his late eighties, alone in the nursing home. It took him a while to get over his wife's death—they'd been married fifty years—but one day when Billy went to see him, he was transformed. He was kidding with the nurses, flirting with the other patients, rolling his wheelchair up and down the hall and visiting with everyone. He was irrepressible. He even had a "girl-friend."

"I am convinced that we can choose joy," writes Henri Nouen in *Road to Daybreak*. He continues,

> Every moment we can decide to respond to an event or a person with joy instead of sadness. When we truly believe that God is life and only life, then nothing need have the power to draw us into the sad realm of death. To choose joy does not mean to choose happy feelings or an artificial atmosphere of hilarity. But it does mean the determination to let whatever takes place bring us one step closer to the God of life.

Mr. Kittrell chose joy, and in doing so he transformed the halls of the nursing home. Patients who were usually sitting lifelessly, heads bowed, were smiling and laughing. The often grim faces of the nurses were lighted up with renewed energy and life. It was amazing what one person could do.

We, too, can choose joy. In our classrooms, in the halls, in the cafeteria, in the teachers' lounge, joy will well up and become infectious . . . if we let it.

Help us choose joy, O Lord, because we know that you love us.

❄ **DECEMBER 4**   **Read Isaiah 44:21-23.**

Dorothy Kazel, a Maryknoll nun who was killed in El Salvador in 1980, used to tell people she wanted to be "an alleluia from head to toe." As someone with a grumpy personality, I like that image.

I experienced one week of feeling that joyful, but it was because of a "mistake"! Billy had left town for a week, and the first night he was gone I was told that rain was forecast for the entire week. Now, I am a decent single parent for short amounts of time, but long amounts of time plus bad weather do me in. I went home absolutely dreading the week.

I woke up the first morning. No rain. I went around humming all day. The second day there was no rain. I sang most of the day. When by the third day there was no rain and no sign of rain, I was ecstatic. The week went well and I think that I was bearable as a mom.

But I had to laugh at myself. The only way I could feel so joyful was if my expectation of something I considered bad was not met. Joy should be the rule, not the exception, in my life!

Often it's that way for us in the classroom, isn't it? We're joyful because something we dreaded or feared might happen didn't come to pass: The class clown behaved himself for a change; a parent-teacher conference with a difficult parent was canceled; it didn't rain on the morning we had bus duty. Yet joy should be the rule, not the exception, in our classrooms—even when things aren't going our way. Our God loves us and forgives us. Let us sing and shout with joy!

Help me, O Lord, to be an alleluia from head to toe.

❄ DECEMBER 5   Read Titus 2:11-14.

I am by nature a crabby person. It has taken me years and lots of teasing by my husband for me to realize that I am a "moanie groanie Joni." Despite all my resolutions to the contrary, my basic nature seems to be negative.

When I am particularly hard on those around me, I have to be reminded that I am really angry at myself and they are in the way. For some reason, the critical spirit I turn on others is even worse when I focus it on myself. So when I read an article in *Weavings* magazine by Wendy Wright called "Hints, Signs and Showings: The Compassion of God," I identified with her observation that "God is greater than your own accusing heart." She went on to say that it is her own heart, not God's, that accuses and judges. God reaches out with loving arms and God steps forth as the heart of a mother who longs to hold her children.

What wonderful reassurance for the part of me that feels utterly unlovable—yet takes it out on others! What comfort for the frightened child I hold in my heart, who fears that there is a limit to love!

In *Memories of God*, Roberta Bondi redefines prayer as "a process of gathering in and reclaiming the lost and despised and wounded parts of ourselves." Instead of trying to ignore that angry, childish voice inside me, I actually embrace it, as I would my own flesh-and-blood child. Instead of denying to myself that the person I am most critical of is myself, I seek to understand why I am so critical. Through prayer I can offer those parts of myself to God for healing.

We are all hurting and wounded creatures, whose need for God's love is like a deep cavern. When we offer that need to God, no matter where or who we are—daily, hourly if need be—God is able to lovingly heal us, bit by bit, until we are new creatures in Christ.

Gather us up, O Lord, all the broken parts of ourselves, and heal us, we pray.

❄ **DECEMBER 6**   **Read Isaiah 54:10.**

Years ago I was in a bad marriage, a very abusive marriage, but I was unable to admit to anyone how very awful it was. Although outwardly I continued teaching, attending classes, and functioning, inwardly I was so torn apart that I was immobilized. I dreaded every morning; getting out of bed took all of my energy. I dreaded returning home every evening because I never knew what faced me: anger, silence, or ridicule.

Finally I made myself write a letter to my parents telling them the awful truth about my life and my marriage. I sent the letter before I could talk myself out of it, but I knew they would be devastated. I thought they would be too upset to respond.

It was only a few days before a special delivery letter came addressed to me. In my father's handwriting it said basically that my parents loved me, had always loved me, and would always love me. Then he added, "Get help."

Perhaps, after all, this is the message of Christ. That God loves us with an everlasting love, but that God calls us to get—and at the same time offers—the help we need for learning how to love ourselves and others. All of us carry around "baggage" of some sort, unfinished business from the pain of living. All of us need mending. God calls us out of hiding and isolation to connect with others and "get help."

That letter—which I still have all these years later—was the grace I needed to move out of my charade and admit that the marriage was failing. I made the call for help.

As I experienced it, grace was both comforting and challenging. It wasn't mushy; it was tough. May we give such grace to others—inside and outside the classroom.

O Lord, thank you for calling us out of our hiding places and showering us with grace and love. Help us to share that grace and love with all we meet.

❄ **DECEMBER 7**   **Read Isaiah 9:2-7.**

During Advent a few years ago, my husband, Billy, called the children down to the front of the church for the usual children's sermon. We had a young visitor that morning who was a special needs child; her parents helped her forward and set her down on the rug with the other children. Her name was Erin.

Billy then told the story of a friend of ours who had been severely depressed. He had suffered through a "dark night of the soul" and had felt God's silence in his life. Though he felt virtually paralyzed by his depression, he made himself volunteer at a camp for the disabled. He was there almost a week. Then he showed up at our door wearing a brightly colored scarf, a big grin on his face, and his hand raised in the air. When we opened the door, he shouted in joy, "Aeeeee!"

He told us that the children in the camp had broken through his depression. Their sheer joy at being alive had awakened his sense of God's presence and had enabled him to see God at work in the world and in his life. He was transformed.

Billy finished the story and the children went back to their seats. Then he started to read the Advent text, preparing us for the coming of the Messiah. Suddenly Erin's hand shot up in the air and she yelled, "Aeee!" Billy stopped and said, "That is an appropriate way for all of us to respond to the news of Christ's coming. Let's all stand and put our arms in the air and yell in joy, 'Aeee!'"

Erin led our entire congregation that morning in a proclamation of joy that shook the very building. And we all learned anew that children *are* our teachers in the faith.

God, let us learn from the children what it is like to be faithful and filled with joy.

❄ DECEMBER 8   Read Luke 12:6-7.

A few years ago my children found a bird in our front yard. It must have flown into our living room window because its neck was broken. While we were tending to it, it died.

We found a shoebox and gently laid the bird to rest inside it. Then my children and their friends decided to have a funeral for the bird. They went off in a little huddle to dig the grave and plan the service. In a few minutes they were ready for the adult mourners to join them.

As we gathered around the makeshift grave, our twelve-year-old friend began by asking if anyone had anything to say. My seven-year-old daughter was the first to speak. "I really didn't know the bird," she said, "but I am very sad it died."

The service moved from testimony to Scripture. Ruth read the Twenty-third Psalm. We all said the Lord's Prayer. The younger children wondered about the bird's mom. Would she know it had died and would she be sad?

Finally the service was over, the little bird buried in our yard. We adults went back inside to reflect on the worship the children had led. They had been so thoughtful, so aware of the comfort offered by Scripture. Where had they learned to put together a service like that? We talked about how much their service had made us aware of the incredible love of God who grieves over one sparrow's fall.

When we came back outside a little later, there were signs taped on the large garbage containers in each yard. The signs, written in bold crayon, said, "Pet funerals. Any animal or bird. Cost: $1.00. Call 278-5540."

Children! Never a dull moment! No wonder God has blessed us with such unpredictable little human beings. They topple all of our smugness. They shake us up. God is teaching us—over and over—to laugh at ourselves and to laugh at life.

And God is reminding us—over and over—how dearly we are loved.

Thank you, God, for loving us and for loving all your creatures.

❄ **DECEMBER 9**　　　**Read Matthew 18:10; Genesis 21:6.**

My first experience teaching Sunday school years ago was a disaster. I walked into a class of three: a five-year-old, a three-and-a-half-year-old, and my own one-and-a-half-year-old daughter. I was armed with materials and crafts and lesson plans. They were doing somersaults around the room.

I was able to settle the two older children down for a few minutes to talk about Jesus' love, while my daughter continued her acrobatics. The older ones seemed to listen attentively—of which I was quite proud. They sat very still and very politely.

Finally, my lesson finished, I asked them what things Jesus would like to see them do to show others God's love. After a long silence the three-and-a-half-year-old said proudly, "Put flowers on dead people's graves."

What a wonderful sense of humor God has—and what better use of it than to knock an arrogant, know-it-all Sunday school teacher down to size! I have never ceased to be amazed at how much humor it takes to be a teacher, Sunday school or otherwise, simply because children are so unpredictable. How else are we to survive besides laughter?

As we laugh, we teach our children to laugh. We teach them that laughter keeps things in perspective. Laughter helps us appreciate when things aren't quite manageable. Laughter helps us delight in each other and in the world.

Sometimes we just have to look at our classrooms and our students until we find something to laugh about. That will keep us going, no matter what.

God, you created laughter to keep our lives in perspective. Let us be willing to laugh.

❄ **DECEMBER 10**   **Read Matthew 25:40.**

I was in the shower one day when I had a revelation. It wasn't a glorious, inspiring revelation; rather, it was a confession. I realized that I did not really love God. Yes, I was trying to serve God, and yes, I believed in God, but I had no sense of loving God at all. It was as if I was doing hard labor for a stern taskmaster and I had decided to get the job done as efficiently as possible.

I was pretty shaken up by this revelation. I talked about it to my husband and friends. I prayed about it. I couldn't shake the feeling that I was simply performing tasks demanded of me without any semblance of love at all.

Advent began shortly after this experience. One of my Advent traditions is to pick a verse from a Christmas carol and write it in my Christmas cards. It takes a good bit of time for me to pick the perfect verse and then to copy it on a bunch of cards, so I usually begin in early December. Dutiful as I was, I picked my verse and started to work, not really thinking about what I was doing.

I sent out about eighty Christmas cards that year, still worrying about my lack of love for God but figuring that I had to keep going anyway. Christmas came and went. We had a nice holiday, and I think it was worshipful. It wasn't until New Year's Eve when I was writing in my journal, reflecting upon the past year, that I grasped the meaning of these words from the verse I had carefully chosen for my Christmas card:

> *How shall we love Thee, holy hidden being*
> *If we love not the world that Thou hast made.*

Loving the world—I could do that! Seeing God in those around me—I could do that! I literally jumped up and danced for joy. Loving an abstract, amorphous God—no—but loving an incarnate God, God in humanity, I could do.

We can love God, and we do, when we love our students, for they are the face of Christ.

O God, may we see your face when we look at others—especially "the least of these."

❄ DECEMBER 11 Read Romans 8:35-39.

I don't think we often realize how much God loves us. We hear the words in church or read them in the Bible, but they pass over us without much effect. If we really believed in that love, wouldn't it transform our lives?

Henri Nouen wrote a description of God that portrays this love:

> Here is the God I want to believe in: a Father who, from the beginning of creation, has stretched out his arms in merciful blessing, never forcing himself on anyone, but always waiting; never letting his arms drop down in despair, but always hoping that his children will return so that he can speak words of love to them and let his tired arms rest on their shoulders. His only desire is to bless.

The "saints" I know, the ones who truly live out God's calling in this world, are those who believe they are loved by God. One of them was converted in his forties by teaching Sunday school. He found himself actually believing the Sunday school literature that talked about God's great love for him. He immediately began to act in lavish love toward others, love that did not make sense to many people. He started giving away most of his money. He would pick up people who were hitchhiking and give them a coat if they seemed cold. He started going up to the elderly housing apartments and taking care of folks—buying them groceries and arranging haircuts, even clipping their toenails when they could no longer see. Through it all he was effusive in his joy. He knew for certain he was loved.

We need to claim that love. Just read the Scriptures and you'll feel it echoing through the ages. The ultimate demonstration of that love was God's gift of his Son, Jesus Christ. This season as we feel God's love in our lives let us lavishly love others, especially our students.

Teach us, O Lord, to love lavishly.

❄ **DECEMBER 12**   **Read Romans 8:18-22.**

Paul wrote a lot about splendor in his letters in the New Testament. In Romans 8, for example, he says, "For I reckon that the sufferings we now endure bear no comparison with the splendour, as yet unrevealed, which is in store for us" (v. 18 NEB). Paul is certain of this splendor, certain that it will be our inheritance as members of the Body of Christ.

Splendor is defined as "brilliance, magnificence, grandeur." It's a word we associate with unbelievable power and majesty—certainly not our feeble and fragile selves! Not even the awesome power of God can give us mortals much splendor!

C. S. Lewis also wrote about splendor. One of the observations he made is that there are no mortals. The people we work with, love, get angry with, and fight are not mere mortals but are either immortal horrors or everlasting splendors. According to Lewis, the daily choices we make slowly turn us into a horror or a splendor. And because our souls are immortal, we are creating what we will be in eternity.

This is sobering if we think of the way we treat others. When my husband, Billy, and I were first married, we worked in a food pantry together several afternoons a week. The first time we worked together I became furious with him. The line of persons waiting for food forked its way through the waiting room, out the door, and down the sidewalk in the cold. But Billy worked as though the person he was waiting on were the only person there. He greeted each one, asked about their day, and asked what choices they wanted in their food basket. Meanwhile I was counting the number of people waiting, antsy and angry that he wasn't more efficient.

I later realized that he was treating each person there as an immortal splendor. With great respect and tenderness he was handing out food as though it were purchased. I don't know if anyone in the line noticed his care, but he was making choices as he worked that were also turning him into a splendor—a splendor instead of a horror.

Rarely does it occur to us that our relationships are defining not only who we will be but also who others will be. In this light, teaching is a very powerful vocation—we are literally shaping souls for eternity. Are we helping to mold splendors or horrors?

What a responsibility we have as mirrors of Christ's splendor on earth!

Help us, O Lord, to claim that responsibility and to treat others as everlasting splendors.

❄ **DECEMBER 13**   **Read Deuteronomy 6:20-25.**

In this passage, Moses is instructing the children of Israel to tell the story, to attribute to God the mighty act of deliverance from Egypt. We are commanded to tell the story of God's working in our own lives both to instruct the children and to remind ourselves to be thankful for all that has been given to us.

But how do we as teachers tell the story? We must find the way we feel most comfortable. It can be through stories we tell in our classroom, not to convert anyone but to share what has shaped us. It may be through holding in prayer all the students we come in contact with, trusting we will see Christ in their faces. It may be in writing about the joys and struggles of teaching. It may be in telling teaching stories to our friends or those in our church. However we choose, our lives will tell the story if we let God work in them.

A young man in our church came forward one Sunday and told his story, a story of childhood abuse, trouble in school, and involvement in drugs. Throughout his elementary school years, he had known one particular teacher. She had loved him tenaciously, had insisted he could choose another road, and had never given up on him. She had modeled through her life that healing was possible. Twenty-five years later he was testifying to the power of her witness in helping him turn from drugs and street crime to the saving love of Christ. And he was telling his story to thank her—a member of our church.

Tell the story. Live the story. It will change someone's life.

Lord God, empower us to tell the story to your honor.

❄ DECEMBER 14   Read Matthew 7:15-17.

"In the last analysis, I have always believed it is not so much their subjects that the great teachers teach as it is themselves." —Frederick Buechner

If you were to think about your favorite teachers, most likely you would find this statement true. I certainly have. I think of my fourth- and fifth-grade teacher, Miss Koepp, who was both stern and loving, calling out of us gifts we did not know were ours. She taught us self-discipline and good work habits when most of us felt scattered and sloppy. Every morning before we began class, she had us stand up for inspection. She'd ask, "Hands? [clean?], Nails? [cut?], Brush your teeth?, Comb your hair?, Hanky?" and we were to show her that we had accomplished these tasks. Even now—thirty years later—I can remember grabbing that handkerchief daily to accommodate Miss Koepp.

Sometimes the gift teachers give is simply being there. My father spent many boyhood years in a tiny Arkansas town. The church his family attended had two youth: my father and the pastor's son. Nonetheless, every Sunday night for years the pastor met faithfully with his "youth group." My father remembers, not so much the content of their lessons, but the faithfulness and steadfastness of a pastor who treated his youth group of two as seriously as he would have a youth group of twenty.

We may be great teachers to some of our students because of our well-organized classrooms or exciting lessons. But I suspect that over time our students will remember who we were and how we cared. Did we stop for a moment after class for a hurting student? Did we mind interruptions? Did we listen? Did we love?

O Lord, help us to offer ourselves to our students, that they may see your love working in us. May we bear good fruit.

❄ **DECEMBER 15**   **Read Colossians 1:11-12.**

I do not come from a Catholic tradition, so when I worked with nuns for three years I learned a lot. I watched them make prayer and praise an integral part of their daily routine. Morning prayers, noon and evening prayers, times of blessing and celebration—all were second nature to these women who had devoted their lives to God.

They had a service to bless their home, to bless our office, to bless me when I became pregnant with our first child. Before any public action, we would lift our work up to God. We celebrated big achievements in our work and little milestones with singing, food, and fellowship.

Their view of aging intrigued me. No one thought of retirement. They just thought of new ministries. At sixty, one went to Africa to live and work, and two headed to Brazil. Life was an adventure to be embraced, no matter what their age.

But the most moving part of their story was that they came from all over the country to live and work in rural west Tennessee. They were committed to teaching the proverty-stricken, mostly black residents of that area to organize nonviolently for services offered in the more affluent white neighborhoods, services like sewage systems and sidewalks, paved roads, and safe bridges. Out of the context of worship, the nuns worked to empower people who had a tradition of being beaten down and ignored. Things began to change. And as leaders emerged from the black community, the nuns moved on.

Teaching is empowerment in its most basic sense, arming our students with the knowledge and skills to take charge of their lives and to improve them—and then, like the nuns, moving on, letting go, embracing another adventure.

Lord, help us to empower our students with love, and teach us when to hold fast and when to let go.

❄ **DECEMBER 16**   **Read Ephesians 3:14-19.**

A friend of mine wrote out Ephesians 3:14-19, a beautiful prayer that describes the love of God. She paraphrased it like this: "With this in mind, then, I kneel before the Father from whom every family in heaven and on earth takes its name, that out of the treasures of his glory he may give you strength and power through his Spirit in your inner being, that through faith Christ may dwell in your hearts in love. And I pray that you, being rooted and established in love, may have power with all the saints to grasp how wide and long and deep is the love of Christ."

My daughter Ruth found this passage folded up so that the only writing you could see was, "how wide and long and deep is the love of Christ." Being conscientious about grammar, she added a question mark and then wrote the answer: "Up past the sky and into space."

Isn't that, at heart, what we want our students to learn from us? That God's love for them flows out past the sky and into space? That the hairs on their heads are all numbered? That God knows each one of them by name?

It is precisely those children who seem the least lovable who need this message the most. The ones with the whining voices or the excuses or the subtle taunts about others. They are the ones we often must will ourselves to love by yearning for their wholeness and health. We don't have to like them, necessarily. But we have to want shalom for them, and we have to want it enough that we will work for it in their lives.

I have struggled with loving a woman in my church for a long time. It is hard to have loving feelings for her because she is very angry and often takes that anger out on me. Out of this struggle, I read William Barclay's commentary on a passage from Luke. Barclay describes love for our enemies as agape love, which means a love of the will, not of the heart. A will that insists upon wanting and working for the wholeness of the other, no matter who that other may be. As we encounter students who are not terribly likable, we must will ourselves to love in this fashion. Will it and pray. Maybe then those very students will experience a love that goes "up past the sky and into space."

Help us love those children who seem the most difficult to love, O Lord.

❄ **DECEMBER 17**   Read Luke 18:15-17.

Jesus was on his way to Jerusalem, preaching as he went. He had just told the story of the Pharisee and the tax collector in prayer. When, amid the preaching, people in the crowds brought babies for him to touch, the disciples tried to hold them back. We can almost hear them saying, "Don't bother the teacher. He is too busy to deal with the children."

Jesus stopped his preaching and gathered the children to him, saying, "Let the little children come to me, and do not stop them; for it is to such as these that the kingdom of God belongs" (Luke 8:16). In fact, throughout his ministry Jesus advocated for the children, healed the children, welcomed the children. He made it utterly clear that to accept the children was to accept him, and to reject the children was to reject him.

When we work daily with children, it can be very difficult to put this command into practice. Some children seem downright unlovable. Yet those are the children who need the all-embracing arms of Christ the very most.

A friend of mine who is a special education teacher for elementary students told a story of Andrew, a rude, nasty-mouthed fifth grader who was extremely bright but was unwilling to do his work. A deeply committed Christian, she tried everything she knew to try to reach him, and he did not respond at all.

The week before Christmas she read Christmas stories to the class daily, ending with *The Hillbilly Night Before Christmas* on the last day of school before Christmas break. When class was dismissed, Andrew lingered. He came up to her and asked, with big tears in his eyes, "Do you think there really is a Santa Claus?" She gave the best answer she could to indicate that Santa Claus is a matter of believing in the Christmas spirit. Then he asked, "Do you think he's never come to see me because I'm so bad?"

Part of the reason that Jesus calls us to love and accept the children is that they keep us off balance and force us to see life from another perspective. Suddenly Andrew's behavior was clear: He thought he was unlovable. The poverty he lived in reinforced his feelings of worthlessness. That conversation enabled his teacher to see past the anger to the pain, allowing her to persist in her efforts to love and accept him.

There are so many Andrews, so many who cry out for love and acceptance. Jesus calls us to open our arms and our hearts to them in his name.

Lord, broaden and deepen my love so that I may embrace all the Andrews I meet today.

❄ **DECEMBER 18**   **Read Luke 5:29-32.**

There once was a cobbler who had waited all his life for Jesus to visit. Finally he received word that Jesus was coming to see him. He closed his shop and made ready, cleaning up everything, fixing a nice meal, finally dressing himself up in readiness. A knock came at the door. When the cobbler opened it, there stood Jesus, the One he had longed to see ever since he could remember. Saying, "I'm so glad to see you," he threw his arms around Jesus.

Just as they sat down to eat, there was another, more timid knock. The cobbler tried to ignore it, but the knocking persisted. Finally he got up, cracked the door, and said loudly and crossly, "This shop is closed! What do you want?" A tattered, dirty beggar stood there patiently and replied, "I'm with him," pointing to Jesus. The cobbler sighed and let him in.

Soon there was another knock. The cobbler, more irritated than ever, went to the door. There stood a woman in very inappropriate dress, obviously a prostitute. Before he could say anything to her, she said, "I'm with him," and pointed to Jesus. The cobbler let her join them at the table.

Soon there was another knock. This time when he opened the door, the cobbler looked with wonder at a long line of ragged, dirty, smelly people stretching down the street as far as the eye could see. All of them were with Jesus.

If we are to "sit at table" with our Lord, we must be prepared to greet those on the underside of society. Among the most vulnerable and powerless in our society are many of the children in our public schools. Do we take joy in their presence? How would we act differently or feel differently if Jesus had a seat in our classroom beside one of the children from the underside?

It may only take one caring, loving individual to make a difference in the life of a troubled child. If we greet these little ones as if they are "with him," we may find ourselves participating in a joyful celebration of the kingdom of God.

Let me realize, O Lord, that each one of my students is accompanied by you.

❄ **DECEMBER 19**　　　　　　　　**Read Isaiah 65:17-25.**

Being the kind of person who always sees the glass half empty, I try to read everything I can about hope. I guess I'm trying to read hope into my life. Particularly in these days preceding Christmas my thoughts often turn to hope.

I once read a wonderful sermon about hope. The first point of this sermon was that hope is a commitment. It is really not a feeling, though we often describe it as a feeling. It is a choice to believe that our lives and our future are in God's hands, and that God is good. We choose this hope even when there is no reason to. We choose this hope despite economics, despite politics, despite our own demons.

Once we choose to hope, we stake our lives on it. We can't do it piecemeal or halfway. We get up, morning after morning, and commit ourselves to hope that day, no matter what happens. To trust that God is at work in us and in the world.

When we read Isaiah we see this hope. It's dazzling. It images a time when all the world will worship God, when all creation will be reconciled. There will be no more weeping.

All people will eat of their own food and tend to their own gardens. The weapons will be beaten into tools for farming. God's love and glory will be revealed to all of us. Isaiah chose to believe that this kingdom would be realized despite all evidence to the contrary.

How can we as teachers be committed to hope? We can imagine our students as healthy, joyful human beings and work toward that end; we can will ourselves daily to expect the best, not the worst, from our students; we can pray passionately to God on behalf of each student.

Lord, let us be prophets of hope in our classrooms.

❄ DECEMBER 20   Read Luke 3:3-18.

Hope begins as a commitment, a commitment despite all the evidence at hand. Hope is also a discipline. If we are truly going to hope, we have to have images of hope and a reason to hope. That's where the Scriptures come into play. We study passages of Scripture because they tell us what to hope. Scripture is a record of great hopes, from Genesis to Revelation.

John the Baptist is a model of the discipline of hope. He followed a radical lifestyle of diet and prayer and preaching that nourished his hope. In this day of easy Christianity, few of us would take seriously John's call to a radical, disciplined hope. Fasting and time apart praying are too difficult for most of us to do on a regular basis. But we *can* commit ourselves to hope as a discipline by studying Scripture daily and praying daily, even if it is only five minutes at a time.

The first year I taught school, it was an hour commute each way. I had to be on the road by 6:30 A.M. I started out listening to the news every morning, but I got so depressed that I turned off the radio and began driving in silence. Soon the silence turned into prayer for the day ahead, for each student I would meet that day. I can't say that it transformed the students, but it did help me face each day with a sense of hope. It helped me see the little things that I might have missed—the eagerness of one student to learn, the willingness of another to do extra work. It became a discipline of hope to watch the sun rise and lift up each person I was teaching.

If we are going to be dedicated, enthusiastic, and effective teachers, we are going to have to be disciplined about hope.

Lord, teach me the discipline of hope.

❄ **DECEMBER 21**   **Read Matthew 5:6.**

Hope is a commitment and a discipline. It also gives us permission to be angry. If we really hope, we are going to be angry. And that is okay—even in this season when we are expected to be "merry."

We are angry because we refuse to be resigned to injustice, dishonesty, oppression, hypocrisy, violence. Things ought to be better than they are. God has promised they will be. Sometimes as we lean into hope for God's kingdom, we feel anger because God's kingdom is still so opposed by the powers of this world.

Job is a story that gives us permission to be angry at God for injustice and suffering. Remember how Job suffers terrible losses—of family, land, servants, money, health? All he has left is his body, covered with sores, and his anger at God. He cannot understand why he has had such terrible misfortune. So he questions God.

Now God does not strike him dead for his questions, though God does get pretty angry at Job for his audacity. "Brace yourself like a man; I will question you and you shall answer me," he thunders (Job 40:7 NIV). When all is said and done, God hears and responds to Job without ever explaining the pain he's been through. But he is there, present to Job in the midst of his pain. In the end, Job's anger is seen as intercession, and God restores to him all he has lost.

In his book *Engaging the Powers,* theologian Walter Wink describes intercession as "spiritual defiance of what is, in the name of what God has promised." We can be angry at the state of things. And we can continually call upon God to right the wrongs of this world and heal the broken. That is what we do with our anger to keep it from festering, and to keep it hopeful.

So when we run into the student we cannot reach, the class we cannot teach, the school we dread driving to morning after morning, we can turn our anger into intercessory prayer and insist that we see God in the midst of it all.

God, we call upon your power to heal this broken world.

❋ **DECEMBER 22**   **Read II Corinthians 5:17.**

Every child can be seen as potential or as failure. The way we see that child may make a big difference in the way that child learns. Educational research has shown this time and time again. It's just hard, sometimes, to appropriate it.

Every morning when I walk my dogs, we pass a very nondescript little house on one of the corners of the block. It used to be owned by an elderly man, who sold it in very bad shape to a young family. One day the house, which had looked so lifeless for so long, was teeming with children. The next day, flowers had been planted in the front yard. The next day a basketball goal had been set up in the backyard. I began to become intrigued about what change I would see the next morning. A porch was built, the bricks were painted, a garden was planted, a back patio was built, a clothesline was hung, and on and on until the house looked very, very loved and lived in.

I once would have dismissed that house as needing to be torn down. I saw no potential there at all. But this family took it and shaped it into a wonderful living space—one step at a time. Even today rose bushes are blooming profusely and a swing has been hung.

Maybe part of the reason this family succeeded in transforming their home was that they saw the potential in that little crouching brick home where others only saw lack. They could envision the changes that could happen. Then they set small, reachable goals that brightened that house and made it into a home.

So it is that we are to look at our students. The one over

there, crouched in his seat. Or that one, daydreaming and fiddling with her hair. Not failure but potential. Potential plus prayer plus hard work. Step by painstaking step until there is transformation.

Let us see with your eyes, O Christ, that we may see the beauty and the possibility of every child.

❄ DECEMBER 23   Read Colossians 1:27.

Years ago when I taught English for grades 8–11 in a rural county high school, I found myself overwhelmed by the number of students I had to teach, the poor facilities, and the lack of textbooks. But what discouraged me most was that I saw myself tending to the students on both ends of the spectrum—the students who were very bright and eager to learn and those students who were unruly, hated English, and tormented those around them. The quiet, unassuming students who did their work without much fuss were the ones who got little of my attention.

At that time in my life I was going through a very messy divorce, so I put aside my pain through an act of will every morning before facing the children and then fell apart every afternoon when I climbed into my car. Though teaching kept me functioning, there were some days when life seemed utterly meaningless. I believed intellectually that God was working amid it all, but I did not feel God's presence.

One night I had what still is the most powerful dream I've ever had. I was out on a lake being pulled across its waters by one of my mediocre students. This student sat in class and never said a word. He was so big that his knees barely fit under the desk and it took him a while to extricate himself from the seat. He seemed utterly embarrassed about himself and his life. But in my dream he was saving me from drowning and was towing me to safety. As I looked up into the night sky, finally able to breathe, I saw the pattern of all the continents and nations of the world lighted up as though I were looking out from the inside of a lighted globe. Everything fit together in an illuminated pattern. It was obvious—

106

and it felt obvious—that God was in control of this beautiful, ordered world. My student delivered me to safety on the other side of the lake, and then I woke up.

That dream has stayed with me all these years not only because of the hope that filled me when I saw God's pattern, but also because of the student who pulled me to safety. Every one of our students has the capacity to "pull us to safety," even the quiet, nondescript ones. It is our task and our call to bring that capacity forth in them.

We give thanks to you, O Lord, for our students and the potential hidden in them.

❄ **DECEMBER 24**   **Read James 2:14-17.**

In the ten years that my pastor husband, Billy, and I have served a little inner-city church; we've seen a lot of changes in the neighborhood, most of them for the worst. Ten years ago most of the homes around the church were single-dwelling homes, lived in for the most part by mothers and their children. Many had gardens and flowers. Almost all the residents sat on their front porches in the evenings, hollering to one another while the children played happily in the streets.

First came an hourly motel just a block away. Then came "drug houses," one by one—houses that started looking unkempt and hosted a lot of folks in and out. Then, one by one, houses started to be boarded up, with a big FORECLOSURE sign on them. Vacant yards became overgrown. Men started hanging out on the street corners. In ten years the neighborhood decline has accelerated, and people don't feel as safe.

The decline was symbolized by the brutal death of one of the neighborhood children a year ago. Found under a pile of dirty laundry, he had been beaten to death. Seven-year-old Jarvis had attended our church. He was very quiet but very bright. His favorite activity had been drawing and coloring in Sunday school. He had a rare but beautiful smile.

I found myself blaming his mother and grandmother, the

neighborhood, the drug houses, everyone—everyone but myself and my church. The truth was that though we had provided a place for Jarvis to come, *he* had made all the efforts. We had not offered rides, invited him or his sisters into our homes, gotten to know him. If those of us who professed to be Christians had not shown that extra love, how could we expect others to?

We had failed Jarvis. As a church we acknowledged it, grieved it, confessed it. We also promised that his death would not be in vain.

As teachers, we may see children like Jarvis. Though our power is limited, we are called by God to be there for those children, to listen, to be present, to care. No doubt we'll have to go the extra mile. But if we, named Christians, do not do this work, no one else will.

Gracious God, prod us into being your presence in the world.

❄ **DECEMBER 25**   **Read I Corinthians 1:27-29.**

When Billy and I first came to our church, we had a very small congregation of mostly older folks with great hearts but minimal monetary resources. When other churches celebrated holidays with lavish bouquets of flowers and banners, we usually had our plastic roses arranged neatly on a while tablecloth to commemorate the occasion.

One day, however, some of us decided that we needed to find some flowers for Christmas. After all, we met in the basement of what used to be a grand old church, and if we really believed that God's Son came and dwelled among us, we ought to be bold in our celebration. We found out that the downtown florists closed by noon on Saturdays and dumped flowers into their Dumpsters. So we decided to go downtown and look for flowers in the Dumpsters behind the florists.

We gathered around one o'clock and found the first Dumpster inside a chain-link fence. The gate was open, and cars were still there, but we wanted to try our scheme anyway. We crept in and I unwittingly climbed into the Dumpster. Sure enough, there were several bouquets of roses, a little squashed but still relatively bright looking. I handed them out and we dashed off. The second Dumpster had the opening on the very top, so we had to climb up and into it, balancing precariously so we didn't land on top of the coffee grounds and "real" garbage. It was worth our efforts. We left with two trunkloads of flowers—enough to fill the basement with more left over to decorate the Sunday school rooms!

The florists got wind of our find and locked up the Dumpsters. But we'll never forget that Christmas when we decorated the church basement with flowers—flowers that had been left for garbage.

This seems a fitting metaphor for teaching. We are to see the potential in all the children. We cannot discard even one single child. The child may be a little ragged or droopy or faded, but with tender loving care, the brightness in his or her face can be restored.

O God, help me to remember the Dumpster flowers—and the children—and hope.

❄ DECEMBER 26   Read Isaiah 58:6-12.

Years ago my husband and I moved to Memphis to serve a broken-down inner-city church. Once a thriving church, bustling with people and activities, it had declined over the years to a handful of faithful people who had weathered the "white flight," the changed neighborhood, the building of an interstate right next door, the falling plaster, the peeling paint, the broken windows.

One of the traditions of this tiny group of people was to gather for devotions before Sunday school. Someone was assigned to do a devotional for the entire group before breaking up into classes—though I remember there being enough people for only one Sunday school class!

I was assigned my devotion week and, of course, I completely forgot until we had gathered, had sung our hymn, and the leader had looked around and said, "Miss Joni will give this morning's devotional." I grabbed a Bible, fumbled for my favorite book, Isaiah, and began to read the above passage—simply because it was familiar.

When I got to the last lines, I burst into tears. Here was the promise that the ancient ruins would be restored. And here I was, standing in the dilapidated remains of what had once been a grand church. Some of my tears were hopeful; most of my tears were despairing. How would this ever come about?

This past Christmas Eve, years later, our congregation met in the "restored ruins" of our church, our renovated sanctuary. We had worked for months, giving up Saturdays and evenings to help paint, clean, varnish, pull out nails, put in nails, you-name-it—to rebuild the ruins. The entire church, from top to bottom, was renewed and restored. As we gathered in front of the stained glass windows with sunlight pouring through, we all read this passage from Isaiah and said, "Truly, God keeps God's promises."

Christmas reminds us that God keeps God's promises. No matter what the ruins—be it in the lives of the children we teach, the situation in which we teach, or our own lives—God's promises *do not fail.*

❄ **DECEMBER 27**   **Read Luke 13:34.**

It's a hard era in which to be a teacher. We seem to be fighting an uphill battle against so many things: drugs, indifference, technology, isolation, abuse, the breakup of families. We are expected to do so much, from teaching manners and values to inspiring, encouraging, and caring for our students—not to mention the actual course work they are required to do. Sometimes it feels hopeless and overwhelming.

In this passage, Jesus is lamenting over Jerusalem. Imagine how he must feel. The very people he has come to teach and save are the most hostile, the most unbelieving. Jerusalem, symbol of the center of all Jewish life, is going to be the place of his death. It is a gut-wrenching cry: "O Jerusalem, Jerusalem! How often have I longed to gather your children, as a hen gathers her brood under her wings; but you would not let me" (13:34 NEB).

We are not going to be able to do it all. We are not going to be able to save every student, motivate every student, even make a difference in every student's life. But the longing is in itself a prayer. The longing for wholeness for those students, our lament as we fail them can be lifted up to God. And God can use even those painful feelings as a form of grace.

A very good friend of mine is a special education teacher in a county high school. She worked diligently with three of her seniors who were failing her class. Despite all of her efforts to build their success, they were convinced that they would fail her class and their senior year. She grieved deeply when they did fail, knowing that they would not be able to graduate. Loving those students, she lamented her inability to change their self-perceptions.

A month later when she was back at school, she saw one of the students in a cap and gown standing with the principal. He waved her over and said to the principal, "This woman is the reason I failed. She's the reason I went to summer school, and she's the reason I'm wearing this cap and gown today."

O Lord, only you can transform our pain for these children into touches of grace.

❄ **DECEMBER 28**   **Read Romans 14:19.**

Years ago when the cartoon character Charlie Brown made the statement "I love menkind. It's people I can't stand," I really identified with his feelings! I've always been big on causes and justice for groups of people, but not too keen on everyday acts of kindness. I have wanted to fight for important things, not fritter away my time on insignificant things.

So, it made perfect sense to me to go talk to a pastor friend about my fear of being a martyr. After all, I knew God was calling me to the big causes, and big causes usually have a martyr. I know he couldn't believe I was serious when I sat down in his office, burst into tears, and sobbed, "I'm so afraid I'm called to be a martyr."

He was very gentle, though, and told me that even martyrs take it one step at a time. They don't wake up and know they are going to give up their lives; they simply make choices that lead them to give up their lives, and as they make those choices they make peace with the fear that they will lose their lives. And true martyrs love others so much that they are willing to lose their lives.

Wendell Berry writes,

> Love is never abstract. It does not adhere to the universe or the planet or the nation or the institution or the profession but to the singular sparrows of the street, the lilies of the field, "the least of these my brethren." Love is not, by its own desire, heroic. It is heroic only when compelled to be. It exists by its willingness to be anonymous, humble, and unrewarded.

Anonymous, humble, and unrewarded—sounds like teaching to me!

Lord, keep our eyes on how we can love the world around us.

❄ DECEMBER 29   Read Philippians 4:8.

I once read of a meditative technique called "benevolent glancing." It's really a fancy way of saying "looking with the eyes of love." The idea was that as we meet people on the street or deal with people in the most mundane situations, we look on them with a blessing in our hearts for them. As we pass people on the street, we silently lift them up to God. This is a form of prayer for others, of intercession.

Last summer I worked in the summer children's program at our church. My own children participated in the program. I had read of this method of blessing others, and I was trying very hard to look upon all the children with a blessing in my heart. Some days it was much more difficult than other days to see past the misbehavior and constant fighting to the gift of the child within.

My son, David, then six, said to me one day, "Mom, when you talk to the kids in the program, your eyes sparkle. Why don't they sparkle like that when you talk to me?"

I thought about that for a long time. I was so busy and pre-occupied with "benevolent glancing" in my dealings with the children in the program that I overlooked the same needs in my own children. They all yearned for it. They all wanted a blessing. "I will not let you go until you bless me," children cry out to us. Without even knowing it, they yearn for our eyes to sparkle when we deal with them.

So much of what we communicate is not verbal. It's in our mannerisms—in the shrug of indifference, in the glance of disgust, in the sigh of despair. But think of the difference when what we communicate is utter joy or delight in being with someone. Think of the difference to our students, troubled and untroubled, if we look on them with blessing and say to ourselves, *Yes, in this child I see the face of Christ!*

O Lord, help me delight in each of my students today.

❄ **DECEMBER 30**   **Read I Peter 2:9-10.**

One of the "disadvantages" of working in an inner-city church is that we don't have it all together. The building itself attests to that: The paint is peeling, one corner of the roof is crumbling in, the air conditioner only cools the worship area. Someone breaks in nearly every week and either takes something or makes a mess. It looks a tad bedraggled no matter how we try to improve it.

During last summer's children's program at our church, there was no air-conditioning in the rooms we used for program activities. The gym was the worst because if we did anything there after 10:30 A.M., we felt as if we were suffocating in the heat. The water fountain provided warm water to drink. The only time we could cool off was at lunch.

But the children kept coming. Never mind the heat, never mind the dilapidated building or the peeling paint, never mind the discomfort. They came. And what amazed me was their enthusiasm. They would happily try to find matching skates from the piles of cast-off skates we'd been donated, and they they'd go skating off—sometimes with two left skates or two right skates—into a steaming-hot

113

gym, laughing and shouting for joy. And if we'd let them, they'd play "ice hockey" with sticks and a volleyball! Their capacity to simply enjoy without commentary made me realize how often I criticize, and how that criticism affects my attitude.

I found myself wondering how many other children would see the skating as a gift rather than complaining because of the dire conditions they were in!

To see life as a gift—to see where we are as a gift—is not always easy. Perhaps like my church, we are in teaching situations that are, at best, difficult. Where is the gift? Is it in the eyes of the children? Is it in the support of fellow teachers? Is it in our grit and determination to make the best of what we have?

And if it is hard to see the gift, thank God anyway, knowing that God will give us eyes to see—like the children.

I name my gifts and proclaim your mighty acts, O Lord, in thanksgiving.

❄ **DECEMBER 31**   **Read James 1:17.**

When we look carefuly at our lives and put aside our petty preoccupations, it is amazing how much grace we see at work in our lives. We only need to have eyes to see.

I remember a gloomy morning years ago when a friend who was visiting took a walk down the alley behind our house with his toddler daughter. He was drinking a cup of coffee as he ambled along behind his daughter, and when he finished he attached the cup to his belt so he would have his arms free to carry her. As they explored the alley, a wizened homeless man, known in that community for collecting trash up and down the back alleys, came up and said hello. The two began to chat about the heat, the dismal state of the world, and the incredible cost of living. When they parted, the old man reached into his pocket, pulled out a dime, and dropped it into our friend's cup, saying, "I sure hope that helps you with your little girl and all."

Glimpses of grace happen with children all the time. I

used to write them down because I didn't want to forget them. It can be something as simple as my son singing to me, "I was born!" or a student dutifully writing a sentence for spelling such as, "I eat a quarter pounder with cheese for lunch."

My church used to have a Wednesday night Bible study. A handful of folks would gather, depressed about the week and commiserating with each other. We'd talk in hushed, somber tones about the text and we'd have heavy-laden prayers about the state of the world. One day, Billy decided to start by having each of us name one blessing that had happened to us in the past twenty-four hours—just one. We sat there quietly for a long time, and then someone plunged in with, "I'm thankful to be alive. That is my blessing." Suddenly the spirit caught on and we began to share the glimpses of grace, the gfits we had experienced. Some folks shared more than one! It was amazing how much that discipline of look-ing for the gifts transformed the entire mood of the Bible study for the years that followed.

Let us look for and celebrate at least one blessing a day. We just might be amazed at how much this simple discipline will transform not only ourselves but also our entire class-rooms.

Lord, I am thankful for this blessing I name in my heart.

January
Reaching Up and Reaching Out
Joan Laney

JANUARY 1 **Read Ephesians 6:10-19.**

y husband, Billy, and I have developed some traditions for seeing the old year out and the new year in. Every year, either on New Year's Eve or New Year's Day, we sit down together and share highs and lows of the past year. Sometimes we have to remind each other of certain events during the past year; sometimes the list of lows is much longer than the list of highs. But we find that by acknowledging them and sharing them, we reflect upon the year and learn from it.

Then we recall what we named the past year. (Sometimes we don't actually remember and we have to look back in our journals.) We try to see if what has happened and what we have done in the year have matched the name we gave that year. The year we named "Year of Boldness," for example, was the year we made a decision to leave one place for another and start new vocations.

Finally we name the upcoming year. After several years of doing this, we have run low on names we are willing to use!

We haven't reused "boldness" because we don't feel very bold. But there have been the year of waiting, the year of patience, and the year of vision. And it is always surprising how often the names really do correspond with how we feel during the year.

I've given up on New Year's resolutions, but I can name my year and try to act accordingly. I can reflect upon the mistakes and joys of the past year and see what I've learned. Those are traditions that work for me.

In this passage in Ephesians, Paul gives us a tradition of arming ourselves for whatever we have to face. He describes the armor of God: truth as the belt, integrity as the coat of mail, peace as the shoes, faith as the shield, salvation as helmet, and the words from God as sword. "Take up God's armour; then you will be able to stand your ground when things are at their worst, to complete every task and still to stand," he promises (6:13 NEB).

I know a devout Christian who "dresses" himself in God's armor every morning before he faces the day. It is a tradition that has borne fruit in his life. He simply radiates faith and love. He completes every task with wholehearted energy and joy. For seventy-something years he has witnessed to those around him in word and in deed.

As we face a new calendar year and the second half of this school year, let us find a tradition to strengthen ourselves in the faith. We can do a yearly appraisal or we can jump right in with arming ourselves daily in Christ.

Lord, help us begin this year with renewed faith, hope, and love.

❄ **JANUARY 2**   **Read Psalm 46:10.**

"Be still, and know that I am God!" (Psalm 46:10). I have always resisted this verse, probably because of the first two words, "be still." After all, I have places to go and people to see. I am too busy to let myself be still—and I certainly would not want anyone to think I was lazy!

A couple of years ago Billy gave me the birthday gift of a weeklong retreat—only this was a retreat of silence. Needless to say, I was not overly enthusiastic. The thought of silence and stillness sounded boring, but I went.

The days were structured with times of silence and stillness, followed by times of silence and writing, followed by sharing what had emerged from the silence. The first day I had to walk during the silence. It didn't work for me to be still. The second day I fidgeted. By the end of the week I was able to sit quietly for two hours and let the stillness nourish me. Somehow—don't ask me how—I was able to know God in that stillness as a peace and a strength I had been too frantic to experience before.

In the stillness I was able to trust God and let go of the worries that consumed me. I was able to lift up and let go of my fierce desire to play God, to control events and people in my life. I was able to feel the order God imposes on my life. I really felt the meaning of the verse, "Be still, and know that I am God!"

Stillness and silence were built into the retreat, but they are not built into my life. That is the challenge. Often I've resolved to sit quietly and recapture the sense of God and have been interrupted or distracted. It is a discipline that I am just learning to appreciate.

If I can set aside ten to fifteen minutes early each morning, I will be able to better center myself for the day ahead and not live in such a frazzled manner. If I imagine it to be time with a God that I love, as I like to spend time listening to my friends, I may be able to value it. It's not so much that God will speak as it is that I will listen—and feel the power of God's presence in my life.

Let me be still, O Lord, and listen to you, I pray.

❄ **JANUARY 3**   **Read Luke 11:5-10.**

This story ends with these familiar words: "Ask, and you will receive; seek, and you will find; knock and the door will be opened. For everyone who asks receives, he who seeks finds, and to him who knocks, the door will be opened" (Luke 11:9-10 NEB).

Somehow we have interpreted this text as the description of God as a cosmic Santa. Whatever we want—be it a parking place, a new lamp, a nice vacation spot, a raise—all we have to do is ask for it in faith. But I think this trivializes the story.

Look again at verse five. The one asking for three loaves wants them for a friend of his. He is not asking for the loaves for himself. He is advocating for another. Jesus is really saying, "If you ask on behalf of others, you will receive; if you seek on behalf of others, you will find; if you knock on behalf of others, the door will be opened."

What a wonderful promise for those of us who teach. We can pray on behalf of our students and God will answer. We don't have to do it perfectly. Think of the story. The friend comes banging on the door at midnight. Like the friend, we call upon God on behalf of our hurting students, and where possible, we call on the community to help.

Prayer allows us access to greater power than we would have alone, and access to a greater love. For that passage is followed by the observation: "If you, then, bad as you are, know how to give your children what is good for them, how much more will the heavenly Father give . . . to those who ask him" (Luke 11:13 NEB).

Gracious God, help us to keep asking on behalf of our students with the certainty that you will answer.

❄ **JANUARY 4**   **Read Matthew 6:9-13.**

Have you ever realized that the Lord's Prayer is subversive? We say it so automatically that it seems tame. It is too familiar to allow us to really hear what we are saying—because we might not want to pray it if we knew what we were praying for!

First of all, the Lord's Prayer is a communal prayer. In our individual-oriented society, that's pretty strange. We pray for the community, not just for ourselves. That ought to shake us up to start with.

We ought to worry when we come to the lines: "Your will

119

be done on earth as it is in heaven" (Matthew 6:10b NKJV). Do we mean that? What if God's will is justice for all people? We may have to do some sharing of our resources. What if God's will is food for the hungry—all over the world—and liberation for the captives? We may have to do some rethinking of stewardship and redesigning of prisons. What if God's will has to do with seeing all peoples as brothers and sisters, so that we no longer dismiss anyone's pain?

"Give us this day our daily bread" (v. 11 NKJV) is a prayer simply for what is enough for today. It's not a prayer of someone who has pantries full of food. It's not a prayer for meat or dessert! It's a prayer for bread, for nourishment that will satisfy us but not sate us. It's also a prayer for the entire world community to have bread—for today, which means whoever prays it takes some responsibility to see that bread gets shared.

But the kicker is this one: "Forgive us our debts, as we forgive our debtors" (v. 12 NKJV). The forgiveness of our sins is contingent upon the forgiveness we show others. We are so used to thinking of God's forgiveness as automatic, wiping the slate clean. But God's forgiveness is related to our ability to forgive. Wow!

The very end of the prayer reminds us that God is sovereign. The kingdom, the power, and the glory are God's, not ours. That is comforting to those of us who struggle to teach. God is ultimately in control and will work all things to his glory.

As Christian teachers, we must pray this prayer on behalf of ourselves and our students. We must implore God to do the things that God has promised to do—in our lives and in the world.

> *Our Father in heaven,*
> *Hallowed be Your name.*
> *Your kingdom come.*
> *Your will be done*
> *On earth as it is in heaven.*
> *Give us this day our daily bread.*
> *And forgive us our debts,*

As we forgive our debtors.
And do not lead us into temptation,
But deliver us from the evil one.
For Yours is the kingdom and the power
and the glory forever. Amen. (Matthew 6:9-13 NKJV)

❄ **JANUARY 5**   **Read I John 3:18.**

Listening is a forgotten art in today's society. It takes so much energy and concentration. How often when someone is talking to us do we make a mental list or plan the next day, feigning interest while our minds are far away?

Many of the ancient Christian writers talked about the art of being present to what is happening. They contended it is a form of prayer to be attentive to the present, not sinking into memory or skipping forward to what's ahead. Since listening to someone, being attentive to their words and feelings, is being present with them, it is a form of reverence. It says, "I am open to who you are right now."

Shirley Temple Black visited my parents' home this past summer and I had the honor of meeting one of my favorite childhood movie stars. We asked her what made her eyes sparkle so in the movies she made. She said simply, "I was totally focused on what I was doing, totally present." The art of being present to others makes Shirley Temple such a winsome character in her movies.

In *A Tree Full of Angels,* Macrina Wiederkehr puts it this way:

> The reason we live life so dimly and with such divided hearts is that we have never really learned how to be present with quality to God, to self, to others, to experiences and events, to all created things. We have never learned to gather up the crumbs of whatever appears in our path at every moment. We meet all of these lovely gifts only half there. . . . Yet the secret of daily life is this: *There are no leftovers!*
>
> There is nothing—no thing, no person, no experience, no thought, no joy or pain—that cannot be harvested and used for nourishment on our journey to God.

May we be present to the children in our care.

Dear Lord, help me to see your presence in the crumbs of my life, your being in those I am with each and every day.

❄ JANUARY 6   Read James 3:1-5.

I am one of those people who often say things before they think about them. My husband calls me the "gum ball machine." Whatever is in my head, I speak. I don't intend to be thoughtless, but I often seem very hurtful.

I was a youth group director at our inner-city church a few years ago. We had quite a large group of youth who lived in the neighborhood and were on the fringes of church, playing basketball in the gym or just hanging around. The associate pastor and I decided to have a lock-in as a way to attract them to church, build Christian community, and have fun.

We planned the lock-in carefully. We even had an admission charge so that the kids would give back something and learn awareness of the world's needs, not just their own. The admission fee for the lock-in was two cans of food per person to be given away in the food pantry.

We had a tremendous repsonse from the neighborhood youth. Even though many were from low-income families, they dutifully brought the canned goods. One young man who had been participating in activities at the church for a while showed up empty-handed. He seemed a bit confused as I stood in expectation at the door, waiting for his canned goods. "Where's your admission fee?" I asked. He stood there. I pointed to the sign and said, "It says bring two canned goods to get in! Can't you read?" With that he turned, gave me a look of hatred and bitterness, and left the church. I didn't see him again for years.

Not only did I shame this young man in public, but I trivialized the very real problem of people not being able to read.

In the letter to James, Paul has harsh things to say about the power of the tongue and the damage it can do. I learned the hard way by seeing the pain my words inflicted on a young man. May all of us teachers speak tenderly and lovingly.

Gracious God, guard our tongues that we may speak in love and kindness to others.

I walk my children to school most mornings. We pass a small, modest house on our way. Both front and back yards are glorious with flowers in the spring, summer, and fall. The woman who used to tend the flowers spent hours working on the yard, pruning the bushes, fertilizing the yard, making sure that everything grew. Whenever we saw her my children loved to say hello and comment on her work. In her forties, she wore a big straw hat as she worked, and she always spoke kindly to the children.

Last spring, however, we didn't see her. No one tended the yard, though the flowers bloomed anyway. We began to wonder where she was. My children missed seeing her and speaking to her. I found out that she died last winter of cancer. When I told my children, they truly grieved. "What will happen to her flowers?" they asked. We realized that we had never known her by name, only by "the flower lady."

This woman's life was heroic, not in a dramatic sense, but in her tenacious commitment to "bloom where she was planted." As long as she was able, she tended her garden, which then witnessed to the rest of us of resurrection and new life. For it is in those small acts of courage day by day that we change others' lives—like planting a garden that refreshes those who pass by.

We teachers may not ever do the dramatic. But our everyday acts of love and tenderness will speak to our students of resurrection and new life. We can tend them, our human garden, so that they will bloom long after we are gone.

Lord, give us the patience and the courage to concentrate on the small acts of love.

❄ JANUARY 8   Read I Corinthians 13:4-6.

"Lord, teach me to be disinterested in my own opinion." This has become one of my favorite prayers as I've gotten older and realized that, as much as I would like to, I do not know everything.

When Billy and I were first married and in our twenties, we had strong, almost rigid opinions. After we had been married a few months, we went on a spiritual retreat. Sister Madeleine was our hostess.

During one of our conversations in which Billy and I waxed eloquent on peace and justice and the evils of the world, Sister Madeleine said in a gentle, loving way, "In my twenties, I thought the problems were with everyone else and I had to solve them. In my thirties, I decided the problems were all within me and I had to solve them. In my forties, I realized that both the world and I were messed up and God's grace is the only thing that gets us through."

I remember those words often, particularly when I am determined to find fault with others. One summer when I taught Vacation Bible School to first and second graders, I had to relearn this truth. In our class of twenty-six active, bubbly children were two very withdrawn children who refused to participate in group activities. One would rip up her art project in order to do another. The other would taunt those children who were cooperating.

Finally I asked the director about the children. She said that both of them were in foster care because of abuse. Suddenly the children ceased to be problems I had to solve and became little people with a tragic past and deep pain. I and my co-teacher worked carefully with them and prayed for them.

By the end of the week, one wrote in big letters, "I love Vacation Bible school." Though their outward behavior didn't change much, our attitude toward them did. Thanks be to God!

Lord, help me be disinterested in my own opinion.

❄ **JANUARY 9**   **Read Ephesians 3:20-21.**

Sometimes God seems to have a marvelous sense of humor. Years ago I lived and worked in a Christian community in a poverty-stricken inner city. There was a neighborhood pool nearby, and several of the children affiliated with the community were on a swim team. There was only one problem: The neighborhood, though full of children, did not have enough swimmers to complete a swim team. It looked like the few that could swim would have to find another team to swim with or forget the competition altogether.

Someone asked the coach if there was an age limit to the swim team participants. The answer was no. We suddenly hit upon the brilliant idea of filling out the team with adults so that the children could compete. All we needed was six adults who could swim.

We discovered that since we were older than all the swimmers, we had our own age bracket. As long as we could finish the race, we could place and get the team points that would help the younger swimmers qualify for the city competition.

The catch was finishing the race because, though all six of us thought we could swim, our definitions of swimming varied greatly. One adult wandered all over the pool during the races, bumping into other swimmers and into the sides of the pool. Three couldn't dive, so they had to start the races from the side of the pool, making their times very slow. The woman who volunteered to do the breaststroke had to wear her glasses while swimming. She swam with her head above water. We were never sure if she could finish one lap, much less a race. Sometimes we wondered if she was moving at all!

But what fun we had. How we laughed at the expressions on the faces of the suburban parents when they saw our bedraggled team. The children—though often embarrassed by our antics—knew we loved and supported them enough to make complete fools of ourselves.

I suspect God loves it when we bend the rules a little for the sake of the children.

Help us to work together for the benefit of the children, O Lord. And keep us laughing so that we can enjoy the goodness you have given us.

❄ JANUARY 10   Read I John 3:18.

How many people who have told you about Christ have really changed your life? How many lectures or sermons do you remember that actually made a difference in your choices?

I suspect that if we are honest, we'll discover that words are not what converted us or changed us or made a difference. For the words to take root, they had to be connected to someone we trusted, or we weren't likely to listen. In fact, the words were probably not as significant as the way the person lived.

Surely this is the case with our students. What we do and the manner in which we do it often catch their attention far more than the words we speak, and our actions enhance or diminish what we say. If we are sharp and condescending, they will hear it in the tone of our voice, no matter what we say. If we show respect when we discipline them, then they won't feel belittled. It's amazing how perceptive they are!

Years ago I taught in an all white community that seemed to pride itself on the fact that no person of color lived or worked there. Being from the city and certain of my open-mindedness, I was scornful not only of this attitude but also of the people in the community. I'm sure that my arrogance was evident in my teaching. But as I got to know each student, I was better able to understand the struggle and tragedy that gave rise to their racism. They were tied to traditions that they themselves did not understand. Their racism was wrong, yes, but so was my arrogance. I realized that we were all in need of a merciful God.

Not surprisingly, during that year I was changed, and as I changed, my students began to trust me. I was saying the same things, but I had a different tone. When I arrived at school early or stayed late, students would come in to talk to me. Then and only then was real education possible. The words became part of the lives we shared.

In her book *Walking on Water*, Madeleine L'Engle quotes Emmanuel, Cardinal Suhard: "To be a witness does not consist in propaganda, nor even in stirring people up, but in being a living mystery. It means to live in such a way that one's life would not make sense if God did not exist."

O God, may we live the mystery of Christ's love.

❄ JANUARY 11   **Read Colossians 1:20; II Peter 3:9.**

I don't think many Christians believe what this verse in Colossians is saying. I'm not sure I do. God has reconciled everything on earth and in heaven through Jesus Christ. *Everything.*

This means that instead of the world being ruled by evil—as it seems to be—it is ruled by love. Instead of all the differences that divide us, we are joined together in that love.

It also means that those we would exclude—be they murderers or homosexuals or refugees or angry youth or even neo-Nazis or Ku Klux Klan members—are included in the circle of God's reconciling love. Nothing and no one is outside of God's reach.

If this is the truth, then why do we live as though it is not? Why do I spend energy focusing on divisions between myself and others instead of working to manifest that reconciliation? Why am I suspicious and judgmental? Clearly the only One to judge is God.

God has made it possible for us to be reconciled in our classrooms—to the bully or the crybaby, to the drug addict or the learning disabled student, to the honor student or the star athlete. All we have to do is recognize it and act upon it so that our students feel the reconciliation that God has already completed. The hard part is over. We have the easy part of believing it into being!

O God, may our classrooms—and our lives—be ruled by love.

❄ JANUARY 12   **Read Galatians 3:28.**

When we read about Rwanda or Bosnia and the ethnic cleansing taking place across the seas, it is easy to despair. Why are people killing other people in the name of Christ? Why are people of the same country turning against their neighbors? It is also easy to dismiss such violence as "over there" and not something we might have to face in this country.

But surely, we teachers know that ethnic cleansing is not out of the question in the United States. Take deep-rooted hatred and distrust for people who are different, add violence in large measure, and there is ethnic cleansing. At the rate our society is going—with its harsh condemnation of the poor and of those who are immigrants—we might be wise to learn lessons from Bosnia and Rwanda.

And we must start with the children, teaching them openness toward one another and patience with one another's differences. They must realize that we are all a part of God's great family.

As I have watched my children grow up, I've noticed that prejudice is not inherent. It is learned. My daughter was six when she came home from school one day and asked me why she was peach. She had suddenly realized that many of the children in her class were another color, and it shocked her. Over the years as my children have seen prejudice, they have been confused, wondering why people would treat others with contempt. How do we explain unfounded and unwarranted hatred to our children?

For the sake of the children and their future we have no choice. We must teach and model tolerance. Lest we dismiss this calling, listen to the words of twelve-year-old Edina as recorded in the book *I Dream of Peace:*

To all children throughout the world:

> I want you to know our suffering, the children of Sarajevo. I am still young, but I feel that I have experienced things that many grown-ups will never know. . . .
>
> No film can adequately depict the suffering, the fear, and the terror that my people are experiencing. Sarajevo is awash in blood, and graves are appearing everywhere. I beg you in the name of the Bosnian children never to allow this to happen to you or to people anywhere else.

For the sake of the children, let us teach tolerance for all.

O God, help us to love one another, for we are all made one in Christ.

While growing up, my family lived in Korea as missionaries for five years. Whenever we asked directions from someone, he or she usually accompanied us most of the way to our destination, especially when we had trouble understanding the directions. We found that even when the person didn't know the way, they would try to figure it out by walking with us, then turn around and retrace their steps!

Accompanying one another on the journey—isn't that what Christian faith is all about? Christ accompanies us, even through death to resurrection. Then he commissions us to accompany others. When we accompany someone who is different from us, it is called solidarity. It means we walk in their shoes for a while. Once we have experienced solidarity with someone, it is hard to dismiss their problems or their pain. We are forced to take them seriously.

Our students can learn to accompany others. My daughter's fourth-grade class had a unit on conflict resolution and peacemaking. During the unit they watched the movie *Gandhi.* My daughter was so overcome by the movie that her hand was the first one raised during the question and answer session afterward. She asked simply, "Am I British?"

If our students learn to accompany others, then the world may change.

O Lord, may we teach our students to accompany one another.

One of the worst school years of my life was the sixth grade. My family had just returned to the States from Korea, and had moved to New Haven, Connecticut. Though we attended a neighborhood school, it was the first year of busing to fulfill court-ordered integration, and the school was in turmoil.

My teacher was violently opposed to busing, but it had been forced upon her; so she carried out segregation right in her classroom. We were divided, the whites from blacks, right down the middle: taught separately, called different names, punished if we interacted with one another. There was an atmosphere of fear the likes of which I had never before experienced. I was an outsider to the other white children and different from the black children, so I sat in my desk at the back of the room and cried silently, day after day.

For many years I wrote off the sixth grade as not being worth remembering. I didn't learn anything except hatred and powerlessness. I witnessed day-to-day injustice and was unable to do anything about it.

Only as an adult have I realized how pivotal that awful year was in my life's experience. It planted within me a seed of awareness of racial prejudice that had not been there before. I heard and saw the ugliness firsthand, and it made me promise myself that if I ever taught school I would treat all my students with loving attention.

All experiences, good and bad, have the ability to teach us. One of the gifts of painful times is learning from them.

Gracious God, give us the strength and the courage to work for justice wherever you have placed us, and help us to learn from even the most painful experiences.

❄ JANUARY 15   Read Isaiah 42:6-7.

In August 1967, Dr. Martin Luther King, Jr., gave an address in Birmingham, Alabama, in which he talked about "divine dissatisfaction" that doesn't accept the wrongs of the status quo. He said:

Let us be dissatisfied until America will no longer have a high blood pressure of creeds and an anemia of deeds. Let us be dissatisfied until the tragic walls that separate the outer city of wealth and comfort and the inner city of poverty and despair shall be crushed by the battering rams of the forces of justice. Let us be dissatisfied until those that live on the outskirts of hope are brought into the metropolis of daily security. Let us be dissatisfied until slums are cast into the junk heaps of history, and every family is living in a decent sanitary home. Let us be dissatisfied until the dark yesterdays of segregated schools will be transformed into bright tomorrows of quality, integrated education. Let us be dissatisfied until integration is not seen as a problem but as an opportunity to participate in the beauty of diversity.

Every teacher ought to possess some of this "divine dissatisfaction." We are in a position of seeing the effects of injustice, prejudice, wealth, or poverty on the children we teach. We see the crushing results of broken homes. We see the dehumanization of our children surrounded by too much technology. Lest that lead us to a sense of despair, we must choose instead to be divinely dissatisfied, channeling our energies into making a small difference in our classrooms.

It's okay for the children to see our "divine dissatisfaction." It will affirm their own perceptions that something is wrong. They can watch us model creative ways of channeling such dissatisfaction—through caring relationships with students, through listening to others, through advocating for justice in the schools and in our communities, and through faithful and persistent prayer.

Lord, give us divine dissatisfaction so that we will not cease working for your kingdom to come on earth.

❄ **JANUARY 16**   **Read Matthew 12:25.**

Imagine a two-mile-wide militarized border between the northern and southern parts of our country. Imagine soldiers facing one another over a concrete sidewalklike border and on military alert—soldiers who could be from the same family looking at one another in hatred and distrust. The cost in human and monetary terms of maintaining such a divide is tremendous, yet for forty-three years North and South Korea have been divided.

When Billy and I visited there, we were struck by the childishness of the situation. It reminded him of a time in college when, in a fit of anger, he divided his room down the middle, not allowing his roommate to cross over the line.

In Korea the disputes are that childish. Whose flag on

which side is bigger? Whose building is taller? It's gone to such lengths that the signs on the north facing the south say things like, "Our president is better."

When our children saw this line separating one section of Korea from another and the soldiers lined up on each side, they were baffled. They wondered why both sides had not been able to work out their problems. They couldn't understand why one soldier hadn't simply stepped over the line and shaken hands with his "enemy." They could not see the situation as hopeless. Perhaps one of the children of the next generation will make peace across that divided land.

Our students will inherit this world, this world of age-old divisions and hatred, this world of childish arguments and refusal to reconcile. We teachers must be willing to help the children learn nonviolent ways of resolving their conflicts with one another or they will perpetuate the violence our generation has thoughtlessly continued. We must teach them to listen, to negotiate, and to work patiently for peace. Most important, we must teach them that God's will is peace for all people.

Lord, wherever there are divisions in our personal lives and in the lives of others, make us all one. Help us to teach our children to work for peace.

❄ **JANUARY 17**   **Read Psalm 126:5-6.**

My grandmother is ninety-six years old. She has weathered a good deal of pain in those ninety-six years. At age thirty she lost her husband in a plane crash. A few months later she lost all her insurance money in the stock market crash. In the space of a year her entire life was shattered, and she picked up her three little girls and moved back home to live with her parents. She got a job as a secretary and went on with her life, never remarrying but putting all of her energies into her family, her work, and her Sunday school class.

If you talk to my grandmother, she will tell you how full of blessings her life has been. She remembers the day of her husband's death as vividly as if it were yesterday, but she has no bitterness about it. Looking back she sees it all as part of God's plan for her life.

In his book *The Great Divorce,* C. S. Lewis writes, "All this earthly past will have been Heaven to those who are saved. Not only the twilight in that town, but all their life on earth too, will then be seen by the damned to have been Hell. That is what mortals misunderstand. They say of some temporal suffering, 'No future bliss can make up for it,' not knowing that Heaven, once attained, will work backwards and turn even that agony into a glory."

My grandmother is living testimony of this. Because of her certainty that God loves her, and because she believes that God is sovereign, she can look back on tremendous pain and see it as redeemed. The agony has been transformed into glory.

We are going to hit hard times sooner or later, because the profesion we have chosen deals with people. We are going to grieve for one student or another, we are going to feel a sense of failure at some time or another, we may even feel as though our world is falling apart. Through it all we will be upheld by a gentle, loving God who is picking up the pieces and weaving them into a beautiful tapestry, integrating the pain and the joy so that, from a distance, they will be a part of the pattern, necessary for the whole.

Please be with us, O Lord, be with us.

❄ JANUARY 18   Read Acts 16:25-27.

Here is the story: Paul and Silas have been imprisoned in Philippi for disturbing the economic equilibrium, and they are singing praises so loudly that the other prisoners can hear them. There is an earthquake that breaks the chains of the prisoners and opens all the prison doors.

What a wonderful story! Instead of cursing the jailers or being angry for their fate, Paul and Silas are celebrating, singing at the top of their lungs. The other prisoners may be bewildered wondering why these men are so joyful. And then—they are set free.

In *A Stone for a Pillow*, Madeleine L'Engle writes:

We all want justice, but if we demand it at the price of love it
will be dark justice indeed. I pray, fumblingly, for those who
have hurt me, for those I have hurt . . . Not a demanding
prayer, just an offering of a timid hope of love. . . . To hold
someone lovingly in my hands, my hands held out to God, is
to share, even in an infinitesimally tiny way, some of the
agony of the cross. . . . Hold out to the love of God those who
have hurt us. . . . Then it's time to move in even closer. To call
on God to bless and transform the enemy within ourselves.

When we call blessings instead of curses down upon those
who hurt and spite us, we free ourselves from the chains of
hatred and violence that imprison us. When we sing with joy
even through the hard times, those hard times cannot
enslave us in bitterness.

All of my friends who are teachers have been hurt by their
fellow teachers at one time or another. Rarely is there a
school with so much support throughout the faculty that
teachers don't occasionally hurt one another. This text suggests that true freedom is singing through the pain—not
holding on to it for future revenge!

*God, break the chains of bitterness that bind us and make us
whole, we pray.*

❅ JANUARY 19   Read Hebrews 10:23.

When my mother-in-law's mother died eighteen years
ago, among the things my mother-in-law, Marge, brought
home was a potted geranium that had belonged to her
mother. It bloomed for a few years and then it died. Marge
was unable to part with the soil or the pot, so she just put
them in the garage for eighteen years. Finally she decided to
throw the dirt away and keep the pot, so she went into the
far back of the yard and dumped the soil out. The soil
landed right beside a drainage area for the yard; whenever
it rained, a good deal of water would gather there. The spot
was also in the sun. That spring, much to Marge's amaze-

ment, there was a large blooming geranium, resurrected eighteen years after it last bloomed.

We often give up hope for what is, in fact, potential that is simply very hard to see. When we first came to our church ten years ago, the church treasurer was a feisty, take-charge woman in her late seventies. She had been treasurer for years. She did not like children one bit, and as children joined the church family, she lectured the parents on their behavior.

During the passing of the peace in worship, which she despised, she would actually push away the children who came to hug her. She treated one six-year-old boy particularly rudely, so he began to avoid her.

This spring, ten years later, she ran up to the boy, now sixteen, during passing of the peace and gave him a big hug. He was shocked. "What happened to her?" he asked his mother later.

Perhaps it was just ten years of experiencing children week after week. I prefer to see it as the work of God. Either way, the story holds within itself the clear message that we must not give up easily, but trust in the miracles of the One who created us.

Lord, teach us to wait for the miracles—in our classrooms, our homes, our churches, and our communities.

❄ JANUARY 20   **Read Lamentations 3:21-23.**

One of my favorite ways to meditate is to say or sing a line or two of a hymn over and over. Over the years one of my favorites has become "Great Is Thy Faithfulness." We used to sing it in the country churches Billy served. The day we moved to the city, a minister friend dropped by. Always the dramatic, he sang "Great Is Thy Faithfulness" in the empty house while we unpacked the U-Haul. His beautiful baritone echoed through the empty house and blessed it, reminding us of a promise God had made to us.

Through the next seven years as we served a tiny inner-city church, that hymn was to be our motto. All that we needed, God's hand *did* provide.

As teachers, we need to be reminded of this: God is faithful. Whatever we need will be provided to us. It may be more patience. It may be more discipline. It may be more money! But we must rely on God to provide it. We might even go so far as to say that if God doesn't provide it, we don't need it!

The words of "Great Is Thy Faithfulness" are actually taken from verses in Lamentations. Throughout five chapters, Lamentations records the grieving of a people for the fall of Jerusalem. But suddenly in chapter 3 comes the assurance: "But this I call to mind, and therefore I have hope: The steadfast love of the LORD never ceases, his mercies never come to an end; they are new every morning; great is your faithfulness" (vv. 21-23).

Never let us forget your faithfulness to us, O Lord God.

❄ **JANUARY 21**   **Read Jeremiah 25:3.**

One of the things I battled with most as an English teacher was despair. Teaching English, particularly grammar, to teenagers seemed futile at best, and hostile at worst! For many of them it had no relevance to their lives, no matter how hard I tried.

Then I read about Jeremiah. In Jeremiah 25:3 he says, "For twenty-three years, from the thirteenth year of Josiah son of Amon, king of Judah, to the present day, I have been receiving the words of the LORD and taking pains to speak to you, but you have not listened" (NEB).

Eugene H. Peterson in *Run with the Horses* elaborates:

> For twenty-three years Jeremiah got up every morning and listened to God's word. For twenty-three years Jeremiah got up every morning and spoke God's word to the people. For twenty-three years the people slept in, sluggish and indolent, and heard nothing. . . . Does that sound like a grim business? Tough sledding? . . .
>
> Jeremiah did not resolve to stick it out for twenty-three years, no matter what; he got up every morning with the sun. The day was God's day, not the people's. He didn't get up to face rejection; he got up to meet with God. He didn't rise to

put up with another round of mockery; he rose to be with his Lord. That is the secret of his persevering pilgrimage—not thinking with dread about the long road ahead but greeting the present moment, every present moment, with obedient delight, with expectant hope: "My heart is ready!"

Jeremiah's willingness to do this day after day, year after year, was a gift to God. He offered it faithfully, whether or not it was "effective" or "successful." Sure he got discouraged. His writing is full of discouragement. But it is also full of the certainty that he is doing what God would have him do, no matter what the consequences might be.

When we get discouraged, we must offer our days to God even more boldly. Then we need to let go and trust God to hold or use our gift—to his glory.

Lord, we offer this day to you with trust that you are acting in our lives.

❋ **JANUARY 22**   **Read II Corinthians 12:9-10.**

My great-grandfather grew up Scottish Presbyterian, a staunch Calvinist. My grandmother remembers him as fiercely religious, rigidly strict, and almost fearful to be around. He became a Methodist minister with a deep booming voice and powerful sermons, but he was not very pastoral. He was a powerful physical presence, tall and dramatic. He was very proud.

At eighty-two he had a stroke that left him blind and paralyzed on the right side of his body. He was bedridden and helpless, he who had once been so self-sufficient and independent. He had to be put into a nursing home.

But this man refused to be defeated. He never complained. He never expressed any self-pity. He listened to sermons on the radio and discussed them, as best he could, with whoever was there. He listened to church music. He took in all the current events, waxing eloquent on what ought to be done. And he was gentled by all that had happened to him so that I remember a wonderfully kind and attentive man who loved to listen

to me tell about school and encouraged me to sing to him—
not the proud disciplinarian my grandmother remembers.

He lived this way for fourteen years. He may have been
more truly a witness in his weakness than he ever was in his
strength.

That is God's promise to us: I can use you—if you trust me,
no matter what. What reassurance that gives us to face challenges both in and out of the classroom!

*Gracious God, remind us that your power is made perfect in our
weakness.*

❄ JANUARY 23   **Read Philippians 1:3-6.**

We experience many failures in teaching. Sometimes it's a
failure to reach a particular student. Sometimes it's a failure
to present the information in a way that excites our students. Sometimes we just fail because we are worn out. We
are tired of the endless rounds of planning, teaching, grading, record keeping, and administrating.

One of the failures I remember most vividly happened
during my first year of teaching high school. One of my students was often absent, and I was never able to reach her
parents by phone or by note. I asked the assistant principal
about this student, and she told me not to worry about her.
She would never follow through on attending school or
doing assignments, according to the assistant principal, so I
should give up on her. I pretty much did.

My final assignment for the class was an autobiography,
and the students worked long and hard on their papers. This
girl was not in school to complete the steps of the autobiography, and I assumed I would just give her an F. To my
surprise, she showed up with her autobiography on the day
it was due. Not only had she done the assignment, but she
had taken it very seriously. She had poured out her story on
those ink-stained pages. Her story was tragic. As I read it, I
wept. I could have been there for her, but I chose not to. She
desperately needed a mentor and a friend.

Yes, we teachers often fail. We say "no" to children who

need us. We say "no" to a system that needs to be changed. We say "no" to ourselves. But the good news is that God never fails. Therein lies grace. What we cannot do, for whatever reason, God can do. This is not an excuse for us to sit by and do nothing. Rather, it is a call to believe in the sovereignty of a God who loves these students far more than we could ever love them and to entrust those we have failed to God's loving arms. Grace picks up where our efforts leave off.

It has been seventeen years since I wept over that student's paper. I still remember her name. I still pray for her, knowing that God will be working in her life despite my failure to do so.

Lord, we lift up our failures, trusting that you can use them for your glory.

❄ JANUARY 24   Read Deuteronomy 30:19-20.

The older I get the more I am struck by the fact that no matter what happens to us, we always have a choice. We have a choice in how we will respond to the events in our lives that are beyond our control. We can choose bitterness or resignation or anger or acceptance or faith. As Victor Frankl wrote in *Man's Search for Meaning,* "The last of the human freedoms [is] to choose one's attitude in any given set of circumstances, to choose one's own way." Sadly, I know many more people who have chosen bitterness or depression rather than trust or acceptance. In our society, that seems predominant.

Years ago I visited Nicaragua at the height of the civil war there. I met women who had lost brothers, husbands, and sons in a war not of their choosing. Many of them were so poor that they didn't even have a single photograph of their lost loved one. Yet they were not bitter. They told their stories tearfully, but they insisted that God was the God of resurrection, so they were refusing to be bitter toward the enemy. The enemy was the United States.

They had every right to hate me, a U.S. citizen. They had every right to be bitter because my tax dollars had funded the means of killing their family members. But because of their faith, they were choosing to trust God in death as well as in life. I'll never forget the rousing choruses of "We adore you, we adore you, we adore you, O Lord" that they sang with fervor, despite their suffering.

As teachers, no matter how difficult the class, how time-consuming the preparations, or how overwhelming the needs of the students, we have a choice: to believe that God is at work or to give up. Our students' faith depends on what we choose.

Help us to choose faith, O Lord, each day of our lives.

❄ JANUARY 25   Read I Peter 5:7.

My daughter went through a period last fall when she was fearful about dying. I remember having similar fears when I was her age and not knowing how to handle them. I talked to her about them. "The only thing I can tell you," I said, "is to pray. Tell God about your fears."

That night when we were saying bedtime prayers, Ruth prayed, "Lord, I am afraid of dying, so please don't let me die. But if I do die, please let me be an angel so I can watch over my family." Then she slept peacefully. She prays that prayer every night, and it keeps her fears at bay.

One of the hardest lessons to learn as we grow up is that we are ultimately not in control. We may do a lot of things to think we are in control; we may even manipulate our lives so that we are as much in control as possible. But we really don't have a whole lot of power.

So we must learn to turn our worries and fears and all that we would control over to God. And we must learn to trust God's providence.

We also must teach this to our students. Their world is going to be so much more technological than ours that they may mistakenly come to believe in the power of humankind. But maybe we can plant the seed of trust, that God is and should be in control and that we can trust our God.

O God, help us to place our fears in your hands.

One of my most vivid memories of religion is the hellfire-damnation sermons of my youth. The sermons were so vivid, so awful in their description of the torments of hell, that I went down to the altar on a regular basis. I also drove my minister father to distraction by frequently asking him if he was sure he'd been saved.

The tragedy of those sermons is that they had it all wrong. They were going to scare us into loving Christ. Imagine! They used fear to intimidate people, mostly children, into salvation.

In a sermon I once heard, the preacher contended that there are 365 phrases of "do not fear" or "do not be afraid" in the Bible, one for every day of the year. Would such a God want us to turn to Christ out of fear? I don't think so.

In *The Active Life,* Parker Palmer discussses fear. "The core message of all the great spiritual traditions is 'Be not afraid,'" he says. "Rather, be confident that life is good and trustworthy. In this light, the great failure is not that of leading a full and vital active life, with all the mistakes and suffering such a life will bring (along with its joys). Instead, the failure is to withdraw fearfully from the place to which one is called, to squander the most precious of all our birthrights—the experience of aliveness itself."

We need to claim each "do not fear" of the Scriptures daily, and then teach and live boldly!

Gracious God, take away the fear that cripples us and keeps us from doing what you have called us to do.

Sometimes teaching feels like walking "in dark places with no light" (Isaiah 50:10 NEB). There are so many demands, and often no clear signal about what is the most important. Do we spend our time with one hurting student or use that time for the entire class? Do we teach to improve the standardized testing scores—which makes everyone look better—

or do we teach what the children will be able to use in their lives? How do we make decisions that are consistent with our faith and yet set clear boundaries so that we don't burn out?

According to this text, we have two choices when it comes to walking "in dark places with no light." We can trust in God to guide us. Or we can kindle our own fire and walk in its light.

Kindling our own fire means that we become self-sufficient and figure it out ourselves, a practical thing to do when we don't have a lot to go on. The problem is that we let go of our reliance on Christ. We decide that we don't really need God. Our decisions arise out of what we want rather than what God calls us to do. Ultimately, our lights go out. We crash, burn out, give up.

In my first year of teaching public high school, I quit in March. I could not go on. The preparation, grading, paperwork, discipline problems, and overwhelming pain of my students were too much for me to bear. I worked from dawn until eleven or twelve every night—and most of the weekends—and it didn't seem to make much difference. There was still work to do, students in pain, little sign of change. I gave up in despair and resigned.

I realized much later that my burnout was because of my "lighting my own fires" instead of leaning on God. I just figured that if I worked harder, cared more, and gave more time I could change both my students and the school! How utterly egotistic! God was calling me to let go and lean on a God who loved those students far more than I ever could. I was being required to "walk in dark places with no light" yet trust in the name of the Lord and lean on my God.

To light our own fires is tempting; to trust in God is extremely difficult. One light will burn on and the other will burn out. Which do we choose?

Light of the world, show us the way.

❄ **JANUARY 28**   **Read Matthew 5:4.**

There are children who often do not respond to anything we teachers do. For some reason they seem intractable, unyielding. Though we feel extremely powerless when we encounter these children, we do have power. We have the power to mourn over these children, to grieve their anger and pain. In the act of mourning we are praying for them. We are yearning for their wholeness. I cannot help but think that this may make a difference in their lives—a difference we may never know about, but a difference nonetheless.

We have to trust that God will take the broken offering of our sorrow for these children and transform it into a touch of grace. We have to trust that looking upon these children with love will gentle them. We have to trust, but we may never know for sure.

If we think back over our own lives, perhaps we can remember persons who lifted us up in exactly that way, persons whose prayers or pain on our behalf made a difference in our lives. And most likely, those we remember never knew how they touched us—*but they did!*

My ninth-grade English teacher was such a person. By the time I entered her class, I was attending my fifth school in five years, and I had decided that I had nothing to lose by misbehaving in class and talking back to the teacher. She was strict and demanding, but she allowed me to stay after school and talk to her; she tutored me through grammar on her own time; she insisted that I behave. I never thanked her for her care, time, and energy. She never knew that I became an English teacher because she refused to give up on me.

Blessed are they that mourn over their students for they shall be comforted.

Lord, help us to trust that our love for those children who seem beyond our reach will make a difference.

❉ JANUARY 29   Read Isaiah 40:28-31.

The Bible is full of waiting. Sarah and Abraham waited for a child and for the fulfillment of the promise. Joseph waited for years in an Egyptian prison before he was released. The children of Israel waited for hundreds of years for deliverance from slavery. The Psalms and the book of Isaiah are replete with admonishments to "wait on the Lord."

Jesus' ministry had many delays, forcing people to wait. As he was heading to Jairus's home to heal his daughter, Jesus stopped to heal the hemorrhaging woman. Meanwhile Jairus's daughter died. Even his close friend Lazarus died before Jesus got there; Mary and Martha waited four days for Jesus to come. Their reproach: "If you had been here, [our] brother would not have died" (John 11:21).

One of my greatest struggles as a parent and a teacher is in having patience—being able to work and wait and trust that my efforts will bear fruit in the lives of the children. Yet waiting is our task as Christian teachers. It makes us relinquish control. When we wait in the biblical sense, we wait for God's action in the world.

An older couple in our church witnessed gently but firmly to the boys in the neighborhood who came to play basketball in the gym but never attended church. The boys would pass through their lives, leave the neighborhood, and never be heard from again. But this couple never stopped their faithful witness, even though it didn't seem to bear fruit.

One day this couple and I were attending an ecumenical worship service when a young man came up and hugged them. He was a member of a church choir, and he attributed his involvement in church and his "going straight" to the witness of this couple. After years and years, their efforts had borne fruit.

Let us have courage and wait on the Lord. Our work *will* bear fruit.

Lord, though we grow weary, you never do. Strengthen us with patience.

❄ **JANUARY 30**   **Read I Corinthians 15:58.**

A few years ago when I was teaching in a public school and was extremely discouraged at the lack of response to all my work, I read a fable entitled "The Weight of Nothing."

"Tell me the weight of a snowflake," a coal-mouse asked a wild dove. "Nothing more than nothing," was the answer.
"In that case I must tell you a marvelous story," the coal-

144

mouse said. "I sat on the branch of a fir, close to its trunk when it began to snow, not heavily, not in a raging blizzard, no, just like in a dream, without any violence. Since I didn't have anything better to do, I counted the snowflakes settling on the twigs and needles of my branch. Their number was exactly 3,741,952. When the next snowflake dropped onto the branch—nothing more than nothing, as you say—the branch broke off."

Having said that the coal-mouse flew off. The dove, since Noah's time an authority on the matter, thought about the story for a while and finally said to herself, "Perhaps there is only one person's voice lacking for peace to come about in the world."

Our work may seem "nothing more than nothing" sometimes. But we must believe that it will make a difference. We must believe in the one snowflake that makes the branch break, even if we are not around to see it.

Lord, we may be "nothing more than nothing," but in time even that makes a difference. Help us to believe.

❄ JANUARY 31   Read Malachi 3:10.

I have always loved rainbows. They are a sign of God's everlasting covenant with us not to destroy humankind. Each rainbow I see is a fresh reminder of that promise.

For years, whenever it was raining while the sun was shining, I'd run outside to see if there was a rainbow. When I was in my twenties and struggling through a failed marriage, it seemed as though there were no rainbows for five or six years. Then one day when I was waitressing at a restaurant, I ran outside during a storm to see a rainbow arching across the sky. Later I told a friend that "the rainbows were back." She replied, "The rainbows were always there. It's just that you've started to look up again."

Yes, the rainbows are always there. As I've had children, I've made a point of looking for rainbows with them. It's amazing how many rainbows children can find. Once we saw three parallel rainbows in grandeur over the mountains.

Another time, in my zeal to tell the children about a rainbow over our house, I ran into the house and tripped over myself, falling flat on my face and scaring my family to death!

"Put me to the proof, says the LORD of Hosts, and see if I do not open windows in the sky and pour a blessing on you as long as there is need" (Malachi 3:10 NEB). When things seem dark and gloomy—when students are not interested in learning, when a difficult student requires constant attention and energy, when the day seems like it will never end—remember that the rainbows are always there. Count those rainbows! Even better, count your *blessings*. As we notice the gifts we are given, we realize that they do indeeed pour down from heaven upon us.

Gracious God, remind us to count our rainbows and to name our blessings, so we never forget that you are good.

February

Making a Difference

Joan Laney

Read Luke 12:34.

ne of the hardest lessons to teach ourselves, much less our students, is the truth of this verse: "For where your treasure is, there your heart will be also" (Luke 12:34). Right before Jesus tells this to his disciples, he reminds them of the beauty of the lilies and of the grass, both of which are clothed by God. "And so you are not to set your mind on food and drink," he tells them; "You are not to worry" (12:29 NEB). And later: "You have a Father who knows that you need them" (12:30b NEB).

When my church first decided to start an after-school program years ago, a young woman in our church felt called to be the director of the program. She lived fifteen miles from the church and had two small children, but she was certain that God meant for her to direct the program. She drove into town daily, her children in tow, to create a program from scratch with few resources. She had many false starts, trouble with staff, problems with the aging building; she had to fight for funds and for materials. But she plugged away until she had a program that used college volunteers as well as paid staff and a multitude of eager, rambunctious children. But what struck me the most about her work was that her heart was in it. She saw the face of Christ in children who could be as rude and difficult as any I'd seen. And because they felt that love, the children kept coming to the church to see Robin. Furthermore, she hung in there tenaciously when all others had quit. God had called her to do this work, and she was going to do it. Throughout the entire time she directed the program, she felt a sense of peace that was incomprehensible to those of us who saw the behavioral problems and the staff problems and the money problems.

Eventually she and her family relocated into the center of the city near the church. Their treasure no longer was the dream of financial success and upward mobility. Instead she treasured God and the children whom God had called her to tend.

What work is God calling you to do today? This week? This year?

Gracious God, put our hearts where they belong.

❄ FEBRUARY 2   Read Mark 9:23.

When I take my dogs for a walk, there is always something to observe. On one route around a nearby college, we no sooner walk beneath some trees than a tiny blue jay dive-bombs the unwitting dogs on the rump, causing them to veer ever so slightly. Then he repeats the whole thing again and again: the angry fussing, the dive, the thump, until the dogs, despite themselves, have altered their route in some way.

The audacity of that bird! It never occurs to him that he can't do the impossible—get the dogs to change where they are going. He never sits up in the tree just complaining, either. He *acts*. He acts with passion and fervor and faith that his actions will make a difference. And though the dogs never do catch on, he alters the way they are headed every time!

Maybe teaching is like that blue jay. We are given students who have their own personalities, interests, and inclinations. To think that we will have any lasting effect on their lives is arrogant. Yet, like the blue jay, we *do* affect their lives. We provide little thumps that help to steer our students on a safer and healthier path.

We have to have the persistence of the blue jay. We have to have the faith that ultimately the little things we do will make a difference in the lives of our students. And then we must thump ahead!

Gracious God, give us the faith to believe that all things are possible through you.

❄ FEBRUARY 3   Read Amos 5:14.

Several years ago Doug Huneke, a Presbyterian minister and religious educator, wrote a book entitled *The Moses of Rovno.* He had undertaken the task of interviewing three hundred rescuers of Jews during the Holocaust to determine if they had any characteristics in common that could be taught to others. He actually discovered ten characteristics that all the rescuers had in common, and he listed them in his last chapter. He encouraged parents to take these seriously so that their children would be compassionate risk-takers as they grew up.

All the rescuers were adventuresome. They were able to present themselves publicly, having done some kind of performing while growing up. They had identified with a morally strong parent. Their homes had valued hospitality and welcoming visitors. But even more interesting, all had been exposed to suffering at an early age and had experienced some form of marginalization themselves. Thus they possessed an empathetic imagination that allowed them to identify with the suffering of others. They were able to recognize and deal with their own prejudices. They had the ability to plan specific ways to help others. And finally, they were convinced that they were not in the struggle alone.

As teachers, we can nourish these characteristics in our students, whether or not they are taught at home. Certainly we can help our students identify with the suffering of others and think of concrete ways to alleviate that suffering. Certainly we can teach them that they are not alone in their concern for justice and right living. Certainly we can teach them that they make a difference and that their lives can make the world a better place.

As Oscar Romero, martyred archbishop of El Salvador, wrote:

> This is what we are about. We plant the seeds that one day will grow. We water seeds already planted, knowing that they hold future promise. We lay foundations that will need further development. We provide yeast that produces effects far beyond our capabilities. We cannot do everything, and there is a sense of liberation in realizing that. This enables us to do something, and to do it very well. It may be incomplete, but it is a beginning, a step along the way, an opportunity for the Lord's grace to enter and do the rest. (Quoted in *Baptist Peacemaker*, Spring-Summer 1994.)

Let us pray for the grace to plant the seeds.

Help us to nurture the young lives in our care, O Lord.

❄ **FEBRUARY 4**   **Read Ephesians 2:22.**

When I visited my parents in South Korea recently, my mother asked me to go with her to her flower arranging class. Now, I'm not much on flower arranging—I just enjoy what others have put together—so I resisted the invitation. But my mother persisted and I found myself trudging along to a flower arranging class, wondering how in the world she'd gotten me there.

The instructor was a tiny Korean woman in traditional Korean dress who greeted us warmly and then took us into a room with flowers and vases where some women were working. As she talked, it became clear that she had several principles: (1) Even one flower, if artfully arranged, can be a flower arrangement; (2) Flowers must be pruned carefully for beauty and for health; (3) Flowers must face upward at all times because that is where they get their nourishment;

(4) Flowers must have space in an arrangement so they will be "comfortable."

As we worked with our flowers, I thought of how much these principles change flower arranging from something I once did automatically—or, more often, didn't do at all—to a thoughtful, caring process that brings out the beauty of the flowers and the artistry in me.

Then I thought about teaching. What if these were guiding principles for teachers? How would they help bring to bloom the beauty in our students? How, for example, would our attitudes change if we considered each student a complete and beautiful whole—like a one-flower arrangement? Then, given the right touches, each student could flourish and bless the world simply by being. Or what if we saw teaching as a combination of loving touch and pruning, helping each student to see what needs changing—a bad habit here, a negative attitude there? Or what if we helped our students to face upward—that is, enabled them to acknowledge God in all things by modeling that in our own lives? And what if we taught each student to claim his or her space, his or her gifts and talents, in order to be comfortable with his or her life?

O God, our students are as diverse and beautiful—and sometimes as unwieldy—as flowers. Grant us the grace to be loving flower arrangers in their lives.

❄ FEBRUARY 5   Read I Corinthians 12:4-7.

One of the things that strikes a North American in Seoul, Korea, is the incredible industry of the Korean people. Everyone works, and everyone takes that work seriously. Everyone does his or her best, no matter how menial the job is.

Whe we went into the Korean markets, we saw this in action. Each vendor might have had just a card table of buttons or fish or jeans, but they were selling their wares with fervor. One woman was squatting there cooking corn to sell; another was frying squid; another selling wrapping paper. A man had set up a shoe repair at the entrance to the subway. An old woman was selling freshly dug gingerroot on the sidewalk. It reminded me of the old saying: "A place for everything and everything in its place."

What if we were to teach this to our students—that each has a place and belongs in that place? It is similar to Paul's discourses in I Corinthians about gifts and claiming our gifts. Sadly, most of us covet someone else's gift! And yet when we claim our own gifts proudly, what beauty there is. Like the Korean market, what beauty and what diversity, from the lady selling buttons to the woman selling flowers by the bus stop.

Lord, let us help our students find their place in this world, we pray.

❄ **FEBRUARY 6**   **Read Mark 9:33-37.**

I wonder who invented competition. Who made it fun to try to outdo someone else at something? As my children grow up, competition is all around them—competition for the biggest house, the most gadgets, the hardest-working parents, the snazziest car, the best grades, the most wins in any sport, and the list goes on and on.

It wasn't until I was an adult that I heard a novel idea: There isn't a scarcity of superlatives. Just because someone I know is very smart does not diminish my being smart. Just because someone does well in a soccer game does not diminish my doing well. Somehow we've been coerced into believing that if someone else does something really well, we are lessened. That is not true.

I love this passage where James and John are arguing over who is going to sit at Jesus' right hand. One of them is determined to beat the other out of that honored position. But Jesus doesn't get into the competition. He redefines what it means to be great, turning the definition completely on its head: "Whoever wants to be first must be last of all and servant of all" (Mark 9:35).

We don't need to get all caught up in competition, nor do we need to encourage our students to do so. Rather, each student should feel as though he or she has a gift to contribute to others. And every gift needs to be seen as integral to the class. Each gift must be celebrated.

I'll never forget my son's kindergarten "graduation." Each student in the class of twenty-six was given a certificate acknowledging something that child did well. Because he is full of helpful information (to some a know-it-all), his certificate said, "The one who knows about a lot of things." I'll never forget the smile on his face—and the smiles on twenty-five other faces as they read their carefully chosen gifts on their certificates.

"Whoever wants to be first must be last of all and servant of all," Jesus says. Then he takes a child and continues, "Whoever welcomes one such child in my name welcomes me" (Mark 9:35-37). Our profession provides us with the opportunities for servanthood—and the children to serve. What a blessing!

Gracious God, help us name the gifts we see in every child who crosses our path.

❄ **FEBRUARY 7**   **Read James 1:16-18.**

When people get beaten down, it's easy for them to become self-pitying. Self-pity generates feelings of helplessness and hopelessness, which can incapacitate. When someone feels unable to act, he or she feels more self-pity, and the cycle continues.

When we first came to our inner-city church ten years ago, it had declined from a thriving 1,200 members in the 1950s to a handful of folks over sixty years of age. The first Sunday Billy preached in the old sanctuary, it looked empty because the few people who attended were scattered all around the cavernous space. Billy was told privately by the powers that be that he could close this church at any time.

The building was in shambles because of lack of money. There was no air-conditioning or heat for most of the building. But the congregation figured they had nothing to lose, so they began ministries to the neighborhood: an after-school program, a food pantry, a clothing sale, neighborhood festivals for children. The church grew a little as a result of all these ministries, and somehow there was enough money to continue financing outreach to the community.

This little church continued in its witness years after the powers that be had decided it might need to close.

In the same city, just around the corner, was another church with declining membership of the same denomination. This church had a fine building with heat and air-conditioning; it had groups renting the space and helping to pay upkeep; it had faithful members and a devoted pastor. But the congregation was never able to claim its power. Whenever the pastor suggested a mission or outreach to the neighborhood, they sighed and said, "We're too old. We don't have enough people. We don't have enough money." And so the church continued with meetings and worship but did not have much contact with its neighborhood. Over the same period of years it lost members through death and transfer, until finally it closed its doors.

Gandhi used to tell the poverty-stricken and oppressed people he worked with in India that no matter how down in the dumps someone might be, he or she always could give a gift of some kind. He felt like the best way to empower people was to make them feel that they could give something to someone else.

The power of this principle can be shown by the lives of the two churches: One said, in effect, we can't do much but we will give something to others; the other one said, basically, we have nothing to give. One lived. The other died.

We must empower our students. No matter how much they fail or how difficult they are to teach, they have a gift to give. It will change their lives to discover that gift—and to give it to someone else.

Lord, may our faith in their gifts empower our students to claim them.

❄ **FEBRUARY 8**   Read Jeremiah 29:7.

For ten years I have complained about our city's heat, humidity, racism, crime, apathy, affluence, and on and on. Then one day I ran across this verse: "But seek the welfare of the city where I have sent you into exile, and pray to the

LORD on its behalf, for in its welfare you will find your welfare" (Jeremiah 29:7).

I confess: I identify more with the exile part of that verse than with its command! I feel exiled in this city, though I know that God has called me to live here and make this my home. I am indicted by the words of this verse because I have not sought its welfare or prayed for it as I have been asked to do—even though my welfare is tied in with the welfare of this city.

Teachers really do have power to seek the welfare of the city because we have access to one of the city's greatest resources, its children. As we actively seek the welfare of the children, we work on behalf of the city. And that is no small task.

It is biblical, though. Our welfare is connected to the welfare of the children we teach. As they learn reverence for life and tolerance of others and identify the gifts they can offer to society, they bring welfare to the city. More than welfare, they bring *shalom*, that wonderful Old Testament word that means wholeness and healing in all its dimensions.

Imagine how the city will change as the children change. Imagine justice and love in the place of anger, mistrust, and violence. Imagine each child growing up to find a place for his or her gifts and talents. God has promised it!

Gracious God, deliver on your promises, we pray.

❄ **FEBRUARY 9**   **Read Isaiah 6:9-10.**

We all live barricaded behind our assumptions—invisible walls that separate us from one another. When I taught freshman composition—that required course so despised by college students—I found that I first had to open up their thinking a little and help them realize how limited their worldview was. Then they could write more authentically.

The assumptions made by students in suburban schools, for instance, are vastly different from those made by students in inner-city schools. In many cities, where one attends school often determines whether or not the school is air-conditioned, has a science lab, offers music or art, or teaches a foreign language. Givens for some students; gifts for others.

As a nation, our society makes assumptions. It rarely occurs to us that we who make up 6 percent of the world's population consume 45 percent of its goods. We assume it is our right to have running cold and hot water, drinking water in our homes, access to swimming pools. We see it as our right to have at least one car, one TV, one VCR, one computer—when in the world's eyes, these are luxuries, not rights.

How eye opening it has been for me to travel to places where people walk everywhere—sometimes four miles to school, for instance; where they carry heavy loads on their backs or heads; where they have to go daily to the well for water; where they eat rice for breakfast, lunch, and dinner; where baths are a luxury; where a day's wage is less than one dollar.

All of us need our assumptions about life to be expanded—if not exploded. As teachers, we must be willing to broaden the worlds of our students. They are growing up in a global society. We can help them to be prepared.

The "catch" is that as we become aware of our own assumptions and then our interconnectedness with others, we become more healthy about our choices, about the difference between what we need and what we want. When we assume responsibility for how our choices affect others, we learn a larger, more inclusive love.

Lord, may we open our students' eyes to their interrelatedness with people all over the world.

❄ **FEBRUARY 10**   **Read John 9:39-41.**

In Korea in ancient times, children of royalty were not allowed outside palace walls. Elaborate gardens were built for walks and exploring, but the children never ventured beyond those walls. The boys were allowed to study; they knew of the world through books. The girls were not permitted formal education. All they knew of the world was what they could glimpse as they rose high on the seesaw or took a turn on the swings.

Imagine growing up with such a skewed perception of the world. The world they knew was only part of the world—the palace, the gardens, the royalty, the servants. Not a realistic portrait of life beyond palace walls.

Some of us or perhaps some of our students have been raised behind proverbial palace walls. We are overprotected. We assume that the world we live in is the only world there is. We don't venture outside of our safe boundaries. We don't think much about other regions of our cities or our county or our world.

Some well-meaning members of a suburban church in our city contacted our inner-city church because they wanted to begin a Saturday morning breakfast for the homeless using our church as a base. They had arranged to come at 7:30 on Saturday mornings, cook breakfast, serve it to the homeless, clean up, and leave by nine. I tried to tell them that most people in our neighborhood, homeless or not, sleep late on Saturdays and so the time needed to be changed. "But people are up early around here," they said, "and they want to get this done and get back home for the day."

Needless to say, the breakfast eggs, bacon, and toast got cold every Saturday morning while the church members drank coffee and wondered where all the homeless people were. They refused to go over the wall!

A teacher once told me that teaching is, metaphorically speaking, like throwing students over a wall. Teachers must help their students grapple with the differences between their perceptions and their experiences, between their theories and the practice of those theories. The best education is hands-on, getting into the dirt and grit of life!

Lord, help us to be willing to go over the wall, and empower us to throw our students over the wall with us!

❄ FEBRUARY 11   Read Psalm 145:8-9.

As we approach the twenty-first century, one of the most important lessons we can teach our students, no matter what their ages, is that we are all interconnected. We know that we are living in a global society, yet we do not really understand the implications of that fact.

The coffee we drink is grown, most likely, in Central or South America, on land that could grow crops to feed hungry children. The sugar we put on our cereal has been harvested by migrant farmworkers who do this grueling work without adequate pay or medical benefits. The clothes we wear—even if labeled "made in America"—are most likely assembled in America from pieces made in factories overseas, factories where women of all ages crouch over sewing machines for hours and hours a day, again without medical care or adequate pay.

As Americans who live a middle-class lifestyle, we endorse injustice without realizing it. We don't want to hurt anyone, but few of us are willing to go without. Unless we grow our own fruits and vegetables in our own gardens, we unwittingly participate in oppression simply by buying the fruits and vegetables so shiny and bright in our grocery stores. It is sobering.

But, realistically, what can we do with this information? We can teach our students that their choices matter. We can teach them that they can garden; they can buy local products; they can boycott products from countries where policies hurt people; they can be aware. They can stop taking for granted what are luxuries for others. And, if they are really serious, we can tell them Gandhi's maxim: "I will not buy what I don't need until all people enjoy what they do need."

Lord, teach us to be good stewards of all you have given us.

❄ **FEBRUARY 12**   **Read Philippians 2:5-9.**

There is often something about teaching that catches us off balance, some unexpected happening thrown into the day's plans or some interruption that causes the day to go haywire. On my first day of teaching, it was learning that not only was I given a trailer for a classroom, but the trailer had no desks for the students! On my second day of teaching, it was being assigned to teach geography instead of English. By the third day at that first job, I was off balance, indeed!

Henri Nouwen calls this displacement. One of my closest friends says it is "getting out of our comfort zones." Whatever it is called, it feels uncomfortable and requires of us skills that we may not think we possess.

But displacement is biblical. Think of Jesus, God in the flesh. What an ungodly thing to do, to put on human form. Not only was Jesus human, but he also associated with not-so-godly folks—lepers, prostitutes, tax collectors, demoniacs, widows, Samaritans. Certainly he chose discplacement. He chose to identify with those who suffered and were outcast from society. He could have spent most of his time in the temple with the religious people doing what was expected of a religious person. But he chose to be displaced.

As Christians, we are called to be displaced. It may mean teaching in an unfamiliar part of town and learning about a neighborhood different from our own. It may mean teaching students from another country or students with physical or mental disabilities. It may mean teaching that requires of us new skills. It may simply mean listening so carefully to the stories of our students that we grieve with them and celebrate with them. Whatever it is, it keeps us just a little off balance.

Maybe we are called to be displaced because it forces us to trust in God. We find ourselves not quite up to the task ahead and we must give up control to God. It also calls forth from us compassion, the ability to suffer with others, the ability to love.

Lord, even if it means being displaced, teach us compassion.

❄ **FEBRUARY 13**   **Read Matthew 7:1-2.**

It was Atticus in *To Kill a Mockingbird* who told his daughter, Scout, that you could not judge anyone until you had walked in their shoes.

How often I've had to relearn this lesson! I am so quick to assume that I know why someone is making the "wrong" choices. I'm great at appraising situations and pronouncing judgment. Rarely do I stop to think of the reasons why someone is acting in a particular way.

When my son began kindergarten in a huge neighborhood school, the transition for him from three half days of preschool to five full days of kindergarten was very difficult. We made a deal that I would go to school during his thirty minutes of lunch and sit with him while he ate. Then he'd hang in there the rest of the day.

Lunch was chaos for these kindergartners. Their teachers received a much-needed break, but the children had no one to help them eat. I found myself peeling oranges and unwrapping packaged foods that they couldn't manage. I encouraged them to eat. I tried to keep the food-throwing and teasing to a minimum.

One child sat there during lunch every day—his untouched tray of food before him—and wept. No one had much patience with him. The children made fun of him. I was so preoccupied with my son that I didn't pay him much mind.

Then one day I asked him why he was crying. He said, "I'm so tired. My brothers keep the TV on all night, and I can't sleep." I asked him where he slept. "On the couch in the living room," he answered.

Imagine what that five-year-old had to deal with daily! Getting up exhausted, going to school, overwhelmed with the desire to sleep. He easily might be dismissed as a crybaby, but he had reason to cry!

Our students—whatever their ages—bring a host of problems and pain to school with them. Our task is to try to walk around in their shoes for a while. It might teach us to love.

Gracious God, teach us to try to understand others—especially our students—rather than judge them.

❄ FEBRUARY 14   Read Matthew 25:31-46.

This is an all too familiar story. We know how Jesus describes the Last Judgment and how he will separate the sheep from the goats. We know the criteria; we know the specific acts Jesus names. We know all that.

What I had not noticed about this text until recently was the difference between the righteous and the unrighteous.

The righteous were unaware that they had fed or clothed or visited or tended to Christ. The unrighteous, in stark contrast, had been very aware of what they did for Christ, for they say, "When was it that we saw you hungry or thirsty or a stranger or naked or ill or in prison, and *did nothing* for you?" (Matthew 25:44 NEB, italics added). "We just never saw you there, Lord," we can hear them protesting.

The righteous are not self-conscious. The deeds they do spring forth from their love of God and are concrete acts of mercy, not abstract theology. God loves them, so they love others. That's all there is to it.

The unrighteous are very self-conscious. They are perfectly willing to serve Christ, but for some reason they don't happen to see Christ in the faces of the least, the last, and the lost. They may see Christ in their churches or in the safety of their own communities, but they are not willing to venture out where the need is and meet Christ there.

The righteous are actually surprised that they are righteous! The unrighteous are surprised that they are not! The tables are completely turned.

Unfortunately, I identify with the unrighteous in this story, those who mean well, profess the Christian faith, have all sorts of good things to say about God in the world, even thank God for blessing them so—and yet forget to carry out the small acts of mercy for those on "the underside" of life. We forget even to look for those on the underside of life—after all, they don't show up in our neighborhoods very often.

But no matter where we teach, we will run into the least, the last, and the lost. Let us have eyes to see the Christ and to act in love and mercy toward him in them.

O Lord, give us eyes to see and hearts to act.

❄ **FEBRUARY 15**   **Read Micah 6:8.**

In the passage where this verse is located, Micah is asking, "With what shall I come before the LORD, and bow myself before God on high?" (Micah 6:6a). He is asking how he can best serve God. He offers to bring burnt offerings, thousands of rams, rivers of oil, his firstborn—all to please God. In modern terms, he would be willing to give his wealth, his land, his business, even his children to show his love for God.

But what is the Lord's response? "What does the LORD require of you but to do justice, and to love kindness, and to walk humbly with your God?" (Micah 6:8).

God is not as interested in a great show of love, in dramatic worship, in huge offerings, as God is concerned with how we behave—in those acts of justice and mercy that we show daily. God calls us to do justice—not just talk about it; love kindness—take those tiny acts of thoughtfulness seriously; and walk humbly with God.

As a parent and a teacher, I have the most difficulty with kindness. Sometimes simply speaking kindly to my children or my students takes more energy than I can muster. When I had to type my husband's Sunday bulletins, I even made a Freudian slip when I typed into a prayer, "Thank you, Lord, for your loving kindmess."

The importance of kindness has not been lost on my daughter, however. One day when I was in a particularly grumpy mood, she disappeared for a while and then reappeared. She had made me a "kindness crown." "Wear this, Mom, and you will be filled with kindness," she promised. O how I wish that were true!

Simple kindness says so much to our students. It tells them they matter to us. It indicates that we respect them. It points beyond us to God.

May we do justice, love kindness, and walk humbly with you, O God.

※ **FEBRUARY 16**   **Read Hebrews 13:1-2.**

Teaching requires hospitality. We may not want to give it, but it certainly is asked of us. We have to be open to intrusions and interruptions, to unexpected visitors, to demands of students. That openness is hospitality.

Hospitality is the art of stoppping what we have planned and ministering to another. Think of Jesus' hospitality. He would be on his way to a quiet place and the crowds would follow, interrupting. He never sent them away. He was on his way to heal Jairus's daughter and the hemorrhaging woman touched his cloak. He stopped.

A few years ago I had to canvass the neighborhood around the church. Friends of mine who had carried out similar surveys in middle-class neighborhoods told of not being welcome at very many homes they visited. So I was anticipating a good bit of door-slamming when I set out.

At almost every house I was not only welcomed, but asked to come inside. It was summer and very hot, so many folks asked if I needed a drink of water. I was invited into homes where the entire family lived in two rooms; it didn't matter. I was a stranger, and they were showing me hospitality. One woman even had all the members of her family answer my questions to help me along!

Hospitality in the classroom means students feel welcome. They know that this is their place, whether they are in kindergarten or ninth grade. They know that their needs matter. They feel important, as I did sipping water in those neighborhood homes.

Lord, teach us to be hospitable, to open our hearts and our lives to the unexpected and the interruptions.

❄ **FEBRUARY 17**　　　　　　　　　**Read Philippians 2:1-4.**

Two years ago, a brutal ice storm hit our city. I woke up in the night to the sound of loud popping that sounded like gunfire. My son, then one and a half, called from his crib, "Hey, Mom! What's happening?" When we peered out of the window, we saw ice draping the world outside. The pops were tree limbs crashing to the ground.

We were without heat or electricity for several days, as was most everyone in the city. So we went to a home of a friend who had heat and a gas stove for cooking. We pooled the food we had and sat out the ice storm together. In fact, the entire city did just that. Community sprang up in the midst of crisis.

Why do we wait for a crisis to become a community with our neighbors? Why can't we sustain that kind of caring, supportive spirit during the good times? Why do we lead such isolated and too-busy-to-care lives?

One of the greatest needs I see in children is their need for community, for a network of loving, caring people who help them make sense of their world and help them feel safe. Community teaches them that we can depend on one another and work together. Sure, it is hard work, and we make mistakes and hurt one another, but forgiveness is also a part of community.

We can build community in our classrooms by making them places where children can learn to love and trust, by encouraging them to do group work, and by accentuating the gifts of all rather than the gifts of just a few. Why not do it before a crisis hits!

Lord, you have called us to be a community to each other. Empower us to build up our common lives in your name.

❄ **FEBRUARY 18**   **Read Mark 9:14-29.**

Have you ever noticed that prayers in the Gospels are rarely pious, "church" prayers? There's the quiet touch-prayer of the hemorrhaging woman, the loud shouts of the demons, the calls of the lepers to Jesus from afar off. There is the pushy Syro-Phoenician woman who won't take "no" for an answer and the persistent woman pounding away at the unjust judge's door until she drives him to distraction. And who can forget Jesus' prayer in the Garden of Gethsemane when he sweats drops of blood? If anything, prayer in the Gospels is unlike any of the stiff, formal words we find ourselves praying in church. It is, rather, cries of agony and need to the Son of God—for healing, for wholeness, for justice.

In this text, a father has brought his epileptic son to Jesus' disciples for healing. But when Jesus comes upon the scene, the disciples are arguing with lawyers and the boy is not yet healed! Jesus calls for the boy and asks his father about the disease. In telling Jesus about the convulsions, the father adds passionately, "But if it is at all possible for you, take pity upon us and help us" (Mark 9:22 NEB).

Jesus exclaims, "If it is possible! Everything is possible to one who has faith!" (9:23 NEB). At that the boy's father cries out in anguish, "I have faith! Help me where faith falls short" (9:24 NEB). Jesus then rebukes the unclean spirit, and the boy is healed.

Later the disciples ask Jesus privately why they were unable to heal the boy. Jesus replies, "There is no means of casting out this sort but prayer" (9:29 NEB).

Who prayed? Jesus rebuked the unclean spirit. Who prayed? The disciples argued with the lawyer. Who prayed? The crazed-with-grief and desperate father when he said, "Help me where faith falls short."

We will not have enough faith to touch all of our students, to model love to all those around us, to do much changing of the world. But our prayers, like that of the father, will be enough for God's power to work in us: "I believe; help my unbelief."

O Lord, help us where our faith falls short.

❄ **FEBRUARY 19**   **Read Mark 7:24-30, 9:14-29.**

As teachers, our spiritual life is not an option. If we are going to stand before children day in and day out, we must have a vital and living faith.

Think of the stories in the Gospels where a parent's faith leads to the healing of a child. There's the uncouth Syrophoenician woman who runs after Jesus, begging him to heal her demon-possessed daughter; who refuses to take no for an answer. There is the father of the demon-possessed boy who cries out in anguish, "I believe; help my unbelief!" (Mark 9:24 NRSV). There is the centurion whose faith is so great that he asks Jesus simply to say the words and his daughter will be healed. The lives of their children depend on their own faith—and their persistence.

So it is with the students we teach. Not only do we model our faith through our actions, but also our prayers on their behalf may be the means of their healing and wholeness. We cannot underestimate the power of our intercessions.

I had not been a fervent believer in the power of prayer until I read a sermon by Bishop Desmond Tutu from South Africa in *Sojourners* magazine (February 1985). His sermon exhorts North American Christians to pray for the people of South Africa. He gives examples of "an excess of grace" that appears "inexplicably" in the lives of black South Africans struggling to live amid terrible oppression: a man in a jail cell who is being tortured but prays for those who are torturing him; a man whose home is going to be bulldozed who is able to thank God for his love. Then he asks, "How is that possible except that you here have prayed [them] into that state of grace?" He goes on to say that knowing they are not alone means so much to those who are oppressed, and that we should never allow others to tell us that what we are doing is insignificant. "Let them know that the sea is made up of drops of water," he writes.

We must pray for our students by name day after day. We must make that a part of our vocation as teachers. If prayer can topple the South African system of apartheid, then we know it can change the lives of those we teach.

O God, this day I lift before you the names of the students who need you, that you will transform their lives.

❋ **FEBRUARY 20**   **Read Ephesians 6:18.**

Several years ago I visited Greece with my grandmother. We went on a tour of the places where Paul had preached and done his ministry.

Although the stories about Paul were powerful and walking the stone-rubbled roads Paul had walked made him real, the spiritual impact of the trip for me was when we visited a monastery perched atop a tall mountain. It looked like it would blow off any minute, but it had been there for years.

Our guide told us that the monks in this monastery had given their lives to pray for the world. I'll never forget her words: "They believe that their prayers have kept the world from destroying itself."

Two things struck me: First, I had never realized that fervent prayers may have saved us time and time again from mass disaster. The second was: What a vocation! What a call! What a gift to the world! *What power!*

I know I don't often consider God's power in my life. It would rattle me too much. But if I think of the commitment of those who pray for us all day long, maybe I can summon the energy to pray for a little while. And as a teacher, maybe I can pray for one student a day—or one class a day, calling upon the power of God that can truly save.

Lord, teach us to pray without ceasing.

❄ FEBRUARY 21   Read Psalm 138:1-2.

An Oriental custom that intrigues me is bowing. Bowing is simply the lowering of one's head in deference to another. Whenever someone says hello or thank you in Korea, for example, they bow. In martial arts classes students are taught to bow to the instructor and then to bow to their opponents before and after an exercise. It is a gesture of respect: more than that, it is a discipline, because sometimes custom requires that you bow when you don't really feel like it.

Imagine what would happen in our classrooms if every morning we greeted our students with a bow—and they bowed back. Imagine what would happen in a classroom debate or even an argument between students if they had to bow before they stated their opinions and again when the exchange was over. It's hard to fake a bow. Maybe that simple discipline would interject a sense of respect into the classroom. It might even force all of us to stop for a second and acknowledge the other person as important.

If we take the symbolism a bit further, think of what happens when we bow our heads in prayer. We may not feel respectful or in awe of God, but that's what the gesture means. It says, "I am your servant; you are my God." It makes us pause momentarily and acknowledge God.

Let us bow before our students, O Lord—at least in our hearts.

❄ **FEBRUARY 22**　　　　　　　　　**Read Genesis 1:31.**

One of my children's favorite books is *Charlotte's Web*, the wonderful tale of a spider named Charlotte who saves a pig's life. After I read it aloud to them for the first time, my then five-year-old son asked me every time he saw a spider, "Mom, is this Charlotte?"

Whenever I would find a spider or other bug in our home, my children would beg me not to kill it. "Remember Charlotte," they'd cry, until we finally agreed on a compromise. We would catch the bug—whatever it might be—and throw it back outside where it belonged. I just didn't want any insect-critters in my territory.

Despite myself, my children have taught me reverence for life—even bugs! And that is an important lesson. For we are all vital to the well-being of our planet, even the most despised insects.

Last year my daughter's class attended a three-day intensive seminar on "Earthkeepers." They went off to the woods to learn about the environment and the interrelationship of life. One of the most powerful exercises that the children participated in was when they each were assigned the role of a particular insect or animal. They were then strung together by thread to create a giant web of life. Whenever one animal or insect in the web was eliminated, a huge hole was torn in the web, a tear that affected the entire web. It dramatized for the children the fact that every creature is essential to the well-being of the earth.

It may be hard for us to teach appreciation of spiders or insects, but we can teach reverence for life. We can model to our students that life is more important than technology or "progress," and that we are entrusted with this beautiful world.

Lord, let us live reverently toward all of your glorious creation.

❄ **FEBRUARY 23**　　　　　　　　　**Read Exodus 20:8-11.**

One of the Ten Commandments that is most often overlooked is number four: "Remember the sabbath day, and keep it holy. Six days you shall labor and do all your work.

But the seventh day is a sabbath to the LORD your God" (Exodus 20:8-10a). Keeping the Sabbath is an integral part of worshiping God, according to this commandment. It means that we trust God with our labor enough to rest. It means that we symbolically give control to God, not our work. It means we let our tired souls and bodies rest in the grace of God one day a week.

Besides going to church, I never thought that much about the Sabbath until I took a two-year Bible study course. One of the questions asked of us repeatedly was about how we were celebrating and honoring the Sabbath. It prodded us to take the Sabbath so seriously that we would change our habits completely. Most of us saw Sunday as a day to do all that had gone undone all week. We were challenged to stop it all and spend time in church and with family, not worrying about the list of undone things, but turning to God in faith that they would get done—another day.

We shared our struggles about keeping the Sabbath throughout the study. Sometimes people felt unbelievably renewed after allowing themselves to rest. Sometimes the pressure to do some work overwhelmed them and actually made them depressed. We all agreed that it was a powerful discipline and an even more powerful symbol. Was God sovereign in our lives or not?

We teachers must take rest seriously. When we deal so intensely with children, we are emotionally frayed, if not spiritually emptied by the end of the week. We deserve a Sabbath. We *need* a Sabbath—if for no other reason than to remind ourselves that the job of God is already taken!

Gracious God, help us allow ourselves to rest and trust that you will carry on our work while we are being renewed.

❄ **FEBRUARY 24**   **Read Psalm 51:1-4.**

I've struggled for years with the traditional confessions of sin that are found in many hymnals. Sometimes they seem so vague that they don't confess enough. Other times they are too moralistic, as if sins are simply the trite little things like smoking or drinking, and not the larger injustices like war and violence. I know confessing is essential to my life as a Christian, but it's difficult for me to know *how* to do it.

Then I read an article in *Weavings* magazine by Deborah Smith Douglas. She suggests a method of self-examination and confession that rings true to me. In looking at our daily actions and interactions, she suggests asking ourselves: "In what . . . was I drawn to God? Did I meet God in the joy or pain of others? Did I in some way bring Christ into my world? Did anyone bring God to me? Did I reach out to someone in trouble or sorrow? Did I fail or refuse to do so? . . . Is there any concrete event of the day which revealed some part of my life that I am withholding from God?"

As teachers, we might ask ourselves: "Did I see God in my students today? Did I in some way bring God to them? Did any of them bring God to me?"

Suddenly sin has become tangible, not abstract—a concrete action I failed to do or did wrongly toward another and thus toward God. Suddenly I am able to identify where I fail to see God in the faces of those around me. I am able to identify where I fail to see gifts in my own life and where that failure is sin.

And I understand now that confession opens my grudging, constricted heart to others. I put Jesus back into the faces of those around me, those I love and those I struggle to love. At least for one day. And that's enough.

Forgive me, O Lord, for the things I have done wrong and for the things I have failed to do.

❄ **FEBRUARY 25**   **Read Luke 6:41-42.**

Our church has a Wednesday evening fellowship meal, a time when church and neighborhood folks sit down and eat together. One evening a retired man in our congregation came to the dinner and sat down across from Bobby. Bobby is an alcoholic who takes care of several elderly people in the neighborhood, but who is often very disheveled looking. The retired church member, good-hearted but opinionated, immediately commented on Bobby's breath. Bobby responded by picking up his stick and threatening to hit him.

At this point, the church member asked another member to call the police. "He's just a derelict," he said. "He ought to be arrested." When my husband, Billy, pulled him aside to talk to him, he suddenly burst out, "My son is an alcoholic, and I don't know what to do about him. They say I'm propping him up, but I just don't know what's right." His pain and anger at his son had been focused on Bobby instead.

So often the things in others that we rail about are the things we ourselves agonize over, the secrets we fail to acknowledge, our own demons. We must clean our own house, not only for our mental and spiritual health, but also for the health of our relationships with others. As long as we have unfinished business to deal with, we will accuse others instead of facing ourselves. And that does not work well in teaching.

Often when I get irritated with a student or someone else, I have recognized some undesirable quality in the other person that I also possess. I have to stop, make my own confession, and address the issue rather than focus all my attention on someone else's problem. Nothing could be more difficult for me to do! Yet unless I take care of my own problems first, I am ill prepared to help my students address theirs.

Gracious, loving God, please enable us to see our own problems honestly and give us courage to address them.

❄ FEBRUARY 26   Read Ephesians 2:10.

How we do things is just as important as getting them done. This reminds me of the monk Brother Lawrence, who believed that we were to do all things for the glory of God, whether it be washing dishes or grading papers.

We Americans tend to be distracted and distractable. We see life as divided into "important big things" and "insignificant little things." It is easy for us to rush through the details—sometimes sloppily—to get to the big events. Or we attend so to the future that we are unaware of the present. The Korean people, however, give their absolute attention and care to the present moment.

While in Korea, I was struck repeatedly by the care the

people gave to small details. When we bought something, the shop owner would wrap it in beautiful paper with such care that it looked like a present. When we sat down to eat, the food was prepared as though it were a work of art. There would be flower arrangements with the most unlikely combinations of flowers—in the most unlikely places. And shops as tiny as card tables were arranged in painstaking order.

It reminded me of the spiritual:

> *O You gotta get a glory in the work you do,*
> *A Hallelujah chorus in the heart of you.*

O God, may we get a glory in our teaching—for your Son Jesus' sake.

❄ FEBRUARY 27   Read Psalm 103.

When I was a teenager, I sang in a youth choir in Atlanta. Though I was in it because of my friends, it was a religious education despite my efforts not to get any religious education! We learned songs that used words from the Psalms, and these songs still return to me all these years later.

One of the songs used words from Psalm 103. Occasionally, when I least expect it, these words will crop into my brain: "As for man, his days are as grass: as a flower of the field, so he flourisheth. For the wind passeth over it, and it is gone; and the place thereof shall know it no more."

Then the music as well as the Psalm changes: "But the mercy of the LORD is from everlasting to everlasting upon them that . . . keep his covenant" (Psalm 103:15-18a KJV).

Here we are, a speck of dust in the vast scheme of things. And arching over us is this steadfast, never-changing love— not only for us but for our children's children, for the line of history that follows us.

It's important that we realize how very finite we are. It is also crucial that we acknowledge the passionate love of a Creator who has numbered the hairs on our head, who encompasses all of us in his hand, who redeems past, present, and future. If this faith is the cornerstone of our lives, then we need not fear. Our work will not be in vain.

Gracious and loving God, keep us aware that without you we can do nothing.

❄ **FEBRUARY 28**   **Read Matthew 7:24-27.**

This is a very intriguing story, especially because it follows the Sermon on the Mount in Matthew, after all the Beatitudes and the admonishments from Jesus about the lifestyles of the kingdom people. When I taught Sunday school, I'd sing with the children, "The wise man built his house upon the rock," and then sobbingly, "the foolish man built his house upon the sand," collapsing to the floor to dramatize the end of the foolish man and his house.

Jesus says that those who hear his words and act on them are like the wise man. Now think about building a house upon a rock. It is hard work. The house has to be anchored to the rock somehow, so the rock has to be drilled. In contrast, building a house on sand is easy. Even little children can dig into the sand!

So the first choice is between building the difficult house or the easy house. The wise man anticipates not only the difficulty of building his house, but also the storms that will follow. The wise man is prepared for the storms.

The foolish man, on the other hand, chooses to build the easy house and also fails to account for the storms. He has a "God will bless me" philosophy. We can deduct from the story that his house was indeed impressive. Jesus says, "The rain fell, and the floods came, and the winds blew and beat against that house, and it fell—and great was its fall!" (Matthew 7:27).

To teach in the name of Jesus is to build upon rock. It is hard, backbreaking work. It doesn't get much positive feedback. It certainly doesn't bring a lot of monetary reward. It is work that faces many a storm. But if it is work done in the name and spirit of Christ, it will stand. This is God's promise to us.

Remind us, O Lord, that your work will stand, and help us carry on.

173

March

Shining Routines

Anne Marie Drew

MARCH 1 Read Luke 24:13-35.

he Victorian poet Gerard Manley Hopkins had a deep affection for nature. In his poem "God's Grandeur," he announces: "The world is charged with the grandeur of God." The poet's vision allows him to see and feel the very heartbeat of creation. So much so that he realizes that even though "generations have trod," the world still flames out like "shining from shook foil."

In March, when dreariness can overwhelm us, when Christmas break is long forgotten and summer vacation is yet a mirage, we can become deadened to the life of God that surrounds us. Our daily routines can become so bone weary-ing that we are insensitive to their importance.

It is good to remember in this month, that every single act we perform, every routine we repeat can be done for the glory of God. The light that shoots out from "shook foil" is brilliant and sudden and piercing. We are duty bound and Spirit bound to remain keenly aware of the life that breathes through even the dullest March day.

So when the snow turns to slush and the March winds make

us hold tight to our books and papers, it is good to remember that the face of our risen Lord beckons us. Like the disciples on the road to Emmaus, we will be surprised by his presence if we are open to the possibilities of shining routines.

Lord of all our routines, reveal yourself to us.

🌂 MARCH 2 Read I Corinthians 13.

I don't remember very much at all about the book *Heidi,* except that I enjoyed reading it. One scene pops into mind fairly frequently, however: the scene in which Heidi is forced to wear all of the clothing she possesses in order to go on a long journey. She wears layers and layers of uncomfortable clothing.

When I taught in elementary school, bundling and unbundling students for the cold weather made me think of Heidi. Between boots and scarves and mittens and coats and face masks, I could spend the better part of a half hour getting my charges ready to go home at the end of a day. To neglect the task would have been to risk their health.

It was often trying, however, negotiating wriggling feet into stiff boots and coaxing resistant arms into bunched-up coat sleeves. Endless patience and kindness were required.

If at the end of every day I had hurried through these "coat" sessions abruptly and briskly, I would have generated anxiety and distress in the little ones charged to my keeping. They would have gone home with an uneasiness they might not have been able to name but certainly could have felt.

Mother Teresa suggests that we perform small tasks with great love. End-of-the-day routines such as this may be a small task, but great love is required to make them an act of charity rather than a chore.

God of love, imbue our every action with charity.

🌂 MARCH 3 Read Matthew 17:1-8.

As Jesus' transfiguration made clear, appearance conveys a powerful message. A note I collected from one of my students drove home this same point in another way.

I normally rip up any collected notes and pitch them into the wastepaper basket, without comment.

Every now and then, I must confess, I do give in to the temptation to read the scribbled missives. Call it sinful curiosity, if you will, but on rare occasions, I succumb.

Having retrieved a note from Becky, I read it as I walked to the wastepaper basket. I could hear Becky gasp as she watched me unfold the piece of notebook paper.

Intended for her best friend, Heather, who sat across the aisle, the note read: "Who dresses this woman? That suit is gross. She looks like she just rolled out of bed."

The note was disrespectful and rude—but correct. That morning I had tossed on an old suit and hadn't paid much attention to my appearance. I had been negligent.

Getting dressed for school can become so routine that we don't even think about it. Have you ever thought, however, that attention to our appearance is one way of caring for our students?

Transfigured Lord, keep us mindful of our appearance.

 **MARCH 4**   **Read John 10:1-16.**

I can still see the Bethlehem tour guide, squatting in front of the cave, imitating the posture of a shepherd. "See?" the guide said. "Once the shepherd got his sheep in the cave for the night, he'd sleep here at the opening. They couldn't stray during the night because he guarded them. And no foxes could get in to harm them."

Continuing his explanation, the guide said, "Every day when the sheep went in and out of the cave, the shepherd would run his hands over them, checking for bruises or cuts, talking to them. They got to know his voice. He paid attention to every one of them every day."

Standing there in that Bethlehem sheepfold, I thought of a principal I'd once worked for. She insisted that every teacher stand at the classroom door at the beginning of every class.

"Greet every student every day," this administrator

insisted. "They need to know you are paying attention to them. Don't sit at your desk between classes. Get on your feet and stand at your door, welcoming your students."

That principal was making us good shepherds. Standing at our classroom doors to greet our students can be tedious beyond words; but as we stand there, the best Shepherd of all is standing right beside us.

Tender Shepherd, help us guard your sheep.

🌱 MARCH 5   Read Matthew 4:13.

If you blink, the passage will slip by. You will miss the humdrum of daily existence reverberating through the few words. Matthew tells us that Jesus "made his home in Capernaum." Think about the hundreds of daily details connoted by those nondramatic words.

We do, after all, tend to think of Jesus' life as a fairly dramatic one; however, his existence, like ours, was filled with monotony. The New Testament captures the startling events of his life, but the Gospel writers also make ample reference to Jesus' sleeping and eating and walking and praying and fishing.

Sometimes when I'm performing a teaching duty I dislike, like collecting permission slips, I call to mind the monotony of Jesus' existence.

Collecting permission slips for field trips seems like such an inordinate waste of time to me. We all know that in our litigious society, even the most carefully worded permission slip will not save a school system from a lawsuit in the case of student injury. But year after year, field trip after field trip, we send home and then collect these little pieces of paper.

I wonder whatever happens to the millions of permission slips that have been collected for decades.

Permission slips are a nuisance for me. You have your own pet peeves. But there is no task, no routine so tedious that Jesus Christ is not present.

He is with us always.

Praise God for our Savior's indwelling presence.

177

Close your eyes and imagine the sensuous nature of the dinner party John describes: the smell of the rich Mediterranean food mingling with the ointment's fragrance; the feel of Mary's hair against Jesus' skin; the voices filling the air with laughter and argument and conversation. Jesus' world was alive with sights and sounds and smells and touches and tastes.

When he went to dinner parties, he smelled and ate rich Mediterranean food. In his walks, his feet felt the stones and rocks of the hilly terrain. The loud cries and shouts of the marketplaces filled his ears. We dilute our understanding of our Savior's existence when we ignore his sensuous existence.

People sometimes think of classrooms as anything but sensuous. That's a view I have never shared.

I find a particular joy, for example, in opening a new box of chalk. There is a very real, very tactile pleasure in opening a box, with all those fresh pieces of chalk lined up. Inevitably the first piece removed from the box has a distinctive smooth coolness. Sometimes a piece of chalk is already broken.

But the simple act of going to the supply cupboard and retrieving a new box of chalk is a pleasant routine for me. More than once, I have thanked the Lord for such simple, sensuous pleasures.

What simple, sensuous pleasure are you thankful for today?

Thank you, Lord, for the gift of our senses.

 **MARCH 7**   **Read Ecclesiastes 4:9-12.**

My husband and I used these verses from Ecclesiastes in our wedding ceremony because they speak so pointedly to the strengths of marriage. However, the verses speak to teachers as well. We teachers need each other, almost as much as spouses need each other.

I certainly needed my colleagues during the siege of the raisin boxes.

Somebody in the cafeteria thought the little boxes of raisins were a good idea. I guess they'd been on sale at a food warehouse, and the dietitian bought hundreds of them for the school lunch program.

But you know what happens when hundreds of kids get their hands on hundreds of raisins, don't you? Of course you do. The raisins get thrown all over the lunchroom. Food fights erupt.

My week at lunch duty coincided with the week of the raisin boxes. When the first few raisins started flying, I calmly went over to the offending students, removed their remaining raisins, and warned them about their behavior.

Then a particularly rambunctious group of students moved a huge trash container about four feet from their table and started "shooting hoops" with the raisin boxes. Before long several other tables joined in with the pickup game of raisin-box basketball. I needed help. So I summoned the assistant principal to help me restore order.

I rely on my colleagues for so much: advice about ideas, articles, a sympathetic ear. And in very practical terms, I need their help when there is a situation I cannot handle.

How have your colleagues been of help to you this year? Express your thanks by offering your help to them in some way.

We praise you, God of the threefold cord.

🌱 MARCH 8   Read Isaiah 55:10-13.

The prophet Isaiah reminds us that our comings and goings are governed by the Almighty. I don't often get the chance to see the comings and goings of my students, but there is one routine that gives me just such an opportunity: bus duty.

One week out of the school year, I stand guard while the students clamor onto the buses after school. I don't have to do much except stand by as an adult presence.

The students, as they come bounding out of the school, have a zest and energy that are sometimes missing from my early morning classes. Even the chance to see them in coats and scarves helps me to see them in fresh ways.

The ones who drag themselves onto the bus as if reluctant to go home give me cause for concern.

I am an invisible presence, of course, in this routine. No one pays any attention to me. However, I am glad for the chance to see all these creatures of God as they work their ways home.

And as they leave, I pray with the prophet Isaiah that they will be "led back in peace" (Isaiah 55:12).

Lord Jesus, continue to watch over our arrivals and departures.

 **MARCH 9**   **Read Matthew 6:26-33.**

One of the traits I most cherish in Jesus is his unrelenting insistence on purity of heart and intentions. His followers must stay focused on the love of God. Nothing else matters.

I was on my way to ride my horse today when I drove by a little boy, stationed in his front yard at a small picnic table. Wrapped up in a heavy coat and scarf, he was holding a sign that said CANDY BARS FOR SALE. The day was so cold and uncomfortable that I wasn't very sure that I wanted to ride my horse. I was even less sure that I wanted to reverse the car to buy candy, but I did.

When I asked the little fellow why he was selling candy, he said, "I have to sell two boxes for school or I get in trouble." I bought five candy bars.

There is something a little degrading about candy sales. Only the rare student relishes the task. Most dread it.

And most teachers do not relish collecting the money and getting caught up in the competition between different classes. Who can sell the most candy bars? Who will win the pizza party? Who will get their class picture in the paper as the winning team? Such activities can obscure our primary role as teachers.

In what ways can you seek first the kingdom of God in your classroom?

Lord Jesus, remind us to seek first the kingdom of God.

🌱 MARCH 10   Read Proverbs 22:15.

Proverbs provides so many useful pieces of wisdom, tested and proven over the ages. It's hard to disagree adamantly with any of the advice offered in chapter 22. Yet I have never believed that the fifteenth verse gives us absolute freedom to inflict corporal punishment. Oh, a quick swat to the bottom of a toddler can be efficient and effective; however, physical punishment of older children is another matter.

Years ago when I was teaching eighth grade, I discovered a wooden paddle in my classroom closet. It was a big thing with cutout holes to make the swats especially painful. Knowing I would never use the paddle, I asked one of my colleagues what to do with the offensive instrument. "Oh, give it to me," he said. "Mine got stolen last year. And I'll need it."

One day this same colleague came to my classroom door and said, "I need you as a witness. I'm going to paddle Dwayne. Can you leave your class for a few minutes and come into the hall?"

"I can't," I answered.

"Why?" my colleague asked. "You know the school board won't let me touch this kid without a witness."

"I think paddling is wrong, and I will not be a witness to it," I told him.

He shrugged his shoulders and got another teacher to serve as a witness.

I do believe we should support each other as teachers. I would never intentionally undermine a colleague's authority. Yet I believe paddling students is such an assault on a student's dignity, such an abuse of our power, that I cannot, before God, serve as a witness to such an event. Perhaps paddling students does not trouble you, but you might have difficulty with other teaching routines. Can you identify such routines that force you to question your very beliefs as a teacher?

Lord, grant me wisdom.

 **MARCH 11**   **Read Genesis 2:15.**

Many people mistakenly believe that human beings only had to work *after* the fall of Adam and Eve. A quick glance at Genesis dispels that notion. Part of the sheer, innocent joy of Adam's existence was his role as the caretaker of the Garden of Eden. Adam's delightful responsibility was to make the Garden look nice.

We share Adam's role as caretakers when we "keep and till" our classrooms. The other day I visited a classroom and happened to look up at the ceiling. There, painted on individual acoustical tiles, were scenes from literary works. One student had used pastels to capture Poe's Raven. Another painted a bright red *A* on a woman who must have been Hester Prynne. Yet another had painted a tombstone with two names on it: Romeo and Juliet.

I was struck by the ingenuity of the teacher who allowed her students to so decorate the classroom.

As a college student, I scoffed at the methods classes that taught us how to create decorated classrooms. As a teacher, I've come to understand their importance.

Not only do fresh bulletin boards and growing plants and catchy posters make a room look welcoming; they foster an environment in which students can take chances and risks. Such attention to classroom appearance conveys a very direct message to students: "You matter enough to me that I will spend time making my classroom attractive."

We do not serve dinner guests leftovers. We do not give used gifts as birthday presents. We do not attend church in dirty clothes.

There are certain behaviors that convey attention and caring. Attractive classrooms are one of them.

What care is needed in your classroom this month?

Lord, eternal caretaker of our souls, make us good keepers of your gardens.

🌱 MARCH 12   Read Matthew 12:5-6; Mark 2:25-26.

We may not think of Jesus as an avid reader, but clearly he knew the Old Testament. In his book *Inheriting the Master's Cloak*, John Wijngaards explains that Jesus knew many of the Old Testament texts by heart and often quoted them in his teaching. Our Lord knew the power of the written word.

Something as ordinary as a textbook can provide fresh reminders of the vital importance of reading.

I have here on my desk, for example, a copy of *Sketches*, a fifth-grade reader. A quick glance at the inside cover indicates that four years ago Jimmy used the book. The following year the book was issued to Timothy. Then last year Meagan used this particular copy of the standard textbook.

Whenever I distribute textbooks and instruct students to inscribe their names inside the front cover, I think of all the previous students who've used the text. In the years when we issue new books and students have to be cautioned to take special care with the fresh editions. I wonder about all the students who will one day use the text. Jesus himself was once a young boy learning to read.

And what he learned through reading helped give him the courage and strength to complete his mission.

How good it is to be reminded of the importance of *our* mission.

Lord, who is the master reader, thank you for giving us a Savior who lived the power of the written word. May we share an enthusiasm for reading with our students.

🌱 MARCH 13   Read Mark 5:25-34.

People did not always know how to get close to Jesus, so they resorted to awkward and sometimes embarrassing maneuvers to reach him. The woman with a hemorrhage must have been extremely self-conscious and nervous as she tried to touch Jesus' cloak. The subsequent commotion she caused would certainly have embarrassed her further. Yet Jesus did not rebuke her. In fact, he healed her.

Teaching provides us all with ample awkward moments, such as the first day of school, parent-teacher conferences, and open house. As a junior high school teacher, one of the most awkward out-of-step moments for me is chaperoning school dances. Between feeling sorry for the wallflower students who seem glued to their chairs and watching in horror the suggestive gyrations of the more advanced students, we teachers occupy an odd spot as chaperones. Often we drag our spouses along, and they end up commiserating with the other spouses about the wasted evening that could have been spent elsewhere.

Still, attending such an event keeps us in touch with the painful social realities of being young. I don't know about you, but I never really enjoyed a school dance when I was in school. And my quick appraisal of today's school dances leads me to believe that most of our students don't enjoy them much either.

But attendance at such events is part of growing up and learning to relate to the opposite sex. And for all the awkwardness and embarrassment, school dances give both us and our students a needed chance to step away from the desks and the chalk.

Whatever your awkward moments may be, remember that God can work miracles despite your discomfort!

Lord of awkwardness, thank you for your steadfast presence.

 **MARCH 14**   **Read Luke 5:1-6.**

Scraping bubble gum off desks is a pretty dismal task, wouldn't you agree? If we are unable to identify the culprit who deposited the gum in the first place, we have little choice but to clean up the mess ourselves. To neglect the task would be to invite bugs and ruined clothing and class disruption. So we force ourselves to complete the task.

Simon and his friends obviously did not want to lower the nets again, as Jesus so instructed. They were weary, as we often are, from hours of seemingly fruitless labor.

More than one teaching routine puts us in Simon's position. However, our spiritual muscles can be strengthened by applying our spirits to an unpleasant task. If we pray as we scrape gum, if we meditate as we wash chalkboards, if we give praise as we pick litter off the floor, we can transform any ordinary task into a chance for increased grace.

God does not desert us because we have to stop teaching long enough to pick up the candy wrappers on our classroom floor. Had Simon refused to lower the nets just one more time, he would have missed the chance to know his Savior. We have to train ourselves to be ever aware of the indwelling presence of our God.

How can you begin today?

Lord, keep us faithful in the midst of unpleasant tasks.

 **MARCH 15**   **Read Isaiah 7:14.**

On his deathbed, John Wesley, founder of the Methodist movement, roused himself from his near coma to utter these words: "The best of all is God is with us." Those words simultaneously convey the truth of Christmas and Easter. Our God is Immanuel, a God who is with us—even on our bad days.

One of the worst things about teaching is that there is nowhere to hide on our bad days. If an early morning tiff at home has left us feeling sour and grumpy, we still have to stand in front of the classroom. If we feel the flu coming on but just can't justify taking another sick day, we still have to put on a brave front and teach.

The saints give us marvelous examples of courage—men and women who persevered through physical pain and emotional suffering in order to do great things for God.

John Wesley, a man whose deep spirituality links him with such men as Ignatius of Loyola, fought through horrific hardships just to do God's will. He lived his life in the classroom of the world, so to speak. And sometimes that classroom was unrelentingly merciless.

I remind myself of Wesley's words when I do not feel like teaching. When having to move through my normal routine seems impossible, I remind myself of the only truth that ultimately matters: God is with us.

Praise Immanuel.

 **MARCH 16**   **Read Mark 9:33-37.**

When the dentist walked in, he stayed totally out of my view. Seated at a desk three feet behind my head, he asked me the usual dental history questions. I was seated in the dental chair facing away from him. When it came time to clean my teeth, he completed the entire procedure without once looking at me. I was so bothered by the spatial arrangement, I never returned to that particular dentist.

As teachers, we know the spaces we inhabit exert a powerful influence on human behavior. Sometimes we arrange student desks in groups of four or six. Sometimes we line them up in rows. We experiment with the position of our own desk, placing it at an angle or at the side or back of the room.

I once thought it would be nice if my students could all look out the window in English class, so I turned all the desks to face the wall of windows. I'm sure I don't have to tell you how long that experiment lasted. I couldn't compete with the playful squirrels and passing cars that lurked outside the windows.

Jesus Christ had a keen sense of physical space. He knew when to go inside, when to gather his disciples, when to enfold a little child in his arms. He also knew when to seclude himself.

As teachers, we need to develop our Savior's awareness of physical space.

Lord, thank you for knowing when to gather us in and when to let us go.

 **MARCH 17**   Read Matthew 26:17-19;
                                      Mark 14:12-16; Luke 22:7-13.

My college roommate, who died at the age of thirty-five from cancer, was born on Saint Patrick's Day. She was one of the most imaginative and dedicated teachers I've ever met. She never let a holiday go by without working a celebration of some sort into her lesson plans.

On Saint Patrick's Day, she'd encourage her students to bring something green to class for show-and-tell. On Valentine's Day, she made individual valentines for each of her students. Even on holidays that seemed minor to the rest of us—like Groundhog Day, for example—Sharon would find an innovative way to work the occasion into her class.

Such innovations took time, of course, and energy and endless dedication. But Sharon's classroom had an atmosphere of goodwill and creativity and well-being. Much of that atmosphere came from the observance of "holidays," because the little celebrations helped to break the potential monotony of daily routine.

With Sharon's death, hundreds of students lost the opportunity to be taught by this tireless professional. Although I can never match her creativity, I do try to imitate her attention to holidays. In doing so, I also remember that Jesus celebrated special days. Although the sober events of Holy Week obscure the Passover celebration Jesus shared with his apostles, Matthew, Mark, and Luke all make clear that special preparations were made for the special feast.

Let us always remember that the varied richness of the calendar gives us ample cause to celebrate.

Lord, increase our ability to celebrate.

 **MARCH 18**   Read Matthew 1:18-24.

In the traditional church calendar, today is the Feast of Saint Joseph or Saint Joseph the Worker, as he is sometimes called. Joseph is one of those people I hope to meet in heaven. What we know of him intrigues me. A dedicated, faithful participant in the greatest events of the world, Joseph remains a mystery.

We know he had doubts and fears, but he persevered. The fact that he worked as a carpenter, which included stone-masonry work in his time, indicates he must have been a very strong man. Content to be a silent player in the redemption of the world, Joseph completed his appointed duties.

His is a good example for us as teachers. He was a solid worker, who did what was asked of him.

Sometimes we are tempted in our profession, I think, to try and stand out, to get to the head of the class. Most of us were successful students ourselves, so we are accustomed to being the bright, talented ones. But there's not much room in the field of teaching for people who want gold stars on their foreheads for every deed accomplished. Days, weeks, months will pass without our getting a pat on the head or any special recognition.

Nonetheless, our labors are important and will not go unnoticed by our students and our God. As we accomplish our daily tasks, we can grow in the likeness of our Creator.

Lord Jesus, keep us faithful to our appointed tasks.

 **MARCH 19**   **Read Proverbs 31:30.**

I hesitate to reveal this little detail of my spiritual life, but in a series of meditations about the sacredness of ordinary routine, I feel compelled to come clean.

When applying my makeup in the morning before I leave for school, I pray. When curling my eyelashes, I hold the curler in place long enough to say the Lord's Prayer. When applying foundation, I call to mind a favorite Bible passage. The doxology works well during the application of lipstick.

Probably this practice sounds ridiculous, maybe even blasphemous. But if I don't pray well, I can't teach well. I can't do anything well if my prayer life slackens. Sometimes, the only way to pray is to lift my heart and mind to God during daily routines.

Applying makeup has always seemed a horribly vain endeavor but one that I feel compelled to pursue, nevertheless. But praying as I try to eradicate the dark circles under my eyes transforms the procedure into one capable of conferring grace.

Much of our life outside the classroom determines our effectiveness inside the classroom. If we are not people of prayer, we run the risk of being whited sepulchers, like whitewashed tombs (see Matthew 23:27). So while I'm working on my outside face, I try to work on my inside one as well.

Lord Jesus, turn our faces to yours.

 **MARCH 20**   **Read Matthew 21:23-27.**

As a spiritual exercise, choose any one of the Gospels and keep track of how often Jesus was interrupted. He would be preaching, as in this scene from Matthew, and the chief priests and elders would intrude. He would be leaving a town, and the people would present themselves for healing. To accomplish his mission, Jesus needed to be flexible.

The bathroom fires demanded about all the flexibility I could muster.

The fires were as inexplicable as they were life-threatening. Four times in one week, the school janitor discovered smoldering fires in the wastepaper baskets in one of the girls' bathrooms. The school had been evacuated and the fire department called the first time the smoke was detected coming from the bathroom.

Then the janitor discovered the source of the problem. Someone was tossing lit cigarettes into the trash, and the trash was catching fire.

So we were all assigned bathroom patrol to try to discover the culprits. Each female teacher had to forego a prep period in order to patrol the bathrooms. The task, as you can well imagine, was not a pleasant one. Circling in and out of the rest room, checking stalls, rummaging around in the trash, were fairly repulsive albeit necessary tasks.

Two weeks passed without another fire. Then three. The administration decided the threat had passed. And it had. There were no further incidents.

None of us enjoyed patrol duty, but teaching requires the ability to be flexible enough to adapt to changing demands.

What will require your flexibility this day or this week?

Christ Jesus, keep us flexible in the face of multiple changes in schedule.

 **MARCH 21**   **Read Revelation 2:2-3.**

The cola was poured, with lots of the requisite ice. The package of cookies was nearby. It was Saturday morning, and my entire family was gone. The house was empty. I was ready to do battle.

There on the desk in my study was a stack of 125 essays, waiting to be graded.

The first fifteen flew by fairly quickly. The students were responding to a short story, and their responses tended to fall into the usual patterns.

Somewhere after the twentieth essay, I realized my attention had started to wander and I wasn't quite sure how I had arrived at the grades I'd assigned to the last few essays.

So I got up, drank some cola, munched on a few cookies, and called my mom. Then I started again.

By the time my family returned that night, I had worked through about half of the stack. It would take the weekend to finish the chore.

Grading essays is exhausting and tedious work. Even a short essay assigned to five or six different sections of students results in a large stack of papers.

Staying fresh and alert and paying particular attention to each paper are very hard. Yet, as this passage from Revelation suggests, there *are* rewards for our labors.

Lord of light, reward our patient endeavors.

I am married to a pack rat. There, for the first time ever, I've announced the fact to the world. My husband saves everything. I could run up to the attic right now and dig my hand into piles of unopened junk mail from the 1970s. Or I could show you the chicken bones left over from his eighth-grade science fair project. I consider his tendency to keep everything a serious character flaw. My husband does not agree.

On the other hand, I get rid of everything. My kids claim I've caused them lifelong emotional scars because when we move I force them to discard their "prized" possessions. Every season I send clothes to Goodwill, old papers to the recycling bins, unsalvageable trash to the dump.

But, even I have a difficult time discarding notes from former students. I have a box into which I toss the notes and cards I've received over the years. There are Christmas cards, thank-you notes, birthday wishes. When I pore over the cards in my nostalgic moments, my acute gratitude deepens. God has been so good to me. I have known and loved so many decent and vibrant young people.

It's a minor routine of mine, this saving of student correspondence. However, that box of treasures reminds me of why I teach. How gently Jesus phrased the emotional reality: "Where your treasure is, there your heart will be also" (Luke 12:34).

Lord Jesus, remind us that the only lasting treasure is you.

My homeroom was the last to be called to the pep rally. As we entered the auditorium, the noise level was pretty obnoxious. Students were goofing around, hitting each other, calling out across the auditorium.

"Another pep rally," I groaned to myself. "Why do I have to endure these things?"

To be honest, pep rallies are never much fun for me. Willing and even eager to attend sporting functions at school, I genuinely dislike the organized frenzy of pep rallies. Students cheering, athletes sauntering, administrators orchestrating—all such activity seems frenetic and pointless to me.

But I've had to attend several such events over the years. This particular pep rally went more or less as they all did. The student body was wildly supportive of their basketball team, which was about to make it into the semifinals.

I know that it is not necessary that I enjoy or like every one of my professional duties, yet I must fulfill them.

When Jesus speaks in this passage from Mark about taking up the cross, we might think solely of the real tragedies in life: sudden death, terminal illness, financial ruin. And certainly those calamities fiercely test our faith.

In my own life, however, I have discovered that unpleasant duties can be crosses as well. I do not mean to suggest that unpleasant teaching duties are as painful as emotional betrayal or physical suffering; still the daily irritants of life are part of our daily cross. When the weight of that cross seems too much to bear, let us draw strength from faith and hope in our risen Lord.

Help us, Lord, to bear our daily crosses.

 **MARCH 24**   **Read Luke 15:6.**

Jesus often refers to the social nature of our existence. His poignant story of the lost sheep, for example, includes the mention of shared joy. The shepherd calls his friends to witness his good fortune.

Last week, sitting in the teachers' lounge made me think of the great wealth of friendships teaching provides.

Laura stopped at the donut shop on the way in and picked up two dozen donuts. On the same morning, Charlie happened to bring in some freshly ground coffee beans. Everyone in the teachers' lounge that morning seemed in good spirits.

When I dropped in during my prep period, Mary Ann was already ensconced in her usual seat by the window. George was pouring himself a cup of coffee as I entered.

"Want any?" he asked me, holding up his own coffee cup.

"No thanks," I told him as I plopped down in my favorite overstuffed chair.

The casual interaction with colleagues during the school day is a great comfort and joy to me. The daily predictability of the encounters, the rhythm of the conversations, the regular updates on kids and husbands and pets form a vital part of my day.

During my busy times, when I do not make time to drop in to the lounge, my days seem thin, almost anemic. Although only a few of my colleagues are true friends, I deeply value the casual acquaintances I have formed with most of my coworkers. My days and my life would be impoverished without their presence.

How will you share the joy of friendship today?

Thank you, God, for the gift of colleagues.

🌼 MARCH 25   Read Luke 1:26-38.

Today marks the traditional Feast of the Annunciation, that day when Mary said "Yes" to the angel Gabriel. That simple act of remarkable faith changed all of our lives.

Perhaps you have seen, as have I, stand-up comedy routines in which some young comic relives the scene between Mary and Gabriel, only in the reenactment Mary refuses to accept her role. These comic sketches make audiences roar with laughter.

The sketches hit on a clear reality: Mary had many reasons to refuse God's request. Unmarried, very young, probably unused to angelic visits, Mary must have been terrified and uncomprehending, at first. Yet her graceful, strong faith allowed her to understand Gabriel's authenticity and Gabriel's mission. Mary was ready to say yes to God on this monumental issue because her life had been a series of little yesses. She recognized God's call because she had trained her soul to hear God's voice.

It is imperative that we follow Mary's example. When God asks the impossible of us, we will only be able to accept the divine will if we have trained ourselves in the dailiness of our ordinary lives.

The daily routines of teaching give us ample opportunity to exercise the spiritual muscle of acceptance.

Lord, when our faith falters, teach us to say "yes."

 **MARCH 26**   **Read Matthew 21:18-22.**

Have you ever thought about what Jesus thinks about lockers?

If he were walking down a school hallway, would some innocent locker grab his attention as did the fig tree? Would he teach a lesson about a locker?

Assigning lockers in junior high can be quite a challenge.

A very short student, understandably, does not want an overhead locker. A student athlete wants one of the bigger lockers for all of her extra gear.

Lockers are an enigma. In one way they stand for all that is restrictive about student life. Student belongings must be confined into a very small space. The lock on the door belies the reality that school officials can search school lockers.

Sometimes lockers give hints of personality. The pictures taped inside, the relative neatness or messiness of the stacked books, the presence or nonpresence of trash—all shed light on the student who "owns" the locker.

Every year, I watch in amazement as the tiny, metal closets take on personalities of their own. Within days Tammy's locker will need a new hinge because she's slammed it, hard, so many times when she was mad at her boyfriend. The janitor will have to come three times in one week to unstick John's locker because he slams the door so quickly that his coat gets stuck in the door. The notes stuffed into the vents of Gloria's locker by her friends will soon spill onto the floor.

I wonder what Jesus would say about lockers?

Lord, grant us your vision.

Long before angels became a popular fad, people of faith understood the efficacious presence of the unseen spirits. Scores of references throughout the Old and New Testaments remind us—as does this passage from Matthew—of the presence of these watchful sentinels.

Driving to work gives me ample cause to think of angels. I cover 100 miles as I wend my way from my house to my classroom and back again. The routine of getting to work never grows dull for me. Driving so many miles, day after day, does more than wear out my car. It gives me a chance to see God in new places.

Every morning on my way to work, for example, I see parents standing watch as they wait with their children for the school bus. In the rural areas, a mom or a dad will drive down the long lane from the farmhouse to the road in a pickup truck. With the engine running and the kids in the cab of the truck, these parents wait for the bus to arrive.

As I approach the city I see mothers sitting and waiting on the edge of the apartment steps in their bathrobes, coffee mugs in hand. Their kids are oblivious to them, not even turning to kiss them as they scramble onto the buses.

I think of these parents as God's sentinels, because as parents they've been given a sacred trust by God. These mothers and fathers guard their precious children.

I pray that each of our students has such an attentive sentinel.

Thank you, Lord, for earthly and heavenly sentinels.

 MARCH 28   Read Matthew 4:23-25.

So often, I wish public prayer were universally acknowledged as a good and necessary teaching routine. It seems ludicrous to me that we are, by and large, not allowed to pray in public—without offending someone. And certainly praying in schools can prove to be a tricky business.

Once, when I was not teaching in a religious school, a student raised her hand at the beginning of class. "Would it be okay if we prayed today for the people I saw on TV last night?"

"What people?" I asked, stalling for time.

"The ones in that war in Europe. Can't we pray for all those people who are being forced out of their homes?"

"You can pray," I told her. "Anyone is free to pray in silence at any time."

That young girl was so right to be concerned for the victims of war. There are so many people who suffer. Matthew records that early in Jesus' ministry he healed people "afflicted with various diseases and pains, demoniacs, epileptics, and paralytics" (Matthew 4:24).

Prayer should be as routine as breathing. We can never pray enough. Even as we go through our teaching day, we can remember those across the world who suffer acutely. I will always be grateful for that student who understood that part of her daily life in school could well include a lifting of the mind and heart to God. Even when we teach in public schools—where it is illegal to pray publicly—we can develop the disciplined routine of continual prayer.

Lord Jesus, help us to develop the routine of continual prayer.

 **MARCH 29**   **Read Matthew 21:12-17.**

One of my colleagues was a devout Christian, but she refused to join any organized church. There were at least three ministers actively trying to recruit this woman for membership in their respective churches, but she would not join. She always worshiped on Sundays, at different churches. She volunteered for any number of church activities, but she kindly and firmly resisted any attempts to make her a member of an institution.

"I never want Jesus to have to chase me out of the temple," she told me one day. She then explained, "If I join a specific church, then I might be tempted to start doing things their way. Those money changers were just doing what everybody did. They got accustomed to a routine, and it took Jesus' whip to make them move."

As a lifelong church member who cherishes my institutional affiliation, I do not share my colleague's views; however, I think her point is extraordinarily valid. Those money changers, with their hearts hardened by routine, must have been astounded and outraged when Jesus attacked their method of operation. For years, they operated their businesses near the temple. My colleague was right. Only divine wrath could make them move.

What old habits or routines may have hardened your heart?

Lord Jesus, keep us from being hardened by our routines within our classrooms and our churches.

MARCH 30   Read Mark 2:1-12.

The Capernaum paralytic was lucky to have persistent friends. One of my students showed similar persistence.

Over the years, the Junior National Honor Society (JNHS) had developed into the primary organizational unit in the school—planning everything from Christmas bake sales to spring dances. The students selected for the society tended to be both academically successful and socially active.

When the new members were announced and inducted in the fall, Kathy's name was not on the list. A brand-new student, she and her family had moved to the area two weeks before school opened. An unknown eighth grader, there was no chance that the faculty would vote her into the JNHS.

But Kathy was a determined young woman. She came to me and complained—respectfully but pointedly. "Couldn't you guys have checked with my old school or something? I know I was going to make it into the Honor Society there. Isn't there some kind of transfer program?"

Kathy's insistence highlighted a glaring deficiency in our selection process. We had not, truthfully, given her a thought. Her name had not even appeared on the list of potential inductees.

A quick check of her records indicated she was an outstanding student. In our deliberations we should have, at the very least, discussed this new student.

Sometimes our established routines need to be reexamined. Had the paralytic's friends stuck to the routine of using the front door, he would not have been healed.

As symptoms of "spring fever" begin to appear, it's especially important to create interest and energy by replacing some of the old routines. How can you breathe fresh air into the classroom this week?

Lord, thank you for students who challenge our routines. Help me to take the initiative this week to break out of some old routines on my own.

 **MARCH 31**   **Read Matthew 23:27.**

Since childhood I have dreaded the possibility of becoming a whited sepulcher, like a whitewashed tomb. When I'm on the verge of spiritual dryness, I vigorously force myself to reexamine my routines. Many of our routines, particularly our teaching routines, need continual evaluation. If you will forgive me an example that might seem crude, I'll tell you about a mundane teaching routine that needs evaluation.

When my own children were in junior high school, I told them, "If you have to use the bathroom and the teacher refuses to give you permission, just get up and leave anyway. I'll go to bat for you if you get in trouble."

This topic may seem inappropriate in a book of meditations, but, for me, the issue cuts to the core of student dignity. I know from experience the chaos caused by students roaming the halls on the way to the bathroom or by students smoking in the rest rooms. There are many good reasons to restrict student access to bathrooms in our junior and senior high schools.

But our students are human beings. Whether we teach junior high or young elementary students, we cannot and should not seek to control them totally. We are duty bound to make sure that our classroom policies are disciplined but not unnecessarily restrictive. We need to review carefully, every year, our routines. There are always new ways of looking at issues, new perspectives to be incorporated.

If we wish to remain vital in the classroom, we must look for the life inside the routines. We must look at every routine with the eyes of Jesus.

Lord, remind us that there is no routine that falls outside of your jurisdiction.

April

Ordinary People

Anne Marie Drew

APRIL 1   **Read any complete chapter in Matthew.**

If you were a contestant on *Jeopardy* and one of the categories was New Testament Characters, you might feel fairly confident about your ability to supply the correct answers. After all, most of us can supply a list of New Testament names: Herod, Pilate, John the Baptist, Nicodemus—and the list goes on.

But there are thousands of unremembered and largely unnamed people in the New Testament, without whom there would be no history of salvation. So many people who met and touched and loved Jesus are forgotten. Those many others who despised and persecuted him are also largely anonymous. We do not know their names. They are, nonetheless, important.

Likewise, we will forget most of the people we meet in our teaching careers. Try now to remember the name of every colleague you've ever had and memory will fail you. Try to pull up from the depths of your long-term memory the name of every school custodian who's cleaned your classroom, and your mind will be blank. Yet all of those ordinary people formed the fabric of your teaching life at one time. During

April, when spring is taking hold, the book of Matthew can teach us extraordinary things about ordinary people.

God of the universe, thank you for the Gospel of Matthew with its rich chronicle of ordinary people whose lives were touched by our Savior, Jesus Christ.

🌂 APRIL 2   Read Matthew 21:1-10.

In most years, Easter falls sometime in April. Therefore, it seems appropriate to begin our explorations in the book of Matthew with accounts about the ordinary people and extraordinary events of that Holy Week.

In chapter 21 we find a story about the donkey that Jesus rode into Jerusalem on Palm Sunday. The donkey is reported to have told one of his friends, "I couldn't figure out why all those people were cheering for me."

Although the donkey's statement is a silly little one-line quip, it holds a powerful message. The donkey, like us, is the bearer of Christ. His importance came through Jesus Christ. Only the donkey's misunderstanding of his task made him think people were cheering for him.

From time to time we lose sight of our primary role in the classroom. Our own sense of importance can become overblown. Busy with multiple tasks, responsible for scores of students, respected in our communities, we can forget that our existence should be a beacon of light for others.

The donkey's mistake should not be ours. Nor should we repeat the mistake of the crowds on Palm Sunday. As exciting as the triumphal entry into Jerusalem was, the triumph was a temporal one. The real glory, the real triumph, was yet to come. And Good Friday would stand in between Palm Sunday and the Resurrection.

I leave myself this little reminder in my desk drawer, on my lesson plans, and in my grade book: "Seek ye first the kingdom of God" (Matthew 6:33 KJV). I never want to make the donkey's mistake.

How can you be a beacon of light today?

Lord of light, thank you for letting us be bearers of your presence.

APRIL 3   **Read Matthew 26:14-16.**

Lizzy, a woman who taught with me, was separated from her husband. In order to make ends meet, she had to rent out rooms of her house. The house, divided into various apartments, had originally been a boardinghouse. Before things turned sour, she and her husband had planned on opening a bed-and-breakfast.

Lizzy had no practice in being a landlord, and in her desperation for steady income, she made two pretty big mistakes. She did not conduct background checks on her boarders, and she charged far below the going rental rates. Those two factors attracted the wrong types of people to Lizzy's house.

Before long, she had two unsavory men as tenants. Lizzy chose to ignore her uneasiness about the men because they paid their rent on time, and she was almost never home anyway.

Then one day, Lizzy was called to the principal's office. A colleague had given him photos of the men, and their lady friends, going in and out of Lizzy's house. The pictures and the activities depicted were pretty sleazy. The principal, understandably, was concerned for the school's reputation.

Lizzy was deeply hurt that whoever took the photos did not come to her directly. She felt betrayed. Yet she was fortunate. The principal, unlike the nameless chief priests who helped Judas betray Jesus, was not intent on doing her harm. He helped her free herself from a bad situation. Betrayers only succeed with the help of like-minded people.

As you think more about Easter, be attentive to the intentions of those around you. Look for opportunities to help "rescue" others from potentially bad situations. Then reach out with the love of Christ.

Provident God, use us to help protect others from betrayers.

APRIL 4   **Read Matthew 26:36-46.**

Most of us are not intentionally cruel, any more than were the weary disciples on Holy Thursday. Still, like the negligent apostles, we can unintentionally cause suffering. I've learned this lesson more than once.

For example, there was an unspoken agreement among the teachers in our school that we would close windows, turn off the lights, and restore general order to our clasrooms before leaving for the day.

Restoring general order and turning off lights were mindless activities I performed without resistance. For some reason, however, I grew lazy about closing windows.

"Oh, somebody else can just close them," I told myself.

My classroom faced an enclosed courtyard, so there was no chance that a sudden storm or intruders could cause harm.

I never gave my laziness more than a moment's thought, until one night, when I returned late to my classroom after a school play rehearsal.

Walking in, I watched a very short janitor straining to close my windows. About to step up on the radiators to reach the top windows, he blushed when he saw me.

"I'm sorry, ma'am. I have to step up here. My arthritis makes it so hard for me to reach the windows."

I have seldom felt more culpable. My indifference was causing someone suffering. I quickly closed the windows and apologized to the janitor. Needless to say, I've been scrupulous about closing the windows ever since!

Look closely at the people who cross your path today. In what ways can you help to eliminate rather than contribute to their suffering?

Please, Lord, do not let me cause needless suffering.

 APRIL 5   **Read Matthew 26:47-55.**

As usual I was moving through the museum too fast, trying to cover as much ground as possible in too short a time. One picture made me stop moving.

Although I never checked to see who the artist was or what the name of the painting was, the scene it depicted was unmistakable and unforgettable: the arrest of Jesus, the very scene described by Matthew.

In this painting, the soldiers were dressed in armor, as they would be, of course. Jesus in their midst looked vulnerable and susceptible to injury. I suppose if I'd ever really thought about the arrest, it would have occurred to me that a good part of the arresting crowd would be in armor. But I was stunned to look at the painting and think about the warm, soft flesh of Jesus being forced up against the hard, cold metal of the Roman soldiers' armor. Christ looked so defenseless, just like the sheep to which he so often referred.

The painting made me realize that I'm much more like a Roman soldier than I'd like to admit. My armor is sometimes more obvious than my flesh and blood. Sometimes I am like those soldiers, whose indentities are unknown to us. I refuse to be vulnerable like Jesus. Instead, I overprotect myself. And armor is not a very effective teaching tool.

What "armor" do you need to shed in order to become more effective in your classroom?

Lord, you made yourself vulnerable for my sake; please give me the freedom and courage to put aside my armor.

🕊 APRIL 6   Read Matthew 26:69-75.

We all sympathize with Peter. When that cock crowed, he was devastated. Already cognizant of his defection, the crowing bird only served to reinforce his treachery. He turned his back on Jesus Christ, a man and a Savior who would never, under any circumstances, turn his back on Peter. Like Peter, we have all, in our own way, turned our back on Jesus Christ. And when we do, there are always the servant-girls.

It is the presence of the servant-girls that troubles me in this passage. Their comments to Peter echo down through the centuries: "You also were with Jesus the Galilean"; "This man was with Jesus of Nazareth." The echo of his response is even louder: "I do not know the man!" (Matthew 26:69-72).

Our betrayals of Jesus may seem to be private, but they seldom are. Oh, a sin or two may be hidden. Some of our faults may not be obvious to others, but there are always "servant-girls" watching—people who will take note if, in word or deed, we deny Jesus Christ.

What message did Peter's denial send to those servant-girls?

What messages do we send to our students when we behave in ways that are counter to the good news? Our students are our "servant-girls," watching, wondering. Once they know that we are followers of Jesus Christ, they will wonder about any behavior that belies our faith.

Peter was not the only one whose betrayal was a public one.

Lord Jesus, let my words and deeds reflect my undying belief in you.

 APRIL 7   **Read Matthew 27:37-44.**

Mr. Johnson was one of my favorite colleagues during my first year of teaching. I knew very little about him except that he was the typing teacher, he had an adopted daughter, and he was a painter during the summer.

A bit of a curmudgeon, he enjoyed poking fun at my experimental teaching techniques. But he was always a source of good-natured wisdom and common sense, and he seemed pretty unflappable. Moreover, he gave me an irreplaceable insight into the Crucifixion.

During Holy Week, Mr. Johnson and I were casually chatting about the services at our respective churches. He was in a bit of a snit because the cross erected for a Good Friday service in his church did not have a marker on it. "It's supposed to have a painted sign on it," he told me. "The cross is supposed to say, 'This is Jesus, the King of the Jews.'"

"The sign doesn't matter much," I told him offhandedly.

"Oh, yes, it does," Mr. Johnson insisted. "Think about the guy who painted that sign for Jesus' cross. He thought it was important. They weren't killing Jesus because he was a carpenter from Nazareth. They killed him because he was a political threat. They thought he wanted to be king. That sign said it all. I wonder how that sign made Jesus feel?"

Mr. Johnson was a painter, and he understood the importance of signs in a way that I did not. Now I cannot read this passage from Matthew without hearing Mr. Johnson's voice and wondering about the man who painted the sign for Jesus' cross.

Today, think about the sign on the cross. What questions does the sign raise for you?

Lord, keep us alert to new ways of understanding your Word.

APRIL 8   Read Matthew 28:11-15.

I do not believe all of those Roman guards wanted to take the bribes offered them. Having lived through the arrest, the Crucifixion, and the Resurrection, some of those men must have been genuinely moved to faith. Yet fear for themselves and their families made them accept the bribe and circulate a false story about the disposal of Jesus' body.

Fear for self and family is no small consideration. A colleague of mine who routinely teaches *The Diary of Anne Frank* is very honest about her own fears. "If I had lived during the Holocaust," she told me, "I would have kept my mouth shut. If the only way to protect my babies was to turn a blind eye to the death camps, nothing could have made me speak out. I never would have helped out a family like the Franks."

Those Roman guards shared the same concerns. Their families might be executed if they refused to participate in the state's lie about Jesus. They might lose their jobs and their families would starve. The decisions they faced were horrible ones. At least some of them would have known in their hearts that Jesus was Lord, but they would not risk the lives of their loved ones for their own beliefs.

Though we may never face life-threatening faith choices, our faith is tested every day in many subtle ways. Will we succumb to fear, pressure, or the status quo; or will we stand firm? Our students are watching.

Dear Lord of mercy, spare us the fearful trials imposed upon the Roman guards. And when our faith is tested, give us the courage to stand firm in our beliefs.

I love, quite literally, empty school buildings. For me, there is immense pleasure in walking the halls, late at night, when all the students have gone home. I like the sound—this will sound silly—of my heels tapping against the tile hallways. I like the eerie stillness of the deserted cafeteria. The desolate look of the gymnasium is somehow appealing.

But my love of the empty building is predicated on my love of the full building, the building that bursts with people and noise and learning. Late at night when I roam the halls, I hear the echoes of students' voices. I imagine them sitting in their seats. I see them banging their locker doors shut. I remember all the students who've passed through the halls over the years. It is their lives that make the school a vital place to spend my own life.

Empty schools are like the empty tomb of Jesus. The vacant tomb that greeted Jesus' followers on Easter morning signified far more than anyone realized at the time. I sometimes wonder how many of those early, unnamed followers of Jesus ran to the tomb just to see for themselves that it was indeed empty. As those first Christians looked on the emptiness, they would slowly come to understand that the emptiness pointed to abundant life.

Resurrected Lord, we adore your radiant spirit that fills all of our empty spaces.

Honestly now—have you ever read in its entirety the genealogy of Jesus as it is recorded in the first chapter of Matthew? Okay, you may be among the few mortals who've actually read the names, but have you ever paid any attention to real people on the list? Have you ever wondered about their tears and laughter and failures and successes? Have you ever given Zerah or Nahshon or Zadok a second thought? Or are they just names to be gotten through before you get to the "good stuff"?

I'll come clean here. Those genealogical lists have always seemed tedious and unnecessary to me, until now. Now that I've forced myself to pay attention to *all* of the people in Matthew's Gospel. Now that genealogy makes me think of the portrait gallery in a school where I once taught.

Throughout its long history, the school had commissioned a portrait of each of its principals. Ignoring the portraits was easy. None but the most recent portraits meant anything to the current crop of teachers. But each of those principals had affected the life of the school—for good or ill. Every one left an imprint on students. They deserve to be recognized, remembered, revered, perhaps. We are all connected to each other in a circle that never ends.

Dear Lord, thank you for the unending circle of your creation that links us one to the other, that links our present and future with the past.

 **APRIL 11**   **Read Matthew 9:9-13.**

She was pretty and vivacious and young, and the students loved her. A first-year math teacher, fresh from college, Becky quickly won the affections of her junior high students. As assistant volleyball coach, she spent hours of her free time working with students.

Not just the successful students were drawn to Becky, but the troubled kids as well. She had a way of setting them at ease. By the end of the first semester, Becky's classroom was routinely filled with students after school. Single and new in town, Becky had no family to hurry home to, no pressing duties outside of school. She was glad to spend time with her students.

The talk in the teachers' lounge grew more petty the more popular this new teacher became.

"What's wrong with her? Why's she spending so much time with those kids?"

"Doesn't she know those kids are just using her?"

"Tell her to get a life and stop wasting it hanging around this place."

Luckily, Becky's goodwill allowed her to ignore the pettiness and keep doing what she did so well. Like Jesus, who did not limit his attentions to one group of people, this gifted young woman knew that she was called to teach everyone— not a select few.

Like Becky, each of us has special gifts, given to us by God. How is God calling you to use *your* gifts?

Lord Jesus, help us to rejoice in the special gifts of our colleagues and to use our own gifts as we strive to be the best teachers we can be.

APRIL 12   Read Matthew 9:14-17; 11:2-6.

Many of us today have heard the New Testament passages so often that we can become deadened to their impact. We have to remind ourselves that the contemporaries of Jesus were unaware of the salvation history being worked out in their midst.

John the Baptist's disciples, for example, were forced to ask Jesus questions because they did not understand the seeming differences between him and the man they had been following. John's disciples questioned Jesus about fasting, about his very identity. They were confused and did not know whom to follow.

When new leaders emerge in school systems, there are often confusions and questions. School superintendents are replaced. Older principals retire and new ones take over. The teachers who were favored by the former administrators no longer feel confident about their positions. Petty jealousies surface as people move to protect their own little fiefdoms.

Yet, Jesus provides the clear path through such confusions and upsets. "Blessed is anyone who takes no offense at me" (Matthew 11:6). His reply to John's disciples was not dismissive or cruel, but his remarks were pointed, nonetheless. Jesus well understood that his appearance was stirring the waters; however, he also knew that people of faith would recognize him and would understand that he and John were not at odds. They were part of the same mission.

When we think of ourselves as being part of the same mission effort, petty differences and power struggles become much easier to handle.

Lord, help us to bear in mind the identity of our true Leader, so that we can gracefully negotiate any change in temporal leaders.

APRIL 13   Read Matthew 14:1-12.

The grisly horror of the story rivets our attention. The seductive dance of Herodias's daughter mesmerized Herod and his guests—so much so that their judgment was suspended. When the spoiled and willful girl said, "Give me the head of John the Baptist here on a platter," no one protested. But Matthew records a telling observation. "The king was grieved," Matthew writes, "yet out of regard for his oaths and for the guests, he commanded it to be given" (Matthew 14:8-9).

I find myself thinking about Herod's dinner guests. One of them, at least, must have shared Herod's misgivings. Some individual must have known that the horrible nature of the request freed Herod from his oaths. Apparently, no one even murmured in protest. How revolted they must have been when John's bloodied head was brought in on a platter. Then they could see the cost of their silence.

One of the saintliest teachers I've ever known lost his job because he refused to keep silent. Simultaneously lacking in diplomatic skills and blessed with keen judgment and vision, this man repeatedly pointed out the errors of the school board. He had the courage to speak out when many others, like Herod's guests, remained silent. His courage cost him his job, but he did not lose his integrity.

It's not easy to speak out against injustice or wrong choices, especially when our voice is the only one to be heard. But we are never really alone. God stands with us, giving us the wisdom and courage we need.

Lord Jesus, grant us the wisdom to know when to remain silent and when to speak out. Then give us the courage to speak.

I once taught in a private, religious school where the teaching staff was dedicated to the advancement of God's kingdom. No task was too large, no demand too great for these teachers. I have never worked with a more caring, dedicated group. But I became aware of an unconscious tyranny that saddened me and eventually made me resign.

No teacher ever felt free to say, "I need help. I have too much work to do."

The message we received from the administration was clear: Follow the example of Jesus. Give your entire life for the school. And while I believe an imitation of Christ is essential for teachers, I also believe we should imitate *all* of his characteristics.

These passages from Matthew make clear that Jesus asked for help when he needed it. When he saw the crowds before him he was moved with pity. The people were "harassed and helpless, like sheep without a shepherd" (Matthew 9:36). At the beginning of the very next chapter, we see Jesus commission his disciples. He tells them to go after the "lost sheep." Jesus knew he could not accomplish everything alone. If he spread himself too thin, his mission would suffer.

We need to be kind to *ourselves* as well as our colleagues. None of us needs the tyranny that suggests we must wear ourselves out in order to be effective teachers.

Dear Lord, help us discern the difference between imitating you and destroying ourselves.

At the risk of sounding like Miss Manners, I have to say that Jesus seems downright rude to the Canaanite woman in this passage. Surely, one hesitates to disparage the social skills of the Lord, but Jesus is directly and repeatedly unkind to a woman who begs for help.

Look at what he says to her. It's hard not to cringe.

For me, the lesson in this passage comes from her, the woman, the outcast. Jesus is gracious when he chooses to heal her daughter, but it is the persistence of the woman that strikes me. She will not take no for an answer. The Gospel does not assign her a name. We know nothing about her. Still, she's worth our attention.

She reminds me of Gloria.

Goria was a rather eccentric substitute teacher who'd been working in our school system for years. Whenever a position opened up, she applied, hoping to win a full-time job. Because she was a bit odd, no one ever took her seriously. Year after year, the jobs went to someone else. Then one year, on the first day of the school year, a teacher resigned. There was no time to recruit a substitute. Gloria stepped in and poured such energy and life into her classroom that the students themselves petitioned the principal to hire her full-time. Gloria finally won the coveted job.

How have you experienced the importance of persistence in your teaching career? What difficulty or challenge in your life do you need to ask God for persistence in handling today?

Lord, grant us persistence in the face of our difficulties.

 **APRIL 16**   **Read Matthew 18:1-4.**

I want to know who that little child was that Jesus called to him. Was he someone Jesus knew? Did the child resist Jesus' summons at first? When the child returned to his friends and family, did they tease him?

Or perhaps the whole event meant nothing at the time. Maybe it was as casual and offhanded as picking up the newspaper from the front porch each morning. There's a chance that the incident left no impression on the child. There's an equal chance that years later when the child heard of Jesus' crucifixion, he or she remembered vividly this incident.

As teachers, we know why Jesus used a little child as an example. For all their sudden cruelties and temper tantrums, children remain unsullied and fresh. Looking into the faces of kindergartners or first graders is a splendid reminder of all that is good.

Rose Kennedy once remarked that she liked having her grandchildren around because they kept her young. As teachers, we share Rose Kennedy's bounty. We are surrounded by people who are younger than we are.

Often, the face of a child we do not know and will never teach catches our attention as the child swings on a swing during recess or trudges down to the cafeteria for lunch. In these little faces, we can see hope. We see God.

Lord, thank you for the gift of little children.

 **APRIL 17**   **Read Matthew 8:5-13.**

Bob could not separate his personal life from his professional one. In the midst of a nasty divorce, he often told his students about his legal battles. Then, he'd come to the teachers' lounge and repeat to us what he told his students.

"My first period class is just great," he told a group of teachers one morning. "They really care about what's happening to me."

As the student started repeating Bob's struggles to their friends, we grew concerned. Students are not meant to serve as sounding boards for our problems. One of Bob's friends finally made him see that he should keep his personal troubles out of the classroom.

When the centurion asked for Jesus' help, he made reference to his position. "I also am a man under authority, with soldiers under me, and I say to one, 'Go,' and he goes" (Matthew 8:9). The centurion understood that his actions affected others. I wonder how his troops were affected when they heard of the boy's healing. The healing must have touched off strong emotions.

Like the centurion, we do not operate in a vacuum. People watch us. If we bring our personal problems into the classroom, our students will be affected. And like the centurion, we know that the only place to turn in turmoil is toward the One who heals.

Lord Jesus, healer of all wounds, when we are hurting, give us the strength to pursue our professional responsibilities with dignity and grace.

 APRIL 18   **Read Matthew 20:20-28; 27:56.**

I always feel badly for the people who asked Jesus the wrong questions. I'm sure I'd have been one of their number. There would be so many things to ask Jesus, and people could never know for sure how he'd react. The mother of James and John certainly was bold in asking of him this favor: "Declare that these two sons of mine will sit, one at your right hand and one at your left, in your kingdom" (Matthew 20:21).

The request caused indignation and agitation. The apostles did not want Zebedee's sons favored in such a way. This mother must have been hurt by the rebuffs she received.

But look at Matthew 27:56. There she is—present at the Crucifixion, looking on with Mary Magdalene and Mary, the mother of James and Joseph.

Like Jesus' mother, the mother of the sons of Zebedee must have suffered terribly as she watched all of her sons' dreams die, apparently, on the cross with Jesus. Once so sure of Jesus' success that she asked him for favors, she could do little at the Crucifixion but look on in sorrow and grief. Yet, she did not desert Jesus or his followers. She remained faithful in adversity.

What kind of adversity are you currently facing in your classroom? How can you remain faithful as you attempt to deal with this adversity?

Lord, give us the strength of the crucifixion women, so that we may remain steadfast.

 APRIL 19   **Read Matthew 8:14-15.**

Penny, the school secretary, was uniformly pleasant and professional in her dealings with me. Neither indifferent to nor terribly interested in her as a person, I interacted with her only on a professional level. She was the school secretary. That's who she was.

Then I got pregnant. Penny became very interested in me, and I suddenly became interested in her.

Twenty-five years older than I, she told me about how she was forced to quit her job when she was pregnant, in the late forties. She gave me tips to avoid morning sickness. She'd cover my first period class for me if I arrived a few minutes late because of a doctor's appointment. Shortly before the baby arrived, she gave me the invaluable infant car seat.

Until I became pregnant, Penny was simply the school secretary to me—more of a function than a human being. Peter's mother-in-law was relegated to the same fate. She may have only been sick one day in her whole life, but that's the piece of her personal history that's recorded in the New Testament. She's worth thinking about though. She and her daughter, Peter's wife, must have had some interesting conversations. She must have had some strong feelings about Jesus, this man who took her daughter's husband away. How close Peter's mother-in-law was to the heart of Christianity.

Are there people you work with but hardly know? Why not take the first step in getting to know one of them this week?

Lord Jesus, allow us to see the human beings behind the titles.

 **APRIL 20**   **Read Matthew 5:1-12.**

I once sat on the shores of the Sea of Galilee, on the hillside from which Jesus is believed to have delivered the Sermon on the Mount. The time I spent on that lush hillside, gazing out over the crystal, sparkling Sea of Galilee is one of the touchstones of my spiritual existence. Jesus Christ was vibrantly alive and real for me that day.

Sitting on the hillside, I tried to imagine the landscape filled with hundreds and hundreds of people. I tried to catch the echo of their voices, their expressions as they listened to

Jesus speak. The acoustics of the site are remarkable. Jesus' voice would have carried easily to the assembled crowd.

As I sat there, I wondered how many people came to faith that day. How many people responded to the gift of Jesus.

I found myself thinking of all the people I've loved, all my students, my friends, my family. I tried to imagine them sitting there listening to Jesus—and it occurred to me that the closest some of them might ever get to Jesus was me. I carry the image of the sparkling sea and the green hillside within me—and with that carried image comes the profound responsibility of being a representative of Christ on earth.

As Christians, we all share this profound responsibility. How are you a representative of Christ in your classroom, your school, your community, your world?

Thank you, Jesus Christ, for the gift of Galilee. Help us to be your faithful representatives wherever we go.

 **APRIL 21**   **Read Matthew 2:16-18.**

There are some passages in the Bible that I almost cannot bear to read. The only way I can meditate on the slaughter of the Holy Innocents, for example, is to remind myself that my horror pales into insignificance when compared to the pain and terror of those families. Filled with atrocities of all kinds, Herod's life created distress and grief for decades.

Having a baby snatched from their arms and butchered as they watched would be life-ending grief for most parents. Thereafter, they might be able to move through their daily routines, but nothing could erase the unspeakable pain of Herod's outrage.

In our teaching careers, few of us encounter people as evil as Herod. But, as in any profession, occasionally there are mean-spirited people around us. People who enjoy making others suffer. We have all met and worked with colleagues whose bitterness poisoned the school atmosphere. In such situations there is always the very human temptation to reciprocate bitterness with bitterness. However, as Christians we are not allowed to give in to that temptation. We are duty bound, we are love bound, to return charity for bitterness, kindness for mistreatment.

Dealing with "little Herods," people whose worldview is negative and bitter, is a mighty challenge. May we meet the challenge by following Christ's example.

Lord, help us grow in your love so that we can greet evil with charity.

🌷 APRIL 22   Read Matthew 8:1-4.

Several years ago, when my husband and I were suffering through one of the worst periods of our marriage, I was often very distraught during the school day. Somehow I would muster the courage and self-possession to teach, without letting my students know what bad shape I was in.

But when the students were out of the way and I sat in my classroom alone after school, all the grief came washing over me, and I often grew despondent. My friend and colleague, whose classroom was next to mine, always stopped in after school to check on me. She was the only one to whom I confided the truth of my situation. Her quiet compassion and gracious friendship sustained me through a very troubled time in my life. And she never told anyone else about my problem.

The leper in this Gospel passage is instructed by Jesus, "See that you say nothing to anyone" (Matthew 8:4). Who knows if that leper kept quiet? The temptation to tell his story must have been great. What would he tell his friends when they asked about the disappearance of his leprosy?

The ability to keep a confidence is a vital characteristic of an effective teacher. Students and colleagues will not talk to us if they learn we will spread their stories all over the place. And how can we expect them to learn from us if they do not trust us?

Lord who knows the secrets of all hearts, give us the moral integrity to maintain confidences.

APRIL 23   **Read Proverbs 19:20; Matthew 2:1-8.**

In Proverbs we read of the importance of listening to advice and accepting instruction. Perhaps just as important is knowing when to seek counsel. Even Herod, one of the most evil and despicable characters in the Bible, had enough sense to ask questions, to find out all he could before he made his move.

Not only did Herod question the wise men, he also questioned his advisers. In the middle of a dilemma, Herod sought advice from every possible quarter. Some of the men advising Herod might have understood the spiritual significance of the events; others would only see events in political terms.

I had a need for wise counsel when a local college asked me to supervise a student teacher in my classroom. In my initial meetings with the potential student teacher, I became convinced that she and my students would not be well served if she did her student teaching in my classroom. A nice enough young woman, her academic background was weak and she was vocally anti-Christian. Given the religious nature of the school and my students, I did not think we had a good match in the making. A part of me, however, thought it might be good for the students to be taught by someone with an opposing worldview. I knew the decision was not one I could make alone.

So I talked to my colleagues. Together we decided that the pluses did not outweigh the minuses. With their help I was able to make a confident and informed decision.

Do you need the advice of others concerning anything in your life today? Who can be of help to you?

Lord God, make us aware of when to seek the advice of others.

APRIL 24   **Read Matthew 3:7-12.**

The football coach was pretty loud. Not unkind. Not nasty. But he yelled. His shouts and admonitions could be heard all the way from the football field into the school building during his after-school practices.

During the day, when he taught his eighth-grade history classes, he also yelled. His booming voice punctuated all of our classes from time to time. He was a big man, with a voice to match.

Of course, some people were irritated by the noise level. Some teachers grumbled. Some students complained to their parents about the yelling.

One day in the office, I heard the coach talking to the principal.

"Hey," the coach was telling the principal, who'd evidently received a complaint, "even Jesus Christ raised his voice. He didn't spend all his time telling nice, quiet little stories about sheep. Heck, at least I never refer to my students as a brood of vipers."

He was right. Jesus Christ did get animated and even angry. He was perfectly capable of raising his voice when the situation called for it.

We err when we assume that effective teaching has only one face. Some students respond better to a mild-mannered, caring approach. Others are better served by a direct approach. No one style is equally effective. As long as the love of God governs us, our particular teaching styles can differ.

Lord Jesus, train us to hear your voice, no matter how loud or soft it is.

 **APRIL 25**   **Read Matthew 13:54-58.**

Busybodies have always driven me to distraction. People who have nothing better to do with their time than gossip and chatter seem pretty useless to me, I always have to remind myself that God loves busybodies, too. But on some days, to tell the truth, I wish he didn't.

You do know the personality type, don't you? Every church, every school has its share of people who genuinely love gossip. They truly enjoy whispering, talking about people, conjecturing about the relative failings of certain human beings.

Well, Nazareth clearly had its share of busybodies. So we

know Jesus Christ was not spared their prattle. Look at the questions and comments his return to Nazareth raised. His return must have given rise to enough gossip to last for years.

As Christians and as professionals, we are not to be gossips. We are not to be like those Nazareth busybodies who denigrated Jesus by their very words. Gossip, no matter how seemingly innocent, seeks to belittle other human beings. It's a way of saying, as this Gospel passage makes clear, "Just who does he think he is?"

Jesus taught us that every human being has worth and value. If that's true, how can gossip be harmless?

Lord Jesus, guard our tongues.

 **APRIL 26**   **Read Matthew 8:28-34.**

The year Pamela won the state Teacher of the Year Award, the whole school system rejoiced. There was a dinner in her honor. She rode on a special float during the Memorial Day parade. The newspaper ran a Sunday feature on her life. Only good seemed to flow from Pamela's selection. She was a fine and decent teacher, relatively new to the system, and she was richly deserving of the award.

But like the swineherds in the Gospel who grow confused and worried, we do not always know what to do in the midst of unexpected good. Jesus actually expells demons in this scene. The two men are freed to live rich and full lives. That is a great good. But the swineherds lose their whole herd and grow confused. In their confusion and fright, they rouse the entire town, and the entire town asks Jesus to leave.

Pamela was stunned and hurt when two of her fellow teachers wrote to the newspaper, suggesting that her relative newness made her an unfit choice for the award. These teachers, both twenty-five-year veterans, were not unkind in their letter—but very pointed.

Sometimes we can't see beyond our own concerns. Yes, the swineherds had a right to worry about their lost herd. And, yes, the veteran teachers had a right to voice their concerns. Jesus, however, encourages us to focus on the good.

Lord Jesus, ruler of all that is good, help us to rejoice in the good-ness that surrounds us.

 APRIL 27   **Read Matthew 21:33-46.**

Jesus was a Pharisee.

Does that statement startle you? I gasped out loud the first time I heard those words. I was attending a Bible seminar in Jerusalem and the minister was explaining to us that there were four major sects during Jesus' time: Sadducees, Pharisees, Zealots, and Essenes. He explained to us the differences between the sects and then explained that Jesus was most closely aligned with the Pharisees. It makes sense that Jesus, then, would always take them to task. He knew them well. He knew they were the sect with the reputation for having narrowed the Ten Commandments to 613 laws.

As long as I can remember, *Pharisee* has been a bad word in my vocabulary. They ask the wrong questions; make the wrong statements; and generally act like unenlightened, testy fools. Once I understood that Jesus emerged from that group, their animosity toward him became all the more clear. Just as we sometimes fail to see the potential in a familiar student or colleague, so the Pharisees chose not to believe that Jesus was special—the Son of God.

In this incident from Matthew, one of several such incidents in the New Testament, the Pharisees realized that Jesus was "speaking about them." They badly wanted to get rid of him, but they knew he had popular support. Rather than rallying to one of their own who was emerging as singular prophet and Messiah, the Pharisees resented Jesus.

If only they had recognized God in their midst.

If only we would.

Lord Jesus Christ, teach us to recognize the divine, especially in one of our own.

Right now my horse is lame. I spent the morning out in the barn waiting for the vet to arrive. When my horse is ill, he becomes very pliable and dependent. He nuzzles up against me. He stands quietly while I rub his neck. When I apply hot compresses to his swollen leg, he stands still while I wrap the hot towel around him. He knows he needs me. He knows I can help.

When he's acting this docile, I often tell myself, "I wish people acted this way. I wish my students acted this way."

Often people are not direct with their needs. Our students do not tell us when they're in trouble. Our friends and families want us to guess what's wrong so that they don't have to tell us.

Jesus, on the other hand, seems to have had no trouble gettting people to express their needs. Acting like my lame horse who trusts implicitly in my ability to make him better, the crowd in this passage bring a possessed mute to Jesus, confident that he will heal the stricken man.

Jesus was approachable, and people trusted him to respond with mercy. I sometimes wonder if my students and my friends trust my responses to be merciful ones.

Dear Lord, make me more merciful.

A former secretary at our school acted like a guard dog, refusing to let anyone get near the principal. More than once the principal instructed her to let people in to see him, but she continued to act as a gatekeeper.

"He works too hard for his own good," she'd tell a teacher who wanted to dash in to see the principal before school. "Just tell me what you need, and I'll take care of it."

If a student wanted to see him, for whatever reason, the secretary used the same approach. "My job is to save him work," she'd tell the puzzled student. "I can handle anything you need."

Finally, both the school community and the principal grew so frustrated that she was threatened with the loss of her job. The official reprimand stunned her into changing her behavior.

I think the secretary was well intentioned. She was acting like the apostles who scolded the children, and presumably their parents, who wanted to be blessed by Jesus. The apostles thought they were doing what was best for Jesus. They were protecting him. But in protecting him, they were also establishing their own self-importance. They set themselves up as mediators between Jesus and his flock. But Jesus, like the school principal, did not want any mediators.

Isn't it wonderful to know that we have a God of direct access?

Lord, sometimes I forget that I can come to you anytime for any reason. Thank you for your constant, loving presence.

 **APRIL 30**   **Read Matthew 9:18-22.**

I guess it shouldn't surprise me. The Bible is meant to be a source of continual spiritual enlightenment. Still, I continue to be startled when a familiar passage suddenly teaches me something new.

These verses from Matthew are just such a passage. I've known this story for years: The father comes and asks Jesus to raise his daughter from the dead. However, one phrase caught my attention the other day, and its power has stayed with me: "Jesus got up and followed him" (Matthew 9:19).

Perhaps to you the words are not remarkable. To me they speak volumes. I always think of Jesus as the One being followed. He is the Leader, the One sitting on the mountainside, on the boat, delivering sermons. He is the One who decides when the time has come to give himself up to his enemies. Yet, here with this grieving father, the Savior of the world follows rather than leads. The father and daughter desperately need Jesus, but they do not need to follow him. They simply need his help, and Jesus is willing to be of use.

As a teacher who is accustomed to leading, I am grateful

for this new insight. As I try to imitate Jesus Christ, some-times I need to follow rather than lead. I need to be prepared to be of whatever service I can to those in need.

Poring over the Gospels gives me never-ending opportuni-ties to meet Jesus again and again. In the process of meeting him, I encounter the thousands of nameless people whose lives he touched. The encounters make me recommit my life to him.

Praise God for the gift of Jesus Christ.

May

The Gift of Memory

Anne Marie Drew

MAY 1   **Read Luke 22:14-20.**

Jesus Christ so understood the power of *memory* that his greatest gift to his disciples invoked the very word: "Do this in memory of me" (Luke 22:19 GNB). The man from Galilee knew that memories breathe life into us.

As teachers we encounter thousands of students over the course of our careers. Some of those students are imprinted on our memories forever. Their names may fade away. Their faces may blur. Still, some detail of their existence lingers.

Our souls carry the imprint of our students. There will be those precious few who develop into lifelong friends. More often, only a memory remains. We find ourselves recalling a testy confrontation, an offhand remark, a spontaneous action—some minor incident that taught us about ourselves, our students, and our God.

Surely, one of the greatest joys of teaching is the ever-changing mix of students. God lives in each of these young people. Therefore, our chances of learning more about our

Creator, who is infinite love, are boundless. And as we remember our students, our gratitude increases.

This month, as we prepare to say good-bye to another crop of students, let us give thanks for the gift of memory.

Thank you, God, for the vital gift of memory. We are grateful for the opportunity to remember, savor, and even learn from past experiences and relationships.

 MAY 2   **Read Luke 9:18-20.**

With two outrageously successful brothers, Tiffany was the last child of a very prominent family in town. And she was an embarrassment.

A seventh grader in a private, very conservative school, she had never outgrown the toddler mentality of testing the limits. Endless stories circulated about her behavior. She'd skip down the halls singing at the top of her lungs. She'd bring orange peels into class and dump them into a wastebasket so that the whole room started to reek of garbage. Knowing in advance that a movie was going to be shown, she'd bring popcorn for the whole class.

None of that behavior is criminal, but in a very traditional school, she clearly was out of step. When I wrote her name in my grade book at the start of a new semester, I asked God for endurance.

Endurance was not required. Tiffany proved to be a delight.

Her reputation was far worse than her behavior. While I did not relish her little pranks, I came to enjoy her sense of humor. The very eccentricity that made her a misfit acted as leaven in the classroom. And she did have perfect timing. She knew when she'd gone too far.

Whenever we encounter students whose reputations precede them, may we try to keep an open mind.

Lord Jesus, remind me, as you did Peter, to form my own opinions.

Jesus' vision allowed him to see the miraculous potential in six stone water jars. A parent-teacher conference taught me to pray for a share in the vision.

When parent-teacher conferences rolled around, I couldn't wait to meet Georgiana's parents. Something about the girl irritated me. She was—forgive me—one of those bouncy cheerleader types, always perfectly dressed, always smelling of the latest perfume. Surrounded by boys and immensely popular, this thirteen-year-old seemed to embody all the superficial and wrong qualities.

On the night of her conference, Georgiana came in, accompanied by an overweight and disheveled woman. The woman, wearing a faded, torn housedress and flip-flops, introduced herself as Georgiana's mother. She was difficult to understand because she had almost no teeth and her words were garbled. Her body odor was strong.

As we talked, Georgiana patted and joked with her mom. Their relationship emerged as warm and affectionate. Many adolescents refuse to be seen in public with their parents. Yet here was a girl who adored her mother, a mother who would have embarrassed many a young student.

How limited had been my vision of Georgiana.

Lord of life, grant me your Cana vision.

Teachers, like shepherds, do not want any of the flock to stray. But students are not sheep. We cannot control them. Dennis was the first of my students to teach me this tough lesson.

When the principal called me into her office, she closed the door behind us and said, "I didn't want you to hear this secondhand. Dennis is withdrawing from school."

"You can't let him do that," I snapped.

"He and his parents made the choice," the principal responded. "And that's the end of it."

Until this day I wonder what happened to this boy.

A too-old eighth grader who could not really read or write, Dennis was a funny, warmhearted young man. For an entire semester, I'd worked with him during my lunch breaks, tutoring him, trying to break through the stone walls that stood between him and academic success. We both tried, very hard. Still, Dennis's skills did not improve.

His parents knew that his greatest happiness had nothing to do with academics. They withdrew him from school, in order to let him work full-time on the family farm.

It's a painful lesson, but one that eventually every teacher learns: Some students are beyond our reach. The good news is that they are never beyond the reach of God.

Tender Shepherd, guard those students who wander beyond our reach.

 MAY 5   **Read Proverbs 3:1-26.**

These verses from Proverbs celebrate the joys of a long life, faithfully lived. When Megan's life almost ended, I became acutely aware of the precious gift of life.

A perky, freckle-faced little girl, Megan was due to start first grade in the fall. As a kindergartner, she'd been so delightful. The teaching staff looked forward to having her around throughout elementary school.

On a hot July evening, Megan stood on the grounds of a local carnival, talking to her family and eating cotton candy. One of the local riders, whose horse had just been in the parade, asked Megan if she wanted to sit on his horse. Of course, the child said yes.

Just as Megan settled onto the horse's back, some carnival noise spooked the horse and he jumped, tossing Megan to the concrete below. In his fright, the horse stomped on the little girl.

The first medical reports were grim. Megan was not expected to live. Then, inch by inch, she fought back. And she made a full recovery. Now a fourth grader, Megan is a bright reminder of how strong the human will to survive is.

As we look at the young faces in our classrooms each day, let us remember to give thanks for the precious gift of life.

Lord, bestower of life, thank you for instilling in us the will to survive.

 MAY 6   **Read John 8:1-11.**

Jesus' behavior in the scene with the adulterous woman always baffled me. When the angry men dragged the woman before him, Jesus bent down in the sand and doodled. His behavior never made much sense.

One Saturday during a youth retreat, I wanted several students to dramatize the Gospel passage. With its noise and fear and rocks and indignant men and guilty woman, the scene provides ample material for dramatization and then discussion and meditation.

I assigned the part of Jesus to Daren, a very shy thirteen-year-old who was one of my English students as well as a fellow church member.

When it came to the doodling part of the scene, Daren stayed drawing on the ground a very long time. While the indignant men left and went their separate ways, and the frightened woman cowered in a corner, he doodled. When Daren stood up, he looked at the woman and told her gently, "Go and sin no more."

Afterward, I asked Daren what Jesus might have been thinking about as he doodled in the sand. Without pausing, Daren answered, "He was praying so he could figure out what to say."

Of course.

Jesus Christ was not the one-second answer man with instantaneous solutions to every situation. He prayed. He considered. Then he acted.

A good reminder from an eighth-grade "Jesus."

Lord, dispenser of wisdom, thank you for students who teach us about you.

MAY 7   **Read Luke 4:16-22.**

As the reading from Luke makes clear, Jesus knew how to command an audience. An enviable talent.

Eric, one of my students, apparently did not share the same gift. Although eager to capture a part in the school play, he stumbled over lines, perspired profusely, and moved awkwardly on stage throughout two days of tryouts.

I could not cast him in the play. Yet he so desperately wanted to be a part of the Drama Club that I made him my assistant director. One of Eric's tasks was to be a stand-in for absent student actors during rehearsals. As a stand-in, he did not stutter. His body wasn't stiff. He looked like a natural on the stage.

One day, after I'd gotten to know him better, I asked, "Why do you think auditions are so hard for you, when you do so well up there on the stage?"

His reply made me catch my breath.

"I have dyslexia," he said. "I can't read stuff that I've never seen before. But once I know the parts, I'm okay."

I'd been directing plays so long that I'd grown insensitive to the stress "cold" readings can cause. Thereafter, I always made copies of the script available beforehand. In the very next show, I lost a very good assistant director. But I gained, in Eric, a very good student actor.

In these last weeks of the school year, challenge yourself to uncover as many "hidden talents" in your students as you can. What a wonderful last gift to give them!

Jesus Christ, you command both our love and attention. Keep me aware that some talents are hidden ones, and help me to recognize the hidden talents of my students.

 MAY 8   **Read Psalm 47.**

The name carved into the desk was clear and sharp: Greg. First row by the window. Last seat. That's where Greg sat during first period.

As I was closing up the windows one day after school, I saw the fresh carving. The defaced desk didn't bother me as much as the knowledge that I'd have to confront the student about his actions. Greg was sullen and uncooperative on his good days.

The next day before school started I asked Greg to come and see me. Walking him to the desk, I asked him if he knew how his name had come to be carved into the wood.

"Sure," he said. "I did it."

"With what?" I asked, as if the instrument made any difference.

"My compass from math class. It's real sharp."

"Why on earth would you do that to a desk?" I demanded to know.

Greg, an eighth grader who was already six feet tall, looked at me and without any malice or anger, quietly said, "Because I get so bored just sitting here. I have to do something."

After school that day, while Greg sanded the desktop to remove the carving, I felt a real wave of sympathy for him. Clearly he should not have defaced school property. But school *can* get boring, despite our best efforts to be creative, especially as the excitement of summer draws near. And we all know there are days when even we teachers long to be someplace else!

The remainder of the school year doesn't have to be drudgery. Draw upon your students' interests and ideas to think of ways to make each day exciting for everyone—including *you!*

Glorious God, help us to praise you even in the midst of boredom.

 MAY 9   **Read Proverbs 22:6.**

"Did you even bother to read the short story?" I snapped at Jason, who clearly was unprepared, again, for class.

"Yes," he said quietly, lowering his eyes.

We both knew he was lying.

I knew he was dyslexic. I tried to be understanding. But he routinely did not read. Then he lied and said that he did.

It was the lying that bothered me, because I knew a life-long pattern could be forming.

Jason's lying made me think too much of the suffering of my best friend.

My best friend's husband, David, had a series of affairs throughout their long marriage. Even when confronted with evidence, he refused to admit what he'd done. When the couple went through counseling, the therapist pointed out that my friend's husband had started lying as a first grader. Because he could not read, David, like my student Jason, learned to lie to cover his problem. His reading problem festered into a horrible emotional weakness that wreaked havoc on his marriage.

As a teacher, I try to remember that what goes on in my classroom has repercussions for a lifetime. As this reading from Proverbs suggests, we have to remember we are shaping human beings.

Patient God, as I try to be the best teacher I can be, allow me to grant my students the same merciful understanding you unfailingly shower on me.

 MAY 10   **Read Mark 8:22-26.**

My first students cured me of my agricultural blindness. They were farm kids. I was a city kid. I did not know the difference between a dairy cow and a beef cow; a soybean crop and an alfalfa crop. My agricultural ignorance gave my students lots of opportunities for good-natured jokes.

One day when we were working on speeches in class, I thought another one of those jokes had popped up. Ken got up in front of the class and announced, "I am going to talk about how to teach a cow to stand."

Laughing, I said, "Stop goofing around and tell us your real topic."

"That is my real topic. How to get a cow to stand."

The topic seemed ridiculous to me. "Cows already know how to stand," I told Ken. "Why on earth do they need to be taught?"

The class, evidently more aware than I was about the source of my confusion, started laughing.

"They don't know how to stand," Ken insisted. "When you go to 4-H or the state fair, they have to stand in certain ways."

Ken then went on to explain the intricacies of preparing a cow for competition.

I am always grateful for those first students. By teaching me about farming and animals and crops, they helped me see God's world in new ways.

How have your students helped you to see God's world differently this year?

God of all nature, thank you for students who improve my myopia, just as you made the blind to see.

 MAY 11   **Read Joel 2:25-27.**

Angela made me think of this passage from Joel, which celebrates visionaries and dreamers. A star athlete from her earliest school days, Angela entered seventh grade ready to be the point guard for the girls' basketball team. When she "blew out" her knee during one practice, I assumed she would never play basketball again, that her basketball dreams were shattered along with her knee.

I was wrong.

Armed with an indefatigable faith in God and herself, Angela underwent surgery and started a merciless rehabilitation program. Right after the surgery, her knee was attached to a stretching machine that resembled an instrument in the Tower of London's torture chamber. She spent weeks on stationary bicycles, building up her strength. Her goal was not simply to regain the use of her knee. She wanted to play basketball again.

I asked her more than once, "Are you sure a sport is worth all this extra pain and work?"

"It's not a sport," she told me, with a certainty that belied her years. "Playing basketball matters to me more than anything."

The next year, the whole school watched Angela break state records for girls' basketball.

This passage from Joel encourages us to persevere because our good God promises to repay us for "the years that the swarming locust has eaten" (2:25).

What better time of year than the last weeks of school to hear this refreshing reminder!

Merciful Lord, your faithful promises allow us all to pursue our dreams and visions.

🌱 MAY 12   Read Isaiah 11:1-2.

The first phone call startled me.

"I love you," a young, muffled voice said. Then the line went dead.

Just a prank, I thought dismissively.

The next such phone call was troublesome. The same muffled voice announced, "I really like that dress you wore to school today." Again, the line went dead.

Over the next several days, the phone calls came intermittently. Sometimes with declarations of love. Sometimes with inappropriate comments. Sometimes with a remark about an assignment I'd given.

I always hung up immediately.

My middle-school principle wanted to know if I had any idea who the caller might be. I didn't. Not really.

Within one month the phone calls stopped as inexplicably as they started. The minor ordeal was over.

But, the long-term lesson is branded into my professional memory.

Like all human beings, our students are complex and unpredictable. They can form misguided attachments that surprise both them and us.

And while the classroom can foster true friendship, one of our tasks as professionals is to foster the wisdom and understanding of which the prophet Isaiah speaks. Our students are impressionable and vulnerable. We need to take care.

Lord, guardian of all knowledge, increase my wisdom and understanding so that my students may see your reflection in me.

Teisha's above-average reading skills gained her the privilege of working in the library. Once a week, while her fifth-grade classmates were working on reading lessons, Teisha went to the empty school library to reshelve books.

Because the school could only afford a part-time librarian, students like Teisha provided necessary help. For several weeks in a row, however, the librarian complained about sloppy reshelving.

"I don't know what that child's been doing. But when I come in after Teisha's been there, half the books are still in the cart and the ones she supposedly reshelved are in the wrong spots. She's just goofing off."

I visited Teisha during her library time one day, hoping to discover the source of the sloppiness. As I approached the library, I heard Teisha's animated voice. Peering into the library, I saw the little girl seated in front of several rows of desks—reading aloud. Having positioned herself in the librarian's usual seat, Teisha was reading a story aloud to imaginary students, showing them the pictures as she went along.

When I quietly approached her, she looked terrified as she tried to explain.

"I'm just pretending. I'm sorry. I'm just pretending I'm the teacher."

Teisha was enthusiastically mimicking the behavior of her teachers! Timothy's message to new church members reinforces the powerful effect of our example.

Lord, as we model our behavior after you, remind us that our students are watching—even during the "countdown to summer."

"Oh, shut up. Just shut up."

Echoing down the tile and concrete hallway, the student's shrill voice grated against my classroom walls. My own eighth-grade students giggled in embarrassed uncertainty, as I walked into the hall to investigate.

Two other teachers, similarly alarmed by the angry voice, followed me down the hall to the source of trouble.

There, near the outside entrance to the school, a fiercely angry young man was screaming at a woman I assumed to be his mother. "Get out of here! Don't come near me! I don't want to see you!" The spit flew from his clenched teeth as he raised his arm to strike the woman in front of him.

Without thinking, I grabbed his raised arm. The fury in that arm so frightened me that little beads of perspiration popped out on my upper lip and around my forehead. I was trying to control a desperately angry young man.

Within minutes the assistant principal pulled the young man away from me and escorted him and the woman to the office.

I have never forgotten the fury raging inside of that young man—a fury that is as ancient as the enmity that rose up between Cain and Abel.

The fury, of course, signals an intense emotional pain beneath the very visible outburst. Because our students, for the most part, sit tamely in front of us day after day, we don't think about their capacity for fierce emotion. But in their lives outside of our classrooms, their emotions can run wild. Our students are not merely the sum total of their quiz grades and their book reports. They are flesh-and-blood human beings.

God of justice, alert me to my students' emotional pain.

 MAY 15   **Read Matthew 27:3-10.**

We know with certainty that Jesus Christ would have forgiven Judas, but despair claimed the apostle before Jesus had the chance. Suicide deprives its victims and their survivors of any temporal chances. Tragically, some of us have experienced the truth of this after losing one of our students.

MaryBeth's suicide is almost too painful to relate. I apologize if the details seem inappropriately gruesome, but suicide is never a pretty picture.

MaryBeth, a student at our junior high school, went home from school one afternoon and put her father's rifle into her mouth and killed herself. Although she'd been an eccentric loner, none of us had understood the depths of her pain.

When the principal assembled the student body and staff, she encouraged us to be more attentive to each other—to stay alert for signs of suffering. Of course, we cannot prevent every suicide, and we are not finally culpable for the choices others make. But we do have to stay aware of suffering, of pain—particularly that of our young students.

It is so easy in a busy classroom to forget that our students' lives are often seared with tormenting agony. Just as they seldom see us as anything but teachers, so we often fail to see them as anything but students. Yet our students—even those who are just beginning the school experience—are often among the walking wounded, enduring inexpressible grief. Though many of them may never even consider suicide, their pain can cause irreparable damage if too long ignored.

Who in your classroom is in need of the healing power of love? How can you begin to share that love today?

Dear resurrected Lord, help us to be more sensitive and responsive to the pain of our students.

 MAY 16   **Read Isaiah 11:3-5.**

The *World Book Encyclopedia* reminded me of the necessity of forming right judgments. Let me explain.

I had photocopied the page from *World Book* that matched—word for word—the student's paper. David had chosen to write his famous author report on James Whitcomb Riley.

But he had simply copied information straight from *World Book.*

I took David out into the hall, showed him his paper, and said, "You copied your report straight out of the encyclopedia."

He didn't look guilty when he replied, "Yeah. My parents bought me a set of *World Books* last year."

I persisted. "But you know copying out of a book is wrong."

"I just used the books my parents bought me," he repeated.

Baffled by his nonchalant attitude, I decided to phone his mother. "David's having a bit of a problem in school," I told her when she answered the phone. "He copied his entire report straight out of the encyclopedia."

"Yes," his mother replied. "That's why we bought him those books. I made sure he copied all the words exactly right."

Further conversation convinced me that both David and his mother had no idea they had done anything out of the ordinary.

Plagiarism is such a basic academic concept that I assumed the understanding of it was universal. My assumption proved false.

From the earliest grades we begin to teach our students how to test their assumptions. Perhaps every now and then we need to relearn the lesson ourselves.

Jesus Christ, the only true Judge of human action, increase my righteousness and decrease my faulty judgments.

 MAY 17   **Read Psalm 96.**

How often my students give me reason to praise God!

Morning sickness made me so miserable that teaching was impossible. For an entire week, I sat at home, two steps from the bathroom.

Barely two months pregnant, none of my colleagues knew I was expecting. And certainly none of my junior high students did.

When the morning sickness abated, I returned to my classroom, feeling much better and looking, I thought, perfectly normal.

I walked into my first period class just as the bell rang. Shannell jumped up out of his seat and hurried to my desk.

"Here, let me get you a chair—don't want you straining yourself in your condition."

"My condition?" I stammered, trying to control a blush.

"We know why you were gone all last week. We'll take good care of you now," he said, whipping a baby rattle out of his back pocket and handing it to me.

The whole class laughed and clapped in enjoyment of this spectacle.

"Thank you," I said, motioning him back to his seat. "Let's get to work."

Although I was a little embarrassed by Shannell's public recognition of my pregnancy, I was touched by his spontaneous and good-natured gesture.

What reasons to praise God have your students given you this year?

Praise God from whom all blessings, including our beloved students, flow.

🌱 **MAY 18**   **Read Mark 12:13-17.**

"I could have your teaching license revoked for this," the superintendent told me. "Think carefully before you resign."

But I had already thought carefully. Risking my entire teaching career, I turned in my resignation.

My first son had been born in June. In August of that same year, I returned to full-time teaching. From the first day, I knew my decision was the wrong one.

A student—whose name I no longer remember—unknowingly spurred me into righting that wrong. One day as I was dictating spelling words to my seventh graders, I grew distracted and looked up, just in time to catch this student staring off into space. Something about his misty look reminded me sharply of my baby's face. I missed my son so much at that instant that I wanted to bolt from the classroom.

The next day I resigned, against the wishes of my husband and the superintendent. But I never once regretted my decision. I eventually returned to the classroom, but right then I wanted to be with my infant son more than I wanted to teach a roomful of other people's children.

The advice Jesus gives to the Pharisees and the Herodians

in Mark 12 is valuable. We need to learn the proper place for our loyalties. And if we prayerfully determine those loyalties, we can trust we are following the Lord's will for our lives. Circumstances and people are different. Other teachers in my situation would have made other choices that were right for them. In my own life, I have sometimes chosen to pursue my professional goals when others have suggested my choices were wrongheaded. With our hearts and minds trained on Jesus Christ, we will be able to determine our proper course.

Creator of life, never allow me to distort the natural order of charity by placing my students before my family.

 MAY 19   **Read Luke 8:16-18.**

Her name was Beverly. Her plight was one of the worst— a new kid in a junior high school where everyone else had known each other since first grade.

Unresponsive to the normal overtures reserved for new kids, she refused to help with bulletin boards, was not interested in trying out for the school play, had no intention of writing for the school newspaper. She came to language arts class, did her work, and left.

One day in class I noticed Beverly reading James Barrie's *Peter Pan.* I called her up to the desk and asked her to tell me about her reading choice. When I told her of my deep affection for the tale, her eyes lit up.

The next day when I got to school there was a rolled up piece of white paper, tied with a red ribbon. Unrolling the paper, I discovered a full page of black-and-white sketches of the Peter Pan characters. There was Captain Hook and Tinkerbelle and Wendy and Smee. In the tiniest letters Beverly had signed her name at the bottom of the artwork. The sketches remain one of my treasures.

Beverly's artistic talent was just the inroad I needed. She became an invaluable aide on several projects throughout the year, projects that helped her to make friends with her new classmates.

One of the greatest rewards of teaching is helping reluctant students to uncover their hidden "lamps" and then watching the light shine. Take a close look at your students. Which ones have uncovered their hidden lamps this year? Which ones still need your encouragement?

Lord, thank you for giving students like Beverly the courage to take their lamps out from under the bushel baskets. Help me to give them the encouragement they need.

MAY 20   Read Isaiah 43:1-7.

Bumper stickers seem fairly innocuous most of the time. With rare exception they announce the driver's loyalties and loves and politics. True, there are some pretty crass bumper stickers, but more often, we read that one driver loves his dog while another has visited Viriginia and discovered the state is for lovers.

But there is one type of bumper sticker that causes pain. You have seen them. They say things like: "My Daughter Is an Honor Student" or "My Son Is a Merit Roll Student."

Jamie taught me that those bumper stickers are anything but innocuous. This fourth grader struggled to maintain Cs in school. Although a very hard worker, his academic skills were limited. During Jamie's lunch period one day, he was caught by the school janitor in the parking lot. With a wide-tipped black Magic Marker, Jamie was defacing those bumper stickers that announced the academic success of students.

When asked about his behavior, Jamie burst into tears. "I hate those stickers," he cried. "My mom can't ever get one for her car."

Academic success should be rewarded and announced and reinforced. We should, however, never lose sight of those for whom academic success will always be an elusive goal.

As another school year draws to a close, how can you recognize the efforts and abilities of *all* your students?

Vigilant Creator, protect in a special way our students who strug-

gle to succeed in school. Help us to remind them that they, too, are infinitely precious in your sight.

🌂 MAY 21   Read Genesis 42:18-28.

I remember Jenny and the lunch money mystery. The lunch money count had been off for several days. The cafeteria worker in charge of tallying the accounts kept sending me little notes via Jenny, my student assistant. "You are missing $1.05," one note read. The next day's note said, "You are 50 cents short." As this puzzling pattern continued, I tried to figure out what had changed about my system.

Everything appeared normal. I collected the money. Jenny carried the money box to the cafeteria. In place for months, the pattern had worked smoothly.

Knowing that my very responsible student assistant would help me solve this mystery, I explained the problem to her one morning. "Jenny," I said, "somehow we're goofing up the lunch money count. Mrs. Dolan in the cafeteria tells me we're missing a little bit of money each day."

Jenny, a cherubic-faced little blonde, burst into tears that quickly became loud sobs. "Please don't tell them I took it. I'll give it back, I promise."

Jenny? A thief?

The unhappy little girl told me her dad had been fired. Her parents were fighting about money all the time. Afraid to ask them for her regular lunch money, she began stealing.

This child knew her actions were wrong. Together, we decided that she'd help me in the classroom after school to pay back the money she "borrowed."

Take a few moments for prayerful meditation. Ask yourself these questions: Which of my students have economic needs? How does my awareness of their needs affect the way I interact with those students? How can God use me to bring some form of "restoration" into their lives?

God, our provider, just as you did with Joseph's brothers, you can restore what has been stolen. Keep us ever mindful of the economic needs of our students.

Children can be heartlessly cruel. They know enough not to poke fun at their severely handicapped classmates and friends. But elementary school boys and girls can zoom in on minor idiosyncrasies with laser accuracy.

Leah was a third grader whose face was marred by a birthmark. A splotchy hematoma spread out over the bottom half of her right cheek. Very outgoing and popular, she did not appear to be much bothered by the birthmark.

Until one day when her best friend, Connie, got mad at her. Vicious as only third-grade girls can be, Connie yelled across the playground at recess, "Leah's got strawberries smashed on her face!" A number of petty little girls started bringing strawberries to school and leaving them on Leah's chair, in her book bag, near her gym clothes.

With a grace that belied her youth, Leah weathered the storm. She did not complain to any of the teachers. Her schoolwork did not suffer. A number of teachers reprimanded the petty pranksters.

Then, as often happens, the strawberry incidents stopped as inexplicably as they had begun. Friendships resumed. Peace returned.

Leah's ability to weather the undeserved pettiness of others was remarkable—and inspirational.

How have you benefited by the example of one of your students this year?

God bless the little children who lead and teach us by their example.

 MAY 23   **Read Proverbs 14:16.**

Oliver was one of those smug eighth-graders who prided himself on his ability to pass tests without even studying. I'd pass back a test and he'd yell out, "I aced it. Never even read the book."

He was exaggerating, of course. But such announcements

always undermined my confidence. Oliver had no use for English class. "My dad says reading is a waste of time. Won't get me a job," Oliver told the class more than once.

I wished, daily, he and his family would leave the school system. Many times, I bit my lip to avoid saying something inappropriately unkind to this young man.

His personality never did grow on me. His good traits never were clear to me. Even after all these years, the thought of his arrogance rankles me. I was unable, with this student, to transform a negative into a positive.

Still, I treated him professionally and did not give in to my visceral dislike of him.

All memories cannot be good ones. We will not like every one of our students, but we have to treat them all with professional courtesy and respect. Learning to do so increases our growth in our profession and our growth in the spirit.

O Bestower of life, keep reminding us that all of your sheep are indeed precious in your sight.

 MAY 24   **Read Matthew 15:1-20.**

In this passage from Matthew, Jesus insists that the disciples and the Pharisees learn to look at life from a new perspective. Sammy, without knowing it, was similarly insistent. He was earning a D in English. Nothing seemed to spark his interest or help him nudge that D into the acceptable C range.

One day after school my car wouldn't start, and I had already done what I knew to do—raise the hood and peer underneath. As I stood there peering, Sammy came up and asked, "Need some help?"

"Only if you can get this car started," I laughed, never expecting that someone so young could help me out.

"What's it do when you try to start it?"

"Sputter," I told him. "I don't think the battery's dead because it tries to start but can't."

Within five minutes he identified the problem—a wet distributor cap—and started the car for me.

While he worked, he spoke of cams and pistons and spark plugs with enthusiasm and knowledge. His enthusiastic knowledge gave me an idea for an educational unit on automobiles and engines. With Sammy's help, I designed several assignments that required students to research automotive topics, learn automotive terms, and write brief essays on their discoveries.

Not only did Sammy's grade get the boost it needed, but the other students and I also learned something new.

How have you gained a new perspective through one or more of your students this year?

Lord Jesus, thank you for sending us insistent reminders in the shape of our students.

 MAY 25   **Read I John 4:7-21.**

Every now and then a student so tugs at my heart that I have to remind myself that loving my students isn't my primary responsibility. Teaching them is.

Emma provided me with such a teaching challenge. A brown-haired, brown-eyed bundle of energy, this child won my heart the moment I saw her.

Right before Christmas, her battling parents separated and Emma's behavior grew testy and petulant. She'd slam her reading book down on the desk. She'd force her way to the front of the lunch line. And often, she'd fall asleep in the middle of class.

Because Emma was special to me, I grew increasingly worried about her emotional state. And certainly, as a teacher it was my obligation to be concerned. I talked to the guidance counselor and my colleagues about Emma's plight, making sure that we were doing all we could to help.

But a gentle comment from one of my colleagues forced me to reconsider my frame of mind. "There are twenty other students in your classroom. Emma is only one of them. Don't neglect everybody else. They need you, too."

My colleague's advice, though unsought, was valuable. I had spent so much time worrying about one student that my focus was getting blurred. All of my students needed me—to *teach* them.

Even so, without love, I know I cannot be an effective teacher.

Help me, O Lord, to love all my students as you would have me love them.

MAY 26   Read Luke 18:18-23.

A minister's wife and a teacher, I've never thought of myself as rich and seldom found much in common with the rich man in Luke's Gospel. That changed when I found my way to the central city junior high where my friend had invited me to come and teach her honors English class. The class was trying to wade through the school board–chosen play—an abridged version of *Macbeth*.

In discussing the play I told the students that Shakespeare repeatedly used several images. One of those images was that of ill-fitting clothes. Many characters in the play make reference to clothes that don't fit properly or that are uncomfortable.

I asked the students for contemporary examples of ill-fitting clothes.

A hand shot up. "When your pants get too short but your parents can't afford to buy new ones," the student said.

Another girl raised her hand and said, "When my friends get pregnant and they don't want anybody to know, they keep squeezing into their old clothes."

One young man offered this example. "When I get the hand-me-downs from my skinny cousins. I can't button my pants."

In all my years of teaching the play, I had never received such responses. My students tended to remember prom dresses that felt stiff or a new pair of jeans that hadn't been washed enough.

The responses of my friend's students forced me to confront inner-city poverty—a poverty I seldom encounter.

As I reflected on the experience, I realized that perhaps I'm more like the rich man in Luke's account than I might like to think. Jesus calls each of us to be generous—generous in giving and generous in spirit.

How can you be generous today?

Lord of generosity, let me imitate your generosity of spirit.

 MAY 27   **Read Proverbs 31:10-31.**

For reasons that have nothing to do with teaching, I remember Amy. A graceful, well-mannered young woman in my language arts class, she was the daughter of a physician. She played the cello. Once she gave a speech on the necessity of licensing carnival rides. She was one of three daughters.

During parent-teacher conferences, students did not have school—thereby freeing teachers from the double duty of teaching and holding conferences in the same day.

When Amy's mother appeared for her scheduled appointment, we spoke of her daughter's academic excellence. Then I offhandedly remarked, "Oh, you have all three of your daughters at home for these two days. I bet you can't wait for them to go back to school."

This dignified and graceful woman looked at me quizzically, then said, "I have always enjoyed having my daughters at home. They fill it with life. I like knowing that one of them is reading and one is talking on the phone and another is watching TV. I never understand it when other parents want their kids gone." This woman spoke with conviction. Her daughers were treasures to her.

Whenever I think of Amy, as I often do, the memory of her loving mother surfaces. Today I'm grateful for the example of gracious and dignified mothers and daughters who rightly deserve praise.

Lord of life, may I benefit from the many worthy examples of students and parents in my life.

Rick, the class clown, discovered Jesus Christ one weekend during a youth retreat. He made a commitment to the Lord and came to school the following Monday carrying a red-leather-covered Bible.

This formerly jovial boy became very solemn. No matter what question he was asked, he found a way to work the Bible into his answer. The students started teasing him and calling him "the Bible Answer Man."

This solemn change in personality continued for two weeks. I was glad Rick found Christ, but I missed his previously lighthearted presence in my classroom.

One day Rick came to me in real agitation.

"I really miss telling jokes and stuff," he said.

"And I miss your telling jokes," I confessed.

"But Jesus didn't tell jokes," Rick said. "I can't even find anywhere in the Bible where he laughs."

"Of course, Jesus laughed," I told him. "He loved people. He loved life. He didn't walk around looking serious all the time."

"You don't think God would mind if I made people laugh?" he asked.

"Actually," I told him, "I think God would consider it a personal favor if you made people laugh."

I believe God wants us to use all of our talents for his greater honor and glory—even the talent to make others laugh. And I believe that God enjoys our good-hearted laughter as much as we do!

Lord Jesus, teach us how to joyfully use each of our talents for your glory.

In this season of graduations and year-end celebrations, I remember a commencement address I once delivered at the high school from which I graduated. It was one of the most heartwarming and gratifying experiences of my life. In preparation for the speech, I'd asked the principal to send me a list of the names of the graduating class. For months, as I worked on the speech, I prayed over that list of names. Just as I have prayed over every name I've inscribed in my grade book for the last several years.

A colleague of mine gave me the idea years ago. A high school principal, she told the seniors at graduation that as she signed their diplomas, she prayed specifically for each of them. She prayed that they would have long and happy lives and that they would grow in the knowledge and love of God.

So, too, every year as I write the names of my yet unknown students in my grade book, I ask God to protect them from all harm. I also pray that their time in my classroom will benefit them.

Writing names in grade books can become rote over the years, I suppose. Yet the ritual signals a fresh start. New faces. New people. New opportunities to advance knowledge and the kingdom of God.

As I reflect back on this school year and all those before it, I am grateful for all the blessings that have come through new people and new beginnings.

Praise God, who calls each of us by name.

MAY 30   Read Luke 23.

Vietnam. A word that is anything but neutral.

In the early seventies, when my teaching career began, that word was almost like a bullet capable of inflicting great damage.

Memorial Day during those turbulent times was not a joyous occasion. The fallen heroes of past wars had many people to honor their memory. Those who fought and died in the Vietnam War were not easily awarded such recognition.

Troy's father died in the Vietnam War. A Marine colonel who was shot down as he tried to evacuate his fallen troops, Troy's dad had been his hero. On Memorial Day, eleven-year-old Troy and his mother visited the grave of the fallen Marine, leaving behind a small American flag and some flowers.

When they returned the following week, the grave had been desecrated. Vandals had spray-painted, "Make Love, Not War" on the plain, military headstone. The flag had been burned around the edges and pinned underneath a rock.

At the end of the school year, Troy entered a speech contest, sponsored by the local VFW. He spoke about his dad and his sacrifice. In conclusion, he said, "I know my dad fought and died even for those people who tried to ruin his grave."

We cannot forget the men and women who gave their lives in the service of our country, for their sacrifices reverberate with the truth captured in Luke 23 and in Troy's speech about his father.

Crucified Jesus, we honor the memory of those who have given their lives so that we might live.

 MAY 31   Read John 3:1-2.

When Christa McAuliffe died in the *Challenger* accident in January of 1986, the nation's heart broke, in part, because she was a teacher. Her favorite motto, "I touch the future. I teach," forms a portion of her legacy. And those of us who spend our lives in the classroom year after year know those words to be true.

Most of our students will probably forget us, but somewhere down the road, a word or a phrase will call us to their minds. Some little incident will bubble to the surface of their memories, and for a flash of time, they will remember our classrooms and what they learned there.

We will grow old. Our first few years in the classroom will transform themselves into decades. So many thousands of students will have passed through our roll books and our classrooms that we will have forgotten most of them.

But long after we have retired from the classroom and

from temporal life, there will be people walking the earth whom it was our privilege to teach. Our students will help form our legacy.

When I meet God face-to-face, I will thank him for the tremendous and unique privilege of being a teacher.

Good and gracious God, giver of all good things, help us to be teachers who come from God.

June

The Power of Love

Ellamarie Parkison

JUNE 1   **Read Ecclesiastes 3:1-17.**

oday is the first day of my summer break. I didn't set
the alarm this morning. What a luxury! Now I must think
about how to use this time I've been allotted. A *Family Circus*
cartoon recently pictured Dolly explaining time to her little
brother, saying, "You see, yesterday is the past, tomorrow
is the future, and today is a gift. That's why they call it the
present."

Today *is* a gift and should be treasured as such. Perhaps I
should treat this gift as we are advised to use our money: a
percentage for saving, a percentage for charity, a percentage
for investing in the future, a percentage for spending, and a
percentage for maintenance or operating expense.

I guess saving is comparable to resting; I'll give it 33 percent or 8 hours a day. Giving includes such things as church
work, caring for family members, helping friends, and working in community organizations. At 10 percent, that would
be 2.4 hours a day. Investing might include improving my
mind and body as well as using my creative powers for
things such as reading, writing, and exercising. I will give

that 10 percent also, another 2.4 hours each day. During the summer I will "spend" more, doing recreational things such as going to movies, watching TV, gardening, talking with friends and family, and so forth. I'll give that 25 percent or 6 hours a day. Some time must be reserved for maintenance or operating expense—those daily chores of cooking, cleaning, paying bills, doing laundry, and so forth. I'll give that 22 percent, my last 5.2 hours of the day.

Of course, this is only a guide to keep me aware of the value of my gift of time. I will revise it as needed to be practical. How will you use *your* gift of time this summer?

Lord, thank you for the ability to plan. Keep me faithful to my plan. Also keep me flexible and willing to change as needed. But please, Lord, help me to avoid squandering my precious time.

☼ JUNE 2   Read Luke 10:38-42.

I read an article recently about a woman who was reminiscing about her grandmother. As she told how "Gram" had patiently helped her learn to sew when she was a small child, she commented that Gram had probably had to rip out and redo most of what she, as a child, accomplished; yet Gram never let on. It was her final comment that set me to thinking: "Gram let me know that I was worth the time."

Time is the one gift received from our Creator that is doled out in equal portions to each of us. Though some of us live longer than others, we each have twenty-four hours in every day; and the choice of how we use each precious hour makes a tremendous difference in our lives.

Some have lived very short lives but have had a terrific impact on humanity. Jesus is the prime example. He lived a short thirty-three years, and two thousand years later, millions ascribe to his teachings. There are thousands of other examples of persons who lived short lives and made significant contributions to our world. Each time I listen to the inspired and magnificent music of Mozart, I am amazed that all of his music was composed before the age of thirty.

Each of us has time, freely given to us. We can choose to

253

wile it away in meaningless activity, in self-indulgence, in nothingness, or we can choose to use it to make this a better world in which to live. I believe that helping a child to feel valued and loved is a use of time approved by our Creator. May the children I work with know that they are "worth my time."

Lord, thank you for the gift of time. Keep me aware of the value of each moment. Forgive me when I grow impatient and think my mundane affairs too pressing to attend to those about me. Remind me that relationships of love are of lasting values and are built with time and patience.

☀ JUNE 3   Read Luke 6:27.

Each year I hang two slogans printed in huge letters on my classroom walls. One is "Using Your Mind Is Exciting!" and the other is "Think Good Thoughts." I do this in the hope of inspiring my students. Perhaps I put them up as much for myself as for my students. They keep me ever aware of the great joy of using my mind and of the incredible power thoughts have on our achievement and success in life. The thoughts we have shape our personalities. If we think kind and good thoughts, we will be positive and good persons. If we think negative, mean, or unpleasant thoughts, we will grow into negative and mean persons.

Sometimes controlling our thoughts and guiding them into a positive path can be difficult. In fact, it may not always be possible to do on our own. Why is it so much easier to be negative than positive? Why do we find so much pleasure in finding fault with others? Why is harmful gossip so much fun?

When students continually resist all efforts to help them learn or to fit into the class in an orderly way, it's often difficult to think positive thoughts about them. Why be positive about someone who is unruly and disrespectful on a continuing basis?

The power of influencing another with good thoughts is God's power. It is the power of love for another person. It is what Jesus meant when he said, "Love your enemies." Love is a transforming power, and it begins with loving thoughts.

This summer as we take a break from the classroom, let us transform our minds and renew our souls by centering our thoughts and our actions in love.

Lord, teach me to drive negative thoughts from my mind and empower my thinking with love.

☼ JUNE 4   Read Psalm 37:3-9.

I have just returned from the airport where I said good-bye to my husband, daughter, and son-in-law, all of whom are headed overseas, the first leg of their journeys by happenstance on the same plane. When we entered the terminal, the sky was sunny and bright. As I drove out of the parking garage after seeing them off, the sky turned black. Thunder, lightning, rain, and hail pelted the car.

The storm was so intense that the highway was not visible. When the car in front of me hydroplaned off the highway, I pulled over to wait until the weather calmed. It was frightening, not only to be out driving in such severe weather, but also to think of that plane with my loved ones taking off in such weather. I began to worry and fret, thinking only the worst, seeing the headlines in my mind's eye, "Plane Crashes in Storm. All Passengers Perish."

As I walked into the house on my return, the phone was ringing. Dread filled my being as I reached to answer it, knowing this was the bad news. Instead, my husband's voice greeted me. He was safely in Cincinnati, his first stop. They had flown above the storm. A strong tailwind had hastened their trip, and they arrived ahead of schedule. All that worry for nothing. I had failed to put my trust in the Lord—not that something terrible might not have happened; but with faith and trust, God would have helped me handle it.

Worry is a worthless exercise that happens only when we try to be self-sufficient. It is almost a denial of God's power in our lives.

This summer as we replenish our spirits in love and prepare for another year of new faces and new challenges, it's comforting to remember that life is a partnership. We are not expected to "go it alone," nor are we capable of doing so.

Lord, forgive my lack of faith. Help me to trust.

☼ **JUNE 5**   **Read Hebrews 12:1-17.**

It was already hot when I was out walking my little dog, Opie, before seven-thirty this morning. The sun was blazing down on us and the temperature was near eighty degrees. As we trekked along the fifth block of our walk, Opie began to drag behind me, his tongue hanging out and his breath coming in quick pants. Occasionally he would lie down on the sidewalk, looking pathetic and exhausted. I worried just a little. He is a dachshund with very short legs and a heavy, long body. I thought, *This heat is too much for him. I may have to pick him up and carry him home.* At that moment a cat appeared across the way, and Opie sprang to life. No longer lethargic and overcome by the heat and exercise, he lunged forward with tail wagging, ears perked up, and body tense, barking loudly. It took every ounce of strength I could muster to hold him back. I realized then that it was boredom and lack of motivation that were causing Opie to drag along.

How similar is our plight as humans. We so often go along living life in a humdrum fashion. Then along comes a crisis in our lives, and our Christian faith "perks up" as we feel the need of God's loving support and the undergirding of Christian fellowship. How, I wonder, could we incorporate that excitement and fervor for Christian living into our lives on a constant basis? How could we keep from falling into the "ho-hum" trap?

Perhaps the answer lies in loving outreach. If we were to forget ourselves and reach out in love to others in need as Christ suggested, a challenge would be forever before us. Apathy would have no soil in which to grow. Our lives would be so rich in loving others that only God's will would flourish.

For us teachers, even the summer months can sometimes be boring as we try to adjust to a slower, more relaxed pace. How will you escape the ho-hum trap this summer? Look and listen for ways to reach out in love.

Lord, fill us with excitement for living your Word and sharing your love with others.

☼ **JUNE 6**   **Read Proverbs 22:6.**

Each morning as I walk Opie around the block, I pick up trash from last night's fast-food fare—all sorts of paper, Styrofoam, glass, and can containers. We are living in a disposable world, a world where everything must be fast and must happen now. We are discontent if we have to wait for our food or pleasure. We can't even wait until we find a container in which to dispose of our trash.

Ours is a world of external pleasure. We are bored if we have to repeat an activity. We want someone to entertain us. Despite a plethora of toys, games, and TV programs at the fingertips of most children and youth, a common phrase of the age is, "I'm bored. There's nothing to do." Where have we gone wrong?

What can we do to help young folks know that the excitement and joy of life lie in challenging oneself to become a better person and to do one's part to make the world a healthier place for all? What can we do to help them know that only as we give of ourselves for the sake of others do we begin to find satisfaction in life?

Christian teachings of love and service have no meaning to children who have never known love. Our task is to live out those Christian values. We must love the children in our care and, after feeling that love, perhaps their understanding may begin.

Lord, we have strayed so far from your teachings and from your loving guidance. Take us back into your care. Teach us to listen and to follow. Guide me in doing my part to help one child at a time back into your loving arms.

My mother-in-law was a remarkable woman. Having had a leg amputated as the result of diabetes complications, her last few years of life would have been lonely and very confining had friends not visited frequently and regularly taken her to social gatherings. She had standing engagements for morning coffee at a local shop, lunch at a friend's home, and weekly card games. In addition, a steady stream of friends dropped in for a cup of coffee and a chat. Many of the friends were twenty, thirty, or forty years younger than her eighty-plus years. On her birthday, cards poured in from out-of-town and local friends. She received well over one hundred cards on the last birthday of her life.

It was a phenomenon I found mystifying when I first met her, but as time passed, I began to understand. She had a deep interest and caring attitude toward everyone she met. Many of her friends were folks she had met at the bank, the grocery store, the hairdresser, the corner gas station, or the post office. Most were folks she had observed to be in need of some sort, and she had offered to help. If a young couple at the convenience store were hungry and had no money, she invited them home for a good meal. If someone at the gas station couldn't afford fuel, she filled their tank.

We worried about her. When would she offer to help the wrong person? When would someone take undue advantage and perhaps harm her? No amount of concern on our parts would change her ways. She was a loving and caring person who offered kindness to all, without regard for race or status in life. She lived out the commandment "[Love] your neighbor as yourself" (Luke 10:27). Her spirit is a model for me as I seek to be a neighbor both in and out of the classroom.

Lord, thank you for the opportunity to watch someone live the example of being a neighbor to others. Lead me closer to living a life of neighborly love.

Toward the end of the school year two sixth-grade girls became upset over a minor incident and began fighting angrily. The fight was so intense, with hair-pulling and pummeling fists in faces, that the other students, who would normally try to interfere and stop it, pulled back in hushed silence. The teacher has earned her second-degree black belt in tae kwon do and could easily have used her skills to stop the battle. However, she knew that doing so would risk greater harm to the girls. She chose to use more conventional means, such as shouting "Stop" and pulling and pushing them apart.

At that point, in their state of heightened anger, they turned and began pounding on her. When all were finally calmed down, the only person requiring medical attention was the teacher, who had torn ligaments in her hand and required surgery on her shoulder. This was a teacher much respected by her students. The students did not mean to harm her, but were carried away by the intensity of their emotions.

As Christians we are taught to turn the other cheek and, in a sense, that is what this teacher did. She chose to risk harm to herself rather than risk hurting her students. She chose to intercede rather than let them harm each other. Unfortunately, the girls' parents' response to the incident was, "She should not have tried to stop them. She was only hurt because she interfered." They also admitted that they would have sued the teacher and the school had one of their children been injured and the teacher had *not* tried to stop the fight.

After the incident, the teachers at our school were frightened and confused. They were no longer sure what to do when students turn on one another.

We live and teach in a confusing world. It's often difficult to remember what Christ would have us do; and when we do remember, we're often too weak to be faithful to what we know is right. This summer as we focus our thoughts on love, may we ask for the wisdom and courage to *always* act in loving ways.

Guide us, Lord. Help us to feel your love and know your way in situations where the waters are muddied and the right path is not always clear.

☼ JUNE 9   Read I Corinthians 13:1.

We all know how fast the world is changing, but in recent months I've been struck by the fact that the young people I teach live in an entirely different world from the one in which I grew up and, in fact, from the one in which I live now. How old I must seem to them, and how difficult for them to accept my teachings as valid in their world. One day one of the first graders in our school brought home the view children have of adults with a swift punch, saying, "My granny's fifty-one, and she ain't dead yet!"

The students in our school are proficient in the use of computers. Last year we began a "computer pal" program between our sixth graders and the sixth graders of a school across town. The students would compose letters on the computer and send them via modem to their pals at the other school. One day as I was helping students edit their letters for grammatical errors, I was struck by the fact that some of them seemed to be written in "code." Many began with salutations such as "Hey Dude, wuz up? Nothin' chilling," or "Illin' in the fillin' here." They went on to mention rap groups, dances, songs, and TV programs of which I had never heard. Fact is, I was not able to help with spelling because I had no idea what they were trying to say! My next thought was, *I wonder if any of these things are inappropriate for exchange in computer pal letters?*

Our school is in the inner city. Our students live in a world of fear and violence. What is "appropriate" in their world is not "appropriate" in mine. As their teacher, I must be a model of love—a model of kindness, caring, and gentleness—knowing that when they leave the school, many must put on a coat of armor, for gentleness will leave them vulnerable to harm in their violent homes and neighborhoods. As a Christian, I must be a model of love in the world outside the school building—even when I'm far away from the eyes of my students.

Lord, help me to love my students as they are and to glimps
through their eyes, so that I may guide them through their tan-
gled world of changing values into a more gentle and loving way.
And help me to love all I meet, wherever I may go.

☼ JUNE 10 Read Zechariah 8:13b-17.

Make yourself a blessing to someone. I don't know who first said that, but it seems to me a worthy bit of advice. We can be a bless-ing in a number of ways. Sometimes a very small act of kindness is a blessing to someone who is discouraged, sad, or lonely. Every teacher has given a smile at a crucial moment or a word of encouragement to a student feeling dejected. That is a blessing.

There are many people who are blessings in my life. I think of a girlhood friend who for many years has lived in a distant part of the country. We seldom correspond other than at Christmas anymore, yet in an occasional phone call or visit we can take up in heart-to-heart conversation as though we have never been apart.

When I started to write these meditations, I wrote to another friend and said, "Do you have any ideas?" She immediately wrote back with a number of suggestions that she felt would be meaningful to her. She is a blessing to me.

Years ago, when we were having some difficulties with our teenage son, a young couple who were good friends offered to let him live with them for a week or so to give us a bit of distance and time to work things out with him. They were blessings to us.

My list could go on endlessly, as I'm sure yours could. Today and every day it's our turn to be a blessing to someone. Oppor-tunities arise every day. All we have to do is notice them.

Lord, open my eyes to opportunities to be a blessing to someone
and give me the energy and confidence to act on that opportunity.

☼ JUNE 11 Read I John 4:11-12.

A phrase from a sermon I once heard has stayed with me: "Choose to be a love finder, not a faultfinder." It reinforced the fact that my thoughts and actions are always by choice. No one forces me to find fault, though I am often prone to blame circumstances or persons. I can always think what I choose to think. No one is controlling my thoughts.

When someone cuts in front of me on the highway, I can choose to rant and gnash my teeth and call her names, or I can choose to think, *She must be late for something important. I hope she gets there safely.*

When a student continually fails to complete assignments, I can choose to think him lazy, disinterested, unmotivated, or dull; or I can choose to search for the cause of his failure and find a way to help him overcome that lack of interest.

I think of Antonio, a former student of mine, who constantly disrupted class, seldom showed interest, and swaggered to impress all with his "machoness." He tried my patience daily, but how I responded to him was my choice. I could respond with anger, with patience through gritted teeth, or with a loving acceptance for his feelings of inadequacy—for that, I knew, was the reason for his actions.

In the weeks ahead, choose to be a love finder wherever you may go. It may be the best summer you've ever had!

Lord, guide me in my choices. Keep a firm hand on my shoulder and lead me away from faultfinding and toward love-finding in all of the little encounters of daily life.

☼ JUNE 12   Read Luke 20:19-26.

Today I was talking with some youth in our church about who in the congregation they would choose as their leaders. There was little hesitation as they quickly and enthusiastically mentioned three people who would be really "cool." The persons they named are all somewhat quiet, nice, and kind, but they are not persons I would describe as "cool." When I asked why they chose these particular persons, the responses were, "They're just really nice," and "They like us." There was the answer. These people conveyed by their actions and words that they liked young people. *That* is "cool."

We've all heard the familiar saying, "What you do speaks so loudly I can't hear what you are saying." Being jovial, talkative, and playful are fine traits—ones I wish were mine—but not as important as being genuinely loving and caring; and it is these characteristics that are evident as much or more through our actions as our words.

Children and youth are quick to spot phoniness and are discerning of sincerity. If we only pretend to be sincere, our very beings will shout out to tell the world of our pretense. Just as Jesus knew that the spies sent by the scribes and chief priests were insincere, so those with whom we live and work will recognize hypocrisy in us.

Lord, sometimes it seems necessary to pretend. Fill my heart with enough love that such times disappear. Give me an open and loving spirit, especially as I work with children.

☼ JUNE 13   Read I Corinthians 13.

Today I heard an interview on the radio with Gordon Parks, an author and renowned photographer. When speaking about his childhood, he mentioned that he was the youngest of fifteen children. Apparently his family was quite poor, because when the interviewer quipped that there must have been a long line for the toilet, he answered, "We didn't have a toilet." He went on to say, however, that he had been a somewhat spoiled child, because he had fourteen older brothers and sisters who showered him with love and attention and a mother who loved and encouraged him to think of himself as special.

How beautiful! One who was raised in a poverty-stricken home looks back on his childhood as being rich in the important things. That old song is true. The best things in life *are* free. The result of that childhood love and encouragement is a man who has been successful and productive and has brought insight and pleasure to millions through his photography.

All children should have the opportunity to be so loved. As teachers, it is impossible to completely make up for a lack

263

of love in the homes of our children. We can, however, make school a loving and encouraging place to be for our children while they are with us. We can provide activities that heighten feelings of acceptance and self-worth every day. And we can respond to our children's needs with patience and understanding.

Lord, it is a tall order to meet the needs of all my students. Sometimes it is difficult to love them. Often it seems impossible to be patient and loving. Help me, Lord, to be fair and to be open to their needs. Help me to "spoil" them with love, respect, and encouragement.

☼ JUNE 14   Read Luke 6:31; Philippians 4:5.

Visiting at the home of a coworker recently, I felt a sense of uneasiness when her phone rang and she refused to answer it, saying, "I know that's Jan. She can't adjust to living alone after her husband's death and calls me all the time. I get so tired of listening to her that I don't answer the phone anymore." Likewise, I know several people who do not answer their phones but use their answering machines to screen calls, returning only those of their choice. This high-tech age makes it easy to distance ourselves from others.

A young person who has made some poor choices in his life and is now suffering severe consequences said to me, "I feel like I'm going to explode. I just don't know how to handle this. I need to talk to someone, but I have no one to talk to." Psychiatrists' and psychologists' offices are overflowing with people who need someone to talk to. Have we lost the art of listening?

Dietrich Bonhoeffer says in his book *Life Together,* "The first service that one owes to others in the fellowship consists in listening to them." Listening to a friend may be boring, it may be repetitious, it may consume valuable time we have reserved for something else. It is also an act of love. To be unwilling to listen is an act of rejection. It is the opposite of caring. It is the opposite of love. Jesus taught us to love our neighbors as ourselves. I hope that when I have troubles, a friend will care enough to listen to me.

Lord, teach me to be more loving and caring. Help me to put the needs of others before my own. Help me to care enough that I find pleasure in sharing my time with a friend in need.

☼ JUNE 15   Read Matthew 5:38-48.

As I was making the bed this morning, I realized that I had walked around it at least ten times, painstakingly making sure that the sheets, blanket, pillows, and spread were all even and smooth with no wrinkles or bumps. I thought, *Why am I doing this? I am almost late for a meeting, and here I am spending time making the bed look perfect when no one will see it all day.* Am I a perfectionist? Well, yes, in some ways I am. Is that good or bad?

Perhaps it depends on how one is trying to be perfect. When Jesus told us to be perfect, I don't believe he meant that we should do every task perfectly. Rather, he must have been referring to being perfect in following his example and in loving all of humankind.

For us teachers, I believe Jesus meant that we must love that annoying little girl who waves her hand and says, "I need help" at least thirty times a day just as much as we love the perfectly groomed, well-behaved "A" students. It means forgetting transgressions of one day and starting each day anew, without ill feelings about what happened yesterday.

Perhaps we should follow the lead of the children. It seems that no matter how bad a day in the classroom may be, they come in with smiling faces the next morning—all controversies forgiven and forgotten.

Lord, teach me how to be perfect—not perfect in making the bed or doing chores, but perfect in love and in fulfilling your purpose for me. Guide me toward those things that are worthy of perfection. Soften my critical nature and remind me to look for the good in others.

A friend of mine who taught school in an area of economic hardship told me about meeting the mother of one of her students. The woman came in for a parent-teacher conference looking and acting a bit nervous. During the conversation, she confessed to my friend that she could not help her children with homework because she was unable to read or write. She also confided that she was unable to get a job because of these inadequacies and was working as a prostitute to put food on the table. She was not proud of this, but said, "If you had kids and couldn't get a job, what would you do?" As my friend related this story to me, she said, "I had to say to her, 'I just don't know.' I hadn't walked in her shoes."

How quick we are to judge those in different circumstances from our own. How true that if faced with the same hardships as others, our response might well be much different from what we think it would be or would want it to be. Though this woman chose a course unthinkable to my friend, she wanted to provide for her children and shared a hope that her children would be able to have a better life. She wanted them to get an education. Perhaps her confessions to her child's teacher were a plea for help. She was not happy with her circumstance, but she was coping as best she seemed able.

How have I judged others this week? What "specks" do I need to remove from my own eye this week?

Lord, keep me from looking for the speck of dust in my neighbor's eye. Remind me to examine myself carefully before judging others. Fill me with love.

The prophet Micah looked around and saw evil all about him. Public officials were corrupt; the rich gave no thought to the poor; greed ruled the land; fighting, murder, and lying were commonplace. He was disheartened and spoke out for justice and peace, saying, "What does the LORD require of you but to do justice, and to love kindness, and to walk humbly with your God?" (Micah 6:8b).

It sounds simple, until I really begin to think about it. What does the Lord require of me? Micah says, first of all, the Lord requires that I do justice. What does that mean? How can I "do justice"? I notice he did not say *believe* in justice but *do* justice, indicating action. Must I speak out as Micah did against the evils of the day? How can I do that? Perhaps by writing letters to the editor of the local newspaper? Joining organizations that are working for equality in housing? Helping homeless persons find homes or providing food for the hungry? Taking into my home a needy person? Giving my money to a group working for justice? Going to work or live among the poor so that I understand their situation?

I'm sure that doing justice is more than reading the newspaper and feeling sad about the world and community situations. I'm sure it is more than staying in the comfort of my home and praying that God will heal the problems of the community. Prayer, however, may be the place to start. Through prayer, perhaps God will show me how I should be "doing justice"; and through prayer, perhaps God will give me the courage to get out there and do it.

Lord, I am sort of a wimp about getting out and "doing justice." I would rather contribute my money and let someone else rub elbows with the needy. Help me, Lord, to see the needs that are all about me. Help me to understand how I can do my part and, Lord, give me the courage and fortitude to get out there and do it.

 JUNE 18   **Read Matthew 25:31-46.**

Years ago, as a young girl growing up in Michigan, I remember it was not uncommon for men to come to the door asking for a bite to eat. We called them beggars then, and it was always a bit of excitement for us children to have these strangers stop by. My mother would rustle up a full-blown meal to serve them. Sometimes they would do a bit of work to pay for the meal: wash the windows, cut the grass, or chop wood for the fireplace.

These memories had been somewhat forgotten, tucked away in the far recesses of my mind, until we moved to our present location. Now, once again, we have persons frequently knocking on our door to ask for help. It is no longer just men, but women as well. Many of them are homeless.

A young couple came by a few days ago who had been walking for miles. The woman removed her shoes to show me swollen and blistered feet caused by walking in ill-fitting shoes. In addition to giving them sandwiches, which they devoured eagerly on the spot, I gave her a pair of socks to help cushion her feet in the too large shoes she was wearing. It was a small gesture. The socks were headed for Goodwill anyway, and the gratitude I received was far more than I deserved. She acted like a little child on Christmas, so thrilled with that pair of used socks.

I don't know why that young couple are in the predicament they're in. It doesn't matter. The delight on her thin face has been haunting me ever since. It was a humbling experience. I just keep thinking how fortunate I am. Given a different set of circumstances, I could be the one doing the knocking.

Often we teachers don't have to go any farther than our own classrooms to find persons in need. May we have the courage and the compassion to reach out in appropriate ways.

Lord, I am grateful for the many blessings that are mine. Forgive me when I am judgmental of those who are less fortunate. Give me a loving heart, an open mind, and a realization that we are all your children. And help me to reach out in love.

 JUNE 19   **Read Psalm 85:8.**

The kindergarten teacher in our school would routinely take little Tina to the shower and clean her up before class started so that the rest of the class would not ostracize her.

Tina would say, "But I don't need to wash, 'cuz I wear 'fume.'" The "fume" not only didn't cover body odors, but was of a sickly sweet variety that simply made matters worse.

Upon investigation, it was discovered that Tina's home had no running water or heat. The home was a flimsy shack with cracks big enough to see through to the outside. Icicles formed on the inside walls in winter. Working with social service, school officials located a home with heat and indoor plumbing for the family. They refused the offer, however, because the family's pet goat would not be allowed in the new place.

All of us shook our heads and pitied these folks for being so backward and unenlightened. We wondered what our role should be. Some thought we should pursue legal action, perhaps have the children removed from the home and put in foster care or have the house condemned, forcing them to move. The family was living in pitiful circumstances, but they were not unhappy, nor were they unloving. To take the children from their mother would have been heart-wrenching for all of them.

It is so confusing to know the Christian and loving course of action in situations where our values are strongly in conflict. May we always remember to bring such matters to God in earnest prayer and listen for the answer.

Lord, often we are prone to jump to our own ideas of what is "right." Teach us to listen in love.

☼ **JUNE 20**   **Read Mark 10:13-16.**

My husband and I have recently become acquainted with the Ashleys, a family who believes that the essence of the church and of Christianity is a sharing and giving of the heart. They have lived out that sharing and giving in a most generous way.

Several years ago, a friend called to ask if they could help out a teenage inner-city girl who no longer had a home. They agreed, though they had three rather young children of their own. Tamika became a member of their family and stayed with them until she graduated, with honors, from high school. They then helped her go on to college. About that time, a friend of Tamika had similar home problems, and she also became a member of the Ashley family, staying with them until she, too, graduated from high school.

When telling about the girls, Mrs. Ashley speaks of what a blessing it was for their family to be enriched by the presence of these girls. She claims that what they did in taking the girls into their family was no different from what thousands of families do for relatives needing help; the only difference in their case is that they are not related to these girls.

This story warms my heart. It is the true spirit of what I believe Christianity is. If we each love a needy child, the world will be changed as each child, having grown strong in that love, goes out to make the world a better place. What better place to begin than our own classrooms!

Lord, help me to be loving toward all of the children I teach, and help me to give special love and care to those who are denied love in their homes.

☼ JUNE 21   Read Galatians 5:13-14.

We've all heard the story of Rapunzel. An ugly witch was jealous of Rapunzel and locked her in a tower because she didn't want anyone to enjoy her beauty. She told Rapunzel she was ugly, saying, "You look just like me." Rapunzel was not allowed to have a mirror and grew up thinking she was ugly. Then one day a handsome prince saw her looking out from the tower and told her she was beautiful. Rapunzel did not believe him until she looked into his eyes and saw her reflection. For the first time she realized she was not ugly. She saw love reflected in the eyes of the prince and knew that she was beautiful.

Although Rapunzel is just a fairy tale, it holds some food for thought. What sort of reflection do people see when they look into my eyes? Is the love of God reflected there? Do they see a reflection that makes them feel more beautiful? Do the children I teach feel beautiful and accepted when they look into my eyes? How important that reflection is for them if they are to grow up feeling worthy and capable of giving and accepting love.

Lord, it is so easy to forget to be loving. It is so easy to forget how important all of our actions are to those around us. Fill me with your love and let me be a reflection of your loving and caring ways.

☼ JUNE 22   Read Psalm 51.

Last year's promotion ceremony for our sixth graders was an affair of some pomp and circumstance: Students dressed in their finest, girls carried yellow roses, and boys wore boutonnieres. It was an occasion of both joy and sadness. Several of the students had been with us since kindergarten, and saying farewell brought both a touch of sadness and a swelling of pride, for we felt we had nurtured them well.

Perhaps most touching of all, however, was the awarding of a GED diploma to a young woman who had left our school in a similar promotion ceremony eight years before. In the sixth grade, she had reached her full height of six feet and towered above the other children, causing her to be self-conscious and discontent. She put forth a rough exterior, yet on occasion wrote sensitive and lovely poetry revealing a tenderness she tried to hide from view. She dropped out of school as soon as she was no longer required by age to attend. Now the mother of a young child, she earned her diploma through a new program offered to mothers whose children attend school. She was our first graduate of that program. No longer acting tough, she is a soft-spoken young woman, eagerly pursuing a better way of life for herself and her child.

How often in our spiritual lives we fail in our first and second and third attempts. Yet our loving God is always there offering us another chance. We fail and fail again, but never do we hear, "That's it. No more chances for you." God is always there offering love, forgiveness, and another chance. Thank goodness!

Lord of love, thank you for your patient and forgiving nature. Thank you for your willingness to let us stumble and get up to try

271

again. Help me, Lord, to be as charitable to others who make mistakes. May I always be willing to offer love and a second chance.

☀ **JUNE 23**   **Read Matthew 10:26-39; I John 4:18.**

In a heat wave one year in Chicago, more than five hundred people died. One person mentioned in an interview that many of the victims died because they were afraid to open their windows and let the air in. They were like prisoners in their own homes. He explained that in the past, heat waves did not claim as many lives because people would go outdoors and sleep on porches or on the beach. Now people don't feel safe. They are afraid to go outdoors at night. We are living in a world of fear.

Often visitors in unfamiliar places are advised not to look happy, not to look anyone in the eye, and not to speak to anyone—generally, not to draw attention to themselves. We are living in a world of fear.

The area where I teach is known for violence. The police officer assigned to our school will not come without wearing her bulletproof vest because she knows the area in a different way from the way we teachers do. We are living in a world of fear.

Fear is a crippling and debilitating emotion that leads to paranoia. When we live in fear, we become emotionally and spiritually paralyzed. Jesus said, "Do not fear those who kill the body but cannot kill the soul" (Matthew 10:28*a*). It's wise to be cautious in a world of violence, but we can't let fear rule our lives. As followers of Christ, we must remember that we are more than flesh. We must carry on in our mission, believing that perfect love will cast out fear.

Lord, help me to have a faith that overcomes fear.

☀ **JUNE 24**   **Read Isaiah 12:2.**

Love and trust are so intricately connected.

Near the end of the school year, we took our fourth- and sixth-grade students to a camp in the woods for a few days. One of our activities was labeled team adventures. We took part in activities designed to build group cooperation and trust. It began with a walk across a meadow, up a large number of steps, and onto a swinging bridge. A scary experience if one could see, but on this trip we worked in partners, one of whom was blindfolded and had to depend upon the other for guidance.

One child in the group was developmentally challenged and a bit awkward on foot. No one wanted to be his partner, so I teamed up with him. He was terrified, and after a few steps began to cry, saying, "I can't see! I can't see!" Rather than have him totally traumatized, we stopped short of the swinging bridge and traded places. I'll have to admit, I was more than a little apprehensive about having him lead me, for beyond the bridge was a hilly path with rocks, stones, and roots. I was not at all certain this child who was still reading preprimers in fourth grade was capable of guiding me through a rocky, wooded path. I wondered if I would be lucky enough to escape with no more than a twisted ankle.

Well, I learned about trust that day. Nowhere could I have found a more conscientious or trustworthy guide. He held my arm tightly and warned me of every dip in the path. I walked more than half a mile through the woods in total darkness, realizing after the first few feet that my guide was not going to let me get hurt. I was able to relax and enjoy the experiment. I knew I could trust him to guide me safely.

I believe that is what trusting in the Lord is like. We cannot see the path ahead of us, and we want to trust in our own strength and power. When we try that, things often do not go well. But if we put our trust in God, knowing that he loves us and will not let us stumble, or at least will be there to pick us up if we do, we can relax and enjoy our lives here on earth.

Lord, forgive my lack of trust. Help me to grow in my trust of your love and guidance.

 JUNE 25   **Read Psalm 19.**

As I write this, I am sitting with an ice pack on my lower back. The pain was caused by repeated bending and stooping to rid my little garden plot of weeds, prepare the soil for new plants, and put the new seedlings in place. Probably the pain would be less if I had taken more care in the way I bent over, using my legs more than my back, or if I had used a knee pad and knelt down rather than stooped over. But I chose to stoop, and now I suffer the consequences.

Actually, I do not mind the pain. It is almost with some amount of pleasure that the discomfort reminds me of the joy of working with the earth. The tenderness and beauty of the little seedlings and the anticipation of the greater beauty that is to come when they reach full growth and bloom in a profusion of color is tremendous reward—much like the reward of watching students grow and bloom. Somehow I feel in partnership with the Creator, as though I am part of the master plan, doing my small bit to further the beauty of this world. If not a partner, at least I am a caretaker, doing my part to care for a bit of the gift entrusted to me.

That a tiny little seed can grow into a glorious specimen of color and design is amazing to me. Even more full of wonder is the fact that every species is unique and intricate in detail, each with its particular needs: sun or shade, sandy soil or rich soil, lots of water or little water. Most all need nurture and care—not so different from we humans, I guess.

So it is that the pain in my back is humbling, but also joyful—a constant reminder of the wonders of the earth we've been charged to care for.

Lord, the wonders of this world are myriad in number. Thank you for the beauty and variety you have provided for us to enjoy. Let me never take for granted the greatness of your creation. Keep alive my sense of amazement and appreciation for the world's beauty.

 JUNE 26   **Read Matthew 6:25-33.**

Two summers ago, I and a group of educators spent several days atop El Triunfo, a cloud forest in Chiapas, the southern-most state in Mexico. Our living conditions there were primitive, particularly in Palo Alto where we slept on the dirt floor of a mule barn, did our bathing in a cold mountain stream, and carried water a quarter of a mile to the outhouse. We American teachers and students, used to comfort at home, did not consider these things a hardship. It was an adventure and thoroughly enjoyable.

Next to our mule barn was a ramshackle shed that was to be our dining hall. It did not look inviting. What a surprise we had when we stepped inside that shack. Our Mexican friends had turned the little dirt-floored hut into a most cozy and pleasant place. Cans filled with wildflowers were on the tables, candles glowed through openings on small pottery holders, and a red checked tablecloth covered the table boards. One corner served as the kitchen with an open fire over which they cooked a full meal of rice, goat cheese quesadillas, soup, and dessert. All of the food and cooking utensils had been transported by mule and backpack over a difficult five-mile mountain path from our main camp.

As we sat around the table swapping stories and sharing experiences, the feeling was one of warmth and contentment. We lived on El Triunfo for ten days without benefit of our accustomed creature comforts, and life was good.

Now at home, I want my life to be simpler. I want to have time to notice the beauty and wonder all about me as I did at Triunfo. I want time to contemplate ideas and to share thoughts with friends and family. I want to stop rushing from one activity to the next. I want to rid myself of the desire to have more things.

What can you do to simplify your life this summer?

Lord, thank you for opportunities to appreciate the beauty of your world and to know and appreciate friends from another culture. Help us to have the faith we need to live simple lives, trusting you to provide all that we need.

☼ **JUNE 27**   **Read II Corinthians 9:6-15.**

Our trip to the cloud forest of southern Mexico two years ago was a strenuous one. The hiking began with an uphill climb of eleven miles, about half of that in overbearing heat and humidity. Despite the fact that we had been warned to be in good shape for this trip, some older members of the group were unprepared for the arduous uphill ascent. Two persons, in particular, found themselves almost overcome by shortness of breath and palpitations of the heart. As the week progresed with challenging hiking each day, some found it difficult to participate and were often left far behind the rest of the group, a somewhat intimidating experience in an unfamiliar forest where poisonous snakes and large cats, such as pumas, abound.

Of the nineteen participants in the adventure, four were teenage students with a great deal of energy. It was touching to note that Vivian, a fourteen-year-old girl of Chinese descent, often chose to hang back and accompany the older folks who were incapable of keeping up with the younger crowd. She was in no way condescending, but always cheerful and pleasant, seeming to sense that they needed some encouragement. She was mature beyond her years and a delight to know.

When the trip was complete, one of the participants who had noted Vivian's thoughtfulness wrote to her parents to express appreciation for sharing their lovely daughter with us, telling them of her considerate caring for the rest of the group. What a lovely gesture! Why didn't I think of that? How often I forget to express my gratitude for acts of kindness and gestures of goodwill. Not only do I neglect doing this for strangers, but also for those who are near and dear to me.

From now on I will make a concerted effort to show my appreciation and gratitude to others, especially my students. There's no better way to teach than by my own example.

Lord, you have given me so much for which to be thankful. In fact, so great are my blessings, that I begin to take them for granted. Forgive my ingratitude, Lord, and undergird my resolve to show my thankfulness more often.

 JUNE 28   **Read John 21:1-14.**

We had been looking forward to our big end-of-the-year picnic for weeks. My sixth-grade students would be going on to junior high school, and we felt the need for a celebration. Many of the children were from the neighborhood around the school and had never ventured far beyond it. To be going to a large park just inside the city limits on the other side of town would be an adventure. Dawn brought with it a dark sky, and as the time drew nearer for the buses to arrive, it grew darker and lightning flashed. It was the darkest sky I have ever seen. As the storm hit, hail the size of golf balls pelted our windows. We could not go to the park. To say disappointment reigned would be an understatement. The children were devastated.

It was time to be innovative. We shoved the desks against the wall and prepared to have an indoor picnic. Since it was as dark as night outside, we pulled the shades and turned out the lights—a perfect atmosphere for ghost stories. We spread blankets on the floor and ate our lunch. We sang some lively camp songs and played group games. At the end of the day when the storm was past and the sun was peeking out from the clouds, the students were smiling and all agreed it would be a picnic to remember.

How important it is to be flexible. We teachers know the truth of this, for seldom does a day go by in the classroom that some flexibility isn't required. I wonder if we remember to make a conscious effort to help our students realize the need to be flexible, to be willing to adjust to the situation, to change plans when expectations are dashed, to make the best of the situation at hand. It is often difficult for me, and I am sure it is doubly or triply so for children, who live in the present and feel so keenly the unfairness of disappointment.

Flexibility requires *hope,* and like the disciples who had lost their Lord and had fished all night with only empty nets to show for it, sometimes it's hard to hold on to hope. Yet the risen Lord stands on the shore and tells us to throw the net on the other side—to try again, to be flexible, to have hope—and when we do, our catch is even greater than our expectations.

Lord, thank you for the ability to be flexible. Forgive me when I stubbornly hang on to the impossible, refusing to seek an alternate path. Please, Lord, undergird my efforts to be flexible so that I may be an example to others, especially the children in my care.

We teachers often learn much from our students. I'll never forget Russell, who was sixteen when he joined the class in our school for children with multiple disabilities. A thalidomide child, he had no arms and was only twenty-seven inches tall. Undaunted by this, he was determined to be independent. He informed his teachers on the first day that there were just two things he couldn't do for himself. He couldn't zip his pants and he couldn't drink from the water fountain. Russell played baseball and wanted to be treated as though he were six feet tall.

Music intrigued Russell and when he learned that one of the teachers was an accomplished pianist, he wanted her to teach him to play. After rigging up a baby seat that would support him on the piano bench, the lessons began. He played with one foot while the teacher supplied the chords.

Russell was an inspiration not only to his teachers and the other students, but also to his teachers' own children, who listened to tales of his accomplishments and indomitable spirit and were able to meet him on occasion. All learned from him that nothing is impossible to one who has the will to succeed. God has given us a spirit capable of overcoming all of our difficulties, if we but have faith.

Lord, I know that with you all things are possible. Forgive me when my faith is weak. Guide me in strengthening my understanding and my belief.

One afternoon I was watching a T-ball game between two teams of four- to six-year-olds. My grandson was among the players. They were having a wonderful time. Some didn't seem to understand that they were to run to first base after hitting the ball; others had difficulty finding the bases; most didn't know when to run from base to base. None had much facility for fielding the ball; and the outfielders often were rolling around in the grass, enjoying the wonderful breezy summer day without care for what the rest of the team was doing. They responded quickly and eagerly when one of the adults offered suggestions or direction. All were smiling and moving with enthusiasm. When a fielder missed the ball, several others would run for it, often collapsing in joyful laughter as they piled on top of one another.

After the game, I asked my grandson which team had won, and he had no idea. I'm not sure anyone even kept score. These children were playing for the pure fun of it. They have not yet been initiated into the competitive world of adults.

Jesus said we should change and become like little children. I wonder if part of his meaning was that we should enjoy this world that has been given to us. Perhaps he was referring to the idea that we should enjoy each other without always trying to beat "the other guy"—to be the winner, to get the best evaluation, to earn the most money. Maybe there is a message here to relax; maybe the message is to be more humble and less competitive. Maybe the message is to be more trusting and dependent on our Maker, rather than trying to do it all ourselves.

Lord, remind me to be mindful of the little children. Open my eyes to the leassons they have for me and let me be willing to "change my course" to be more childlike in my faith.

July

A Soaring Spirit

Ellamarie Parkison

JULY 1   Read Jeremiah 31:25.

inancial planners often counsel, "Pay yourself first." In other words, put some money away in savings before spending anything else in order to secure some wealth for emergencies and retirement. That is also good advice in areas other than financial planning, especially teaching.

We all know that working with children is an intense and often stressful experience. It requires our constant attention and energy. It is both physically and emotionally draining. That's why it's so important to take time to replenish our souls and minds and bodies: time to relax, time to read, time to pray, time to play, time to exercise. Summer is a wonderful break that allows us to replenish ourselves. But what about the rest of the year? It is difficult to find the time when there are always papers to grade, plans to make, projects to work on, parents to call, and perhaps a family at home to care for.

That's why we must pay ourselves first before paying others. If we spend all our time on the many tasks we have to do, no time will be left for activities to build up the spirit,

280

mind, and body. Just as expenses cannot exceed income on a financial balance sheet, so we cannot give too much without replenishing ourselves. If we neglect time for ourselves, we can become spiritually and emotionally bankrupt—unable to function at our best.

They say it takes six weeks to form a new habit. Start today: Pay yourself first!

Lord, remind me to take time for communing with you, for replenishing my soul and mind. And help me to realize the importance of caring for my body with exercise and good nutrition, so that I may be able to do my best in service to you.

☼ JULY 2   Read Luke 15:11-32.

The African violet on my windowsill appeared to be dead. Most of the leaves had fallen off; those that were left were hanging limp and looking lifeless. I ignored it for several days and finally decided to throw it out. On my way to the garbage, I passed the kitchen sink and thought, *Oh well, perhaps I should give it one more try.* So I took it out of its container and placed it in a bowl of water—a strange and, I guess, radical treatment. I have no idea why I did that. When all of the water had been soaked up, I put it back in its pot. The next morning I was amazed that the leaves were standing up perkily and looking quite alive. A week later, a dozen or more buds appeared, and today, it is so beautiful that a visiting friend asked me if it were real or artificial. I had been following the "don't overwater your African violets" advice I had heard, and the poor little plant was starved for water and attention.

We, too, are sometimes starved for love and attention. Sometimes we feel dead and lifeless inside. We teachers can become so focused on the needs of our students and others that we neglect our own needs, including our need for spiritual nourishment. When that happens, our steps are slowed, our smiles are scarce, our irritability increases, and boredom fills our heads. We are spiritually dead.

My little plant was calling to me, begging me with its lifelessness to rescue it, and fortunately I happened to respond. Our odds of receiving help are much greater than those of the plant. We have a God who will answer our call whenever we ask, a God we can rely on to respond, not as an afterthought or by lucky chance. Our God is always waiting in the wings for our call, ready to instill new life into our inert souls as soon as we are willing to accept it. All that is asked is that we believe, that we have faith. Our God is waiting and ready to welcome us back just as the father rejoiced and welcomed his son who had strayed so far from him.

In this "growing season," get in the habit of nourishing your soul. The Master Gardener is ready and waiting.

Lord, thank you for the mercy and forgiveness you so freely offer to us. Make me willing to admit my mistakes and return home to your love and care.

 JULY 3   **Read Psalm 89:1-8.**

When I think of summer and the opportunity for renewal, I think of vacation. Our family is spending this week at Cloudland Canyon State Park in northern Georgia. The canyon is deep and the hike to the bottom of it is strenuous and tiring for adults, so our little three-year-old granddaughter, Karlyn, found it especially challenging. Park workers have made the trip accessible by building dozens of steps on the steepest parts. Nonetheless, one feels the climb both in the legs and lungs.

Karlyn is an independent little miss, but the steepness of the descent made her willing to accept a hand for part of the trip. Each time we came to a somewhat level section, she let go and announced, "I don't need any help on this part."

We adults travel through life in much the same way, trying to go it alone and do it all ourselves. We teachers, in particular, strive to be self-sufficient, conpetent, and independent. Only when the going gets rough and a little frightening are we willing to turn to God for help and, like a loving parent, that hand of God is always there to offer stability and guidance. How much easier our lives and our jobs might be if we turned to God on a regular basis. If we sought

God's guidance on days of joy and days of humdrum as well as days of stress and days of sorrow, those difficulties might be easier to bear.

Lord, thank you for your constant availability. When we call for your help, there is never a busy signal or a "please hold" response. Thank you for your patience with us when we wait until trouble comes to ask for your guidance, and help us to call on your name more often until we sing of your steadfast love forever.

☼ JULY 4   Read Psalm 104.

This evening we sat on the deck overlooking this amazing 1,000-foot-deep canyon and watched as the sun dipped behind it in a festive display of reds, oranges, and yellows. Now the tree toads are entertaining us with a raucous symphony of sound.

Yesterday we hiked through a cave to a spectacular underground waterfall. While the grandchildren were here, we delighted at the antics of a little chipmunk living in a hollow log beside the cabin, watched as a squirrel timidly came close enough to inspect a fallen piece of cereal, and marveled at the speed of a daddy longlegs racing away from us human intruders.

This summer I have traveled from the historic eastern shore of Virginia and the beauty of Chesapeake Bay to the ruggedness of Alaska, and I am once again in awe of the beauty and diversity of this world we're allowed to inhabit.

Yet I wonder if we let ourselves get into a state of boredom or indifference when there are endless opportunities for pleasure and exploration. New discoveries are reported from labs of science and technology daily. This is a dynamic and exciting world.

When school starts for the new year, I will return refreshed and renewed, in hopes I can pass some of my restored vigor and enthusiasm for life on to my students.

Lord, thank you for this summer that I am privileged to enjoy. May the vitality I feel now continue throughout the school year.

Nudge me, Lord, if I begin to let the stress and strain of the days overshadow the reality of the opportunities you've provided.

☼ **JULY 5**   **Read Proverbs 2:10.**

Today when my neighbors pulled into their drive, the children jumped out of the car giggling and greeted me with "Bonjour, Madame." They had been listening to French language tapes in the car. Earlier today, my daughter called to say how much her three- and five-year-old daughters were enjoying a children's encyclopedia they had just received. She said, "They were so fascinated, we kept reading new articles, and as I was getting them ready for bed, they wanted to know more: more about Africa, more about how we breathe, and more about camels." Last evening a three-year-old friend was visiting us and enjoyed using our computer. Her eyes were aglow and her entire face tinged with excitement as she oohed and aahed at responses on the screen when she clicked the mouse.

How exciting it is to learn! What great satisfaction there is in using our minds, and how fortunate are children whose parents and teachers help them to capture that excitement. Keeping that spark of enthusiasm for learning alive as children progress through school is a challenge.

I remember a teacher I had in college who taught English. I went into his class with some dread, for I had not enjoyed English in high school. I remembered reading such poems as *The Rime of the Ancient Mariner* and finding it pure drudgery. Not so in Mr. Taff's class! He loved the old poets, and as we laughed and cried with him in the study of Wordsworth, Burns, and others, we, too, learned to love those works. When Mr. Taff switched to the music department, his class in opera had to be expanded to several sessions to accommodate his English students who now wanted to learn to love opera.

May I become more like Mr. Taff each year, sharing my enthusiasm for learning with every student I teach.

Lord, help me to keep the love of learning alive within me, that I may in turn pass that joy on to my students.

Brian, a fourth grader who could not read and who was having difficulty communicating orally, came to my classroom door one morning appearing greatly agitated. He was gesturing wildly, and from what I could understand, he kept saying, "There's something . . . There's something . . . I don't know what it is." Because he was so excited, I followed him down the hall to discover the source of his excitement. What I found was two large birds who had somehow found their way inside and, despite open windows, couldn't find their way out. I opened more windows and doors nearby, but the birds just kept crashing against the glass of closed windows. One finally collapsed, and we presumed him dead. The custodian brought a broom and tried to guide the still flying bird to an open window, but the bird refused to change his pattern of crashing into the glass again and again.

A crowd gathered, and we finally managed to get the bird out. He flew away happily and, to our surprise, his "dead" companion rose up and followed.

How often we fall into a similar rut: unwilling to change our ways when a new path appears; unable to convince ourselves to give a new concept a try; resisting different ideas proposed by friends and coworkers. It is so comfortable to stay with the familiar, even though it is sometimes unpleasant or unproductive. All new ways are not better; all new paths don't lead to bliss; all new ideas are not effective; yet how do we know if we resist trying them—if our minds are closed before they begin?

Psalm 96 invites us to sing a new song to the Lord. What will be your new song this summer?

Lord, you sent your Son to show us a new and better way to live our lives. Help us to continue to grow and change into more fully developed Christians. Keep our minds and hearts open to new revelations. Let us not become stagnant in our faith or in the living of our lives.

My mother lost a battle with cancer when I was quite young, almost forty years ago. Some memories have dimmed over the years, but one that is still vivid in my mind is her laughter and the joy she found in the little everyday happenings of life. I remember her saying to me almost daily, "This is the day that the Lord has made; let us rejoice and be glad in it" (Psalm 118:24).

One day, Adam, a fifth grader, came up to me with a million-dollar grin and said, "Today in music I was honored as a Red bird." He was holding a red shoestring, his "red bird ribbon," in his hand.

I said, "What does that mean?"

He beamed as he explained: "I get to do special stuff, like when all the other kids have to sit on chairs, I get to sit on a crate!" Talk about pleasure in a little thing! Somehow our very creative music teacher had managed to make the dubious pleasure of sitting on a crate seem like a great honor.

Our challenge as teachers, parents, and human beings is to look for and create pleasure in the everyday wonders of life. How easy it is to get bogged down with the burdens and complexities and ignore life's little wonders. A few minutes ago, my little dog was trying to tell me he wanted his bed brought downstairs, but I was too busy to listen to him. He disappeared for a while and when I later made my way upstairs, there he was, about halfway down, laboriously pulling his bed down the steps. I couldn't help but laugh at the sight of him, both because of his resourcefulness and because he looked so comical. *That's pleasure?* you ask. Well, it was for me.

Last Sunday I walked around the block with my five-year-old granddaughter. It was the day after her birthday and she had received many lovely gifts, but none so exciting as two robin eggs and a furry caterpillar she found on the walk. She found a stick on which the caterpillar could perch and carefuly carried him home as though he were more precious than diamonds. She couldn't wait to proudly show her sister, cousins, and parents her treasure.

God created a world with millions of opportunities for the living of life. He left us the choices of how to use those opportunities.

Lord, let me never be too busy to enjoy the little wonders of life. Help me to practice taking pleasure in little things this summer, so that next fall I will be ready to watch for ways to help my students have wonders to enjoy.

☼ JULY 8   Read James 2:14-26.

I heard a joke yesterday. It seems a man prayed the same prayer over and over. It was a pleading prayer: "Please, Lord, let me win the lottery just once. If I can win it just once, I will never bother you again." Day after day he prayed that prayer. Then one night he had a dream in which the Lord appeared to him and said, "Look. Concerning this lottery prayer, perhaps you could meet me halfway . . . like maybe you could buy a ticket."

The joke made me laugh, but I began to think how often my prayers are like that. I pray for help and guidance and then I forget that some effort is needed on my part. I just expect God to take over and see that I do whatever action needs to be taken. When I ask that God help me be more forgiving, I have to make an effort to forgive. When I ask for help in being more accepting, I must engage in accepting thought and behavior.

God is all-powerful, but some effort on my part is expected. Just as I can't bring about change in my students without their cooperation, so also God needs my cooperation to bring about change in me.

Lord, forgive my laziness and lack of follow-through. Forgive me for asking for help and expecting you to do all of the work. Give me a little nudge, Lord, when I forget to do my share.

☼ JULY 9   Read Matthew 7:7-11.

Delores and I taught in the same school several years ago. Most of us didn't understand Delores. I guess we were envious of her. She was so perfect. Delores was never ruffled. Her classes always won every school competition, whether it was bringing in food for the hungry, reading books for a Read-a-thon, or behaving in the lunchroom. The children in her class appeared quietly happy and always came out on top in test scores.

Delores herself had a smile and friendly word for everyone she met—and to top it all off, she had fresh flowers on her desk every day and dressed like a page from the latest fashion magazine. When my child was in an auto accident, Delores was the first to arrive at the hospital asking how she could help.

Delores was always the first teacher at school in the morning. No matter how early I got there, Delores's car was already in the lot. I knew she arrived early to plan and prepare for the day, but it was several months before I became aware that a large part of her early preparation was for daily devotion. She arrived early to spend time with God, asking for guidance and help in experiencing the day. She prayed for specific students and for the rest of us teachers. She asked that God's hand be in hers as she led her small charges toward knowledge and understanding.

No wonder she was "successful." She had God at her side, like a co-teacher. That power is available to all of us—anytime, anywhere—if we only ask.

Lord, you are always ready to take my hand. Help me to accept your offer.

 JULY 10   **Read James 5:13-19.**

We teachers devote great time and energy to detecting and correcting the shortcomings and mistakes of our students, but how much time do we devote to our own? We're quick to offer help to our students, but how quick are we to seek help when we need it?

Today I heard someone talking about the effectiveness of Alcoholics Anonymous. He was saying that a major component of that group is confession—admitting that one has a weakness that cannot be controlled by one's own power and that dependence on a higher power is necessary as well as dependence on help from fellow humans. This confession cannot be done in private and kept a secret. It must be a public confession before the group.

The person went on to say that confession is something that doesn't happen for many Christians today, because we do not want to admit dependence on anything or anyone, even God. I guess this is largely true. We Westerners pride ourselves on being self-sufficient and independent. We want to be seen as competent and able to care for ourselves no matter what the circumstance. Yet this is completely counter to Christian teachings.

Without God's help and guidance in our lives, we are not sufficient or complete beings. Our attempts to be independent beings have resulted in a great deal of unhappiness, discontent, and loneliness, causing many of us to turn to alcohol, drugs, or therapists for relief.

What is *your* need today, however large or small? How can you seek help?

Lord, thank you for loving us despite our pretense and denial of our need for help. Forgive us. Take away the shame we feel at admitting dependence on your love and care. Make us more willing to confess our need for your support and the wisdom of your guidance. Our need is so great.

☼ **JULY 11**   **Read II Corinthians 3:18; Romans 12:1-3.**

Tina had been a thorn in my side all year. She was immature, loud, dirty, generally obnoxious, and did absolutely no work. Talking with her mother did little to improve the situation. She failed to complete assignments in class and never did homework assignments. As the year neared a close, I knew she was not prepared for eighth grade, but I saw little benefit in retaining her for another unproductive year; and the thought of putting up with her for another year was more than I could bear. So I intended to promote her and looked forward to saying good-bye.

About two weeks before the term ended, the principal called me in to discuss Tina. It seems that in checking her records, it was discovered that in transferring schools she had been promoted to seventh grade by mistake and should actually have been in sixth. The upshot of this was that she would repeat seventh grade and would be in my class again. It was too late for me to get a teacher transfer, so I considered quitting completely. This I couldn't afford to do, but the thought of having Tina in my class again made me physically sick.

Before the new year started, I did all I could to prepare myself to deal with Tina. I would look for the good in her. I would gear lessons to her level. I would try to like her. No need. *Tina did it all.* She came back the next fall with a new attitude, worked hard, and became my star student that year. Was it my changed attitude? Was it that she was now developmentally ready for seventh grade? Did she simply feel comfortable and realize she now had a chance to succeed?

Working with Tina taught me two important lessons: (1) Don't prejudge, and (2) Never underestimate a person's ability to change. Christ came to give us a glimpse of God's transforming grace in our lives and, with Tina, I saw that transformation at work.

Lord, thank you for the ability to change. Help me to always give my students the benefit of the doubt while also expecting the best from them.

 JULY 12   **Read Hebrews 10:19-25.**

Some years ago my pastor husband and I spent several days in Haiti. While there, we attended a service of baptism on the shore of the sea. Most of the natives who attended had no means of transportation other than their feet, and some walked for two or three days to be in attendance at this special event. Once there, their enthusiasm was contagious. They sang with gusto despite the fact that they must have been exhausted from their long trek across dusty roads and hills.

While in Russia recently, my husband led a Bible school for one hundred and fifty new Christians who came from many miles around to spend their ten days of vacation at a very primitive camp learning more about their faith. They did not walk, but they did give up other recreation and displayed the same sort of fervent devotion to their faith as did the Haitians. They were hungry for knowledge about the word of the gospel.

I couldn't help but feel some shame at my own lukewarm enthusiasm for attending church. It only takes me minutes to get to my church in the air-conditioned comfort of my car. The building has all the modern, comfortable amenities I could ask for. How often on a dreary rainy morning I try to talk myself out of attending. *Wouldn't I rather stay home and lounge around reading the Sunday newspaper?* I ask myself.

It is probably a given that I would not give up my only vacation time to attend a Bible school at a primitive camp, and certainly I wouldn't walk three days in my bare feet to attend a baptism. Why is this? Is life too easy for me? Is it because I have never suffered the privation and hardship that the folks in Haiti and Russia have known for generations? Or am I just lazy?

These are challenging questions for all of us. How will we respond?

Lord, I want to be an enthusiastic Christian. I want to know the fervor and eagerness that new Christians around the world are feeling. Lord, take away my self-centered disinterest and replace it with a spirited search for conviction.

 JULY 13   **Read John 13:34-35.**

One hundred fifty people attended the Bible school my husband led in Russia. They were from churches in twenty-six different communities, so most had not known one another before. When he returned, I heard him remark on several occasions about the eagerness of these people to explore their faith, of the lovely camaraderie that developed, and of the fact that in ten days of living together in somewhat uncomfortable conditions, he heard not one cross word. At the close of the ten days, the director of the campground said, "I am not a Christian, but I want to say, 'You are remarkable people.'"

This group stood out from other groups the camp director had hosted because of their love and caring for one another. This is as it should be. Jesus' words are clear: "I give you a new commandment, that you love one another. Just as I have loved you, you also should love one another. By this everyone will know that you are my disciples, if you have love for one another" (John 13:34-35).

I wonder if people know by observing me that I am a disciple. I wonder if people observing our church groups know that we are disciples. I wonder if our love for one another shows in our actions as it did for those very early Christians and as it did for those Russian folks who for so many years have had to hide their faith or suffer persecution.

It's easy for us to say we are Christians. It's not as easy to live the kind of loving and accepting life Christ calls us to live.

Stay with us, Lord. Keep prodding and reminding us to let your love shine through us to others. With your love, we must be "remarkable people."

☼ JULY 14   Read I Corinthians 13:4a; II Timothy 4:2.

After returning from Russia, my husband talked of the long line he had to wait in to get through customs. It was hot and the procedure was slow. Rather than a line, people approached the desk in a crowd. The process took almost two hours. The thing that amazed me about all of this was that he said, "No one complained." In fact, he said that long lines and waiting are commonplace in Russia; but in the two weeks he was there, he never did hear anyone fussing about the wait.

How different from our country where we demand service and demand it now! I recently noticed a group of customers leave a restaurant in a huff because they had not been waited on seven minutes after they were seated. Impatience seems to have become a way of life with us.

How out of keeping our impatience is with Christian teachings. In the Bible we are exhorted over and over to be patient. We are told in I Corinthians that "Love is patient; love is kind" (13:4) and in II Timothy, ". . . be persistent . . . with the utmost patience in teaching" (4:2). All of us probably heard the old adage "Patience is a virtue" more often than we would have liked as we were growing up.

Is patience an inborn trait, or is it a skill that can be learned? Some are certainly more patient from birth than others. They are those contented, uncrying babies. Others of us come into the world crying for our needs to be met immediately. Still, I believe that with God's help, we each can increase our capacity for patience. God has infinite patience with us, and if we will quiet ourselves and listen, that quality of patience will be eagerly shared with each of us.

Now is a good time to practice patience. After all, we'll need an extra supply come September!

Lord, forgive my lack of patience. Slow me down and quiet me down so that I am able to hear your voice. Show me, Lord, that the world will continue without my hurry. Replace my impatience with calmness and acceptance.

☼ JULY 15   **Read Hebrews 12:11.**

Last week a friend invited me to play bridge. I played a little when I was younger, but I never learned to play well; and I didn't have enough confidence in my ability to accept the invitation. Since then I've had many thoughts about it: *I would really enjoy being part of a bridge group. I wish I knew how to play well. I wish I had stayed with it when I was younger. Why had I been too lazy to learn?* All kinds of negative thoughts. Then I remembered one of my mother's favorite sayings: "You can't learn any younger." If playing bridge is really important to me, I guess I will get my act together and learn to play; if it isn't, I'll just go on halfheartedly wishing I had that skill.

Many of us are that way in our Christian faith. We wish we were better Christians. We wish we were more loving. We wish we were more forgiving. We wish we were more faithful. It is much easier to have good intentions than to actually follow through.

Discipline. I encourage my students to practice it, yet I allow myself to make excuses. I don't know if I'll ever learn to play bridge, but today I will start spending at least fifteen minutes in quiet meditation—not while I'm drying my hair or taking a shower or driving to work, but fifteen minutes in a quiet place without distraction; fifteen minutes of relaxed centering on matters of the spirit. Sometimes it seems impossible to find those minutes in my busy life. I will probably have to make them by getting up fifteen minutes earlier, but I am sure the rewards will be well worth it.

Lord, my intentions are sincere, but sometimes I am weak. Renew my strength if I try to wiggle out of this commitment. Give me discipline to stay on track.

 JULY 16   **Read Proverbs 3:1-10.**

I was talking on the phone to my four-year-old grandson, Dane, yesterday. He told me that his mom was reading the *Goosebumps* books to his older brother and him. He said, "They're pretty scary, but I'm old enough to understand that it is just pretend." I had to smile as I pictured his mom explaining this to him. I'm sure Dane swelled with pride as he thought of himself as "old enough to understand."

It's interesting that when we are very young, the greatest compliment is to be told we are in some way "older" or "old enough"; yet, later in life, to be thought of as older is a put-down, and being thought of as younger than our actual age becomes the ultimate compliment.

If age is the key to understanding, then I am old enough to understand most everything! Unfortunately, I'm not so different from my own young students; acting on my understanding is not always easy. I understand that as a Christian I should love my enemies. I understand that as a Christian I should be forgiving regardless of what wrong is done to me. I understand that as a Christian I should put God first in all decisions and temptations that come my way.

How my humanness gets in the way of living these understandings! The hurts of old wounds make forgiveness so difficult. Loving those who commit terrible injustices seems impossible. Giving of my money to those in need when there are so many things I want often requires more willpower than I have. Only with God's help am I able to act on my understandings.

Lord, help me to be still, listen, and feel your undergirding strength, so that I may be strong in my Christian commitments.

☼ JULY 17   Read I Timothy 4:7-8.

While watching television recently, I saw part of a story of a young man who was attempting to climb the highest peak in North America, Mt. McKinley. It is a highly adventurous, ambitious, and dangerous climb, which few people complete. Several have lost their lives in attempting it. The amazing fact about this particular young man tackling the climb is that he is totally blind. A genetic factor of some sort caused him to lose all sight by the age of nineteen. But he has refused to give up the adventures life has to offer because of his blindness, choosing to work harder to accomplish challenging feats and using his remaining senses to feel the wonder the world has to offer. Equally heroic is the friend willing to be his guide and eyes on his adventures.

Though I don't know either of these young men, it seems that both exhibit a bit of godliness. The one for his undaunting spirit, his willingness to live life to its fullest despite a disability; the other for his willingness to take on the challenge of another's lack of sight, putting his own success and safety at tremendous risk. In fact, I found myself wondering, whose was the greatest adventure? He who climbed without the benefit of sight, or he who carried the responsibility of another's life on his shoulders?

Our adventures may not be as dramatic as climbing high

295

mountain peaks, but the principles are the same. We are to be steadfast and undaunted in our search for godliness in our lives.

Lord, help me to ever strive for higher goals in following your teachings.

☼ **JULY 18**   **Read Proverbs 2.**

Here I am in Alaska, traveling with my daughter, Nanci. Today we went by boat into the Gulf of Alaska, a very cold and windy trip even in July. We saw a great deal of wildlife on the trip—animals who prefer this cold climate and thrive in the harshness of it. Our guide told us that while we might not be enjoying the cold, we should be glad for it, because if it were sunny and warm, the birds and animals we were enjoying would be hiding back in the rock crevices, away from the heat.

We saw hundreds of puffins, a peculiar little black and white bird with distinguished markings, a comical face, a heavy body, and large red webbed feet. Puffins would probably qualify as the clowns of the bird world. They are not especially good fliers because of their heavy bodies and short wings. But they are excellent swimmers. The interesting thing we observed was that they seem to be somewhat gluttonous. They get into the water and eat so much that their short little wings can't pull those fat tummies out. We watched them struggle again and again to no avail.

Perhaps the little puffin does not have the capacity to consider the consequences of its actions, but I do. I know that if I overindulge in food, the least consequence will be discomfort; and if I continue, the consequences will be clothes that no longer fit and unhealthiness. If I squander my time and appear before my class without a lesson plan, the consequence will be chaos or, at the least, apathetic attention and bored students. If I lose my sense of patience and respond to someone in anger, the consequence will be hurt feelings and broken relationships.

I plan to frame a picture of the little puffin, which I am going to place in a prominent place in my home to remind me to consider results before I act.

Lord, with wisdom you have given us the capactiy to think ahead, to realize the consequences of our actions. Help me to use that capacity—to look ahead, to think ahead, to plan ahead—so that my actions are in keeping with your plan.

☼ JULY 19   Read Psalm 56.

On our first night in Alaska, Nanci and I stayed in the Glacier Way Bed and Breakfast, where the owners, Wayne and Janice, welcomed us into their spacious home. Soon after we arrived, Janice, having shown us around and presented us with house keys, left for an appointment. Wayne offered suggestions of sights we might enjoy in Anchorage and then he, too, left for his office.

Here we were, total strangers, being trusted alone in their home. How unusual in this day and time when we are taught by society to trust no one.

To be trusted is a fine feeling. It gives a boost to the spirit. We immediately thought of Wayne and Janice as friends, almost as kindred souls. Why not? They trusted us. They must have thought we were OK folks and we, in turn, thought the same of them.

The Bible often speaks of trust. "I trusted in thee, O LORD: I said, Thou art my God" (Psalm 31:14 KJV). It is often not easy to trust in an unseen God. Many times I find myself thinking I know best or at least that my way is best. I am too frightened to take that "leap of faith" or "leap of trust" across the chasm of the unknown and let God lead the way. Yet, when I do, my spirit is boosted and things go well.

Lord, forgive my timidity, my lack of courage to trust your leadership. Take my hand, Lord, and help me leap across that valley of mistrust. Help me to become a risk-taker, trusting you for guidance and wisdom.

☼ JULY 20   Read Job 11:15-20.

Fishing is an avid pursuit of many in Alaska and the reason many tourists make the trip up here. Though fishing is a sport I have never been drawn to myself, today I saw a small poster which helped me to better understand the allure it has for so many. The poster read,

> The charm of fishing is
> that it is a pursuit,
> elusive, but attainable,
> providing a perpetual
> series of occasions for HOPE.

How we all need such pursuits in our lives, with some challenge to them but also the possibility of eventual success. Life without challenge is boring and humdrum. Challenge without success is frustrating and discouraging.

Looking ahead to the fall, I wonder how I can make the process of learning like a fishing expedition for my students. How can I provide little challenges, elusive but attainable, for them? It will require frequently changing visual displays, regularly throwing out new concepts for them to pursue, offering small and varied challenges to entice all students—the quick and the slow—to participate, being sure that every student experiences enough success to sustain that element of hope, for it is when hope fades that disinterest begins. It is when the challenge is too difficult or too easy that boredom sets in.

Lord, it is a big order, keeping hope alive in all my students. I'll need a lot of prompting. Let me not get so caught up in all of the meetings, testing, grading, and other details that I let the challenging pursuits escape. Keep me alert, Lord, to each student's need for hope.

 JULY 21   **Read Hebrews 6:1.**

Holgate Glacier, much larger than Byron, was on our agenda today. We approached this one by boat, and while it was immense, making large boats near it appear the size of ants, we were reminded that it is now only a tiny fraction of its former size. It once covered all these huge mountain peaks and formed the very sea we were traveling on.

It was an active glacier, and we watched in fascination as it calved huge chunks of ice and threw them into the sea with thunderous force, the sound reverberating in nature's amphitheater of mountains and sea.

We were reminded that our earth is ever changing, still being created. It is not a stagnant place.

Nor are we, as humans, meant to be stagnant, but ever growing, ever changing in positive and loving ways. The earth is rich with opportunities to learn and to become more knowledgeable. Always we have the opportunity to grow in the wonder and power of the love of God. Never do we reach completion or perfection in the living of our Christian faith. It is a mission that requires constant pursuit.

Lord, it is often easier to settle in and take life for granted, to do as I've always done. It takes too much effort sometimes to grow, to grasp new ways, to reach out to the unknown. Sometimes I really don't want to bother. I'm content with things the way they are. I'm not sure that new idea will work, and I'm quite sure I won't like it. Give me a little push, Lord.

☼ JULY 22   Read Philippians 1:20-21.

Today we were preparing to take our first Alaskan hike. Byron Glacier, accessible only by foot, lies about three-fourths of a mile from the road. The path leading to it is through wilderness, but it is a well-defined trail. It was late in the day and raining when we arrived, no other hikers were around and no cars at the pull off. We were determined to see the glacier, so we donned warm jackets and ponchos and headed for the trail. Having been warned several times that there had been bear attacks in the area recently, we carried a can of pepper spray. At the entrance to the trail was a haandwritten sign: WARNING! BEAR IN IMMEDIATE AREA. PLEASE DO NOT HIKE ALONE. We hesitated for a moment or two, then decided to venture forth. We trod forward singing and conversing loudly, so as not to surprise a bear. We saw indications that a bear had recently been on the path, but had no encounters.

The reward for our risk-taking was to stand at the foot of lovely, blue Byron Glacier with spectacular rugged mountain peaks rising high on both sides, a rushing river gurgling below it, and a tiny ray of sunshine blessing the scene. A grand sight well worth the risk! It made me want to bow down and give God glory.

Before the fleeting days of summer have gone, why not replenish your spirit and put new life into your step by taking a few risks? Try something new, go somewhere different, or do something you've always wanted to do. Go ahead, and enjoy the unexpected blessings!

Lord, let me not be careless and foolish in the taking of risks, but let me also have the courage to go forth and take chances for the improvement of myself and others.

☼ **JULY 23**   **Read II Timothy 3:14-17.**

As we were hiking today, Nanci remembered a fact about Alaska that she had learned in a junior high social studies class. I commented that her teacher must have been a good one for her to remember what she had learned so long ago. She disagreed, saying, "Well, he was an entertaining character, but most of what we did in his class was busywork. We copied and memorized lots of lists. Very little of it is useful in my life today."

As the conversation proceeded and I asked who her best teacher had been, she answered without hesitation, "Mrs. VonCannon." "Why?" I asked. "Because she knew and loved her subject and conveyed to us that she really wanted us to learn what she had to teach. She let us know that what she was imparting to us was important to our lives. She thought of different ways to present topics. We did a lot of hands-on experimenting. She never gave up until we had mastered the concepts, and she helped us understand the joy of learning."

As I consider the year ahead, that last sentence will state my goals. I will not give up on any student until concepts have been mastered. I will constantly seek ways to impart to them the joy of learning—learning not only in school, but in all aspects of life; not only now, but throughout life. To stop learning is to stop living.

Lord, keep me faithful to these goals. Bolster me when I try to renege on them. Don't let me give up on my students.

☼ JULY 24   Psalm 78:52, 72; Luke 8:15.

With our Alaska adventure behind us and only a pleasant memory, we had a day to enjoy Seattle together before I headed for home. Dawn presented us with a glorious blue sky, warm sun, and refreshing breeze, so Nanci and I rented a two-person kayak and set out to explore some lakes in Seattle.

We shared the water with hundreds of very tame Canadian geese. Before leaving the boat dock, we had been advised not to feed the geese. It seems that because of the kindness of people in the area, the geese have become dependent upon humans for food. They no longer hunt on their own. They no longer migrate, and they are no longer the proud, independent creatures they once were. They now spend their days waddling up on the beach begging for food. So, in essence, the kindness of people has ruined these beautiful birds.

It strikes me that we who work with children must always be alert to avoid a similar "kindness." Children must learn to be independent. They must be allowed to explore and to make mistakes. I often find myself aching to help or take over and do a task as I watch a child toil over something I could easily do in a second or two. I must remind myself that it is not a kindness to do for children what, with a little struggle, they might do for themselves.

Lord, as I prepare for the coming school year, continue to teach me patience so that I may guide and nurture my students as they struggle and learn. Keep me always aware of the need to "let them go."

Here are some words of wisdom from children and youth:

"Never pick flowers that are growing in someone's garden. That would make them sad. It is okay to pick them if they are growing through cracks in the sidewalk, because sidewalks belong to everyone." (five-year-old)

"Don't look down on a person just because he has green hair and wears a nose ring. He may be a person with a pure and loving heart." (eighteen-year-old)

"Some people just never like new ideas." (four-year-old upon failing to convince siblings to watch his choice of video)

"It's not fair that some people have millions of dollars and live in mansions and some others have to live in shacks and don't even have food to eat. If everybody would share what they have, no one would have to be hungry and homeless." (ten-year-old)

"If everybody who has an extra bedroom let a homeless person stay there, I think every homeless person could have a room to stay in." (nine-year-old)

"If my friend asked me to steal something to prove my friendship, I'd get a new friend." (nine-year-old)

"Sometimes my mom is kind of mean and won't let me do stuff I want to do, but I still think she's the best mom in the whole world." (nine-year-old)

"If adults don't want us to smoke and drink, why don't they stop having cocktail parties where everybody gets smashed in a socially acceptable way?" (seventeen-year-old)

"If I had a million dollars, I'd build a whole lot of houses so all the homeless people would have a place to live." (nine-year-old)

"Churches shouldn't spend money fixing up their buildings. Buildings are not important. They should spend it to help people who need things." (twelve-year-old)

Lord, thank you for the wisdom and innocence of children.

This prayer of Solomon might well be the prayer of every teacher. How we need an understanding heart! I recently heard a speaker say that in dealing with children "we must be not only gentle doves, but also wily serpents." While we love and accept them, we must also be wary of the many ways we can be manipulated into being too easy or too harsh. The understanding heart Solomon asked for was one that could rightly judge between right and wrong, one that would truly understand the truth and act with fairness and justice. As teachers, an understanding heart must also include compassion.

From year to year the faces and names may change, but the prayer remains the same:

Lord, grant me an understanding heart:

> — *When Darien sleeps though the first period class day after day.*
> — *When William leans back in his chair and just stares into space for as long as an hour.*
> — *When Stacy responds in anger, even to comments made in kindness.*
> — *When Michael projects boredom no matter how exciting I try to make the lesson.*
> — *When Tabatha copies from her neighbors at every opportunity.*
> — *When Susanna disrupts the class with her constant movement and talking.*
> — *When Tony antagonizes everyone and tries to pick fights.*

Lord, grant me an understanding heart:

> — *When the parents of these children don't seem to care.*
> — *When all my efforts seem to fail.*
> — *When I am too tired to care myself.*

Lord, grant me a heart with understanding that does not quit.

☀ **JULY 27**   Read Psalm 100:1-2a.

I believe the Lord means for us to be a happy, joyful people. Why else would our Creator have given us the gift of
laughter and the ability to appreciate humor? Laughter is
one of the best ways I know to make a joyful noise unto the
Lord. In fact, research has shown that laughter is therapeu-
tic. It lessens stress and can even be a factor in the healing
of disease.

As a teacher, I've always thought that a day in the classroom was lost if we were not able to have a good laugh
together. To be sure, there are days in the classroom when
tension is high and nothing seems amusing; yet those are the
days we need laughter most. The joke, however, must be at
no one's expense—unless, perhaps, the teacher's. On occasion, I have even made mistakes purposely, just to lighten the
situation and give everyone a chance for a good laugh. It
must be a situation humorous to many but hurtful to none.

As Christians, we have much to celebrate. We know that
God is with us and stands by us, giving us strength and
courage in good times and bad. Celebrate today with the
joyful noise of laughter!

*Lord, when the day seems grim, remind me to look on the "light"
side. Help me especially to be able to laugh at myself and to share
moments of humor and joy with my students. Free me from getting bogged down in the little annoyances of life.*

☀ **JULY 28**   Read Psalm 100.

Someone has described a smile as a "curve that sets a lot
of things straight." Smiles transform faces.

Our family used to patronize a restaurant in which the
waitresses were notoriously sour and grumpy. It became a
game of challenge each time we were there to see if we could
get our waitress to smile. When we were successful, the transformation was amazing. The waitress suddenly became a
person with feelings, even a friend. We got better service, the
meal tasted better, and we all felt happier.

Mother Teresa has said that we should smile at each other—no matter who it is—and that this will help us to grow in love for one another.

Schoolteachers frown a lot. Sometimes it seems as though the main goal in life of all those little bodies is to make us frown. I have a small vertical crease between my eyebrows. It had to have been developed by years of frowning, by what my own children used to refer to as my "teacher look." What a shame! How much happiness and love I could have spread by smiling instead. How many little egos I could have boosted. How much tension I could have relieved. How many problems I could have set straight.

But it's never too late to make a change. Beginning today I will make an effort to smile more often!

Lord, I know the value of a smile. Help me to remember to be generous with my smiles.

☀ **JULY 29**   **Read Matthew 9:24.**

Jesus knew what it's like to be laughed at. Laughter is great when we're in on the joke, but to be outside and feel that we might be the target of the laughter is no fun at all—especially for children. When little children are laughed at, it is often humiliating and can cause irreparable harm to their tender self-esteem.

Some years ago, we were preparing a Christmas pageant at school. My second graders were to present "The Friendly Beasts." They were excited and eager about their roles. Little Charles, our donkey, was perhaps the most eager of all. Naturally I was surprised when he came in the day before the performance and said, "I don't want to be in the play." Tears spilled from his big brown eyes and he began shaking with sobs as he said, "They called me a jackass." "They" probably intended it as good-natured teasing, but to Charles it was serious business. They had attacked his pride. The teasing was aimed at his very vulnerable ego.

Shirley, another student, just hadn't been herself. Her behavior had changed radically, and we teachers were trying to discover the cause. She was reluctant to talk about it for weeks; then one day she finally blurted out her concern. It seemed her father was suffering from severe hypertension and had to limit his intake of salt. When her older sister put a saltshaker on the table at a meal, the other siblings laughed and said, "Oh, trying to kill Dad, huh?" It was a joke, but little Shirley thought it was serious. She was frightened and didn't have the courage to talk to her siblings about it.

Sometimes laughter and joking are innocent and intended to be fun for all, but children do not always understand this; and sometimes we may not recognize the consequences of our own innocent fun. As we seek to "lighten up" our lives and our classrooms, may we remain sensitive to the feelings and understandings of our students, however young or old they may be.

Lord, we want to enjoy life. May our humor and our laughter be in keeping with your teachings, harming no one.

 JULY 30   **Read Job 12:1-10.**

It is a humiliating experience to be laughed at in public—especially in front of one's peers. I remember a painful experience from my own childhood. Being an excruciatingly shy child, it took courage for me to read in front of the class. However, being an avid and good reader, I had a measure of confidence. In the sixth grade, while reading aloud in front of the class, I mispronounced the word *corps*. The teacher good-humoredly explained that the word I had said meant a dead body. The class roared with laughter. I still remember how the heat rushed to my face as it turned beet red and how I wanted to sink into a hole. The incident, which sounds like a small everyday occurrence now, worried me so much that I dreamed about it for weeks and probably did not raise my hand to volunteer in class until I was in graduate school.

Several years ago we took a neighbor child with us to a Wednesday night church dinner. She was about nine years old. It was an informal setting, and after we introduced her, the leader asked where she was from. Her answer was "Allen Road" rather than the expected "Nashville," and the group chuckled. The child was so embarrassed that she would never attend church with us again.

It is easy to thoughtlessly embarrass a child. Often laughter by adults is intended as appreciation of the child's innocence, but the little one has no way of understanding that. Laughter by peers is often intended to be cruel and hurtful, and both can cause damage to a tender ego.

Lord, help me to refrain from laughter when children make mistakes and to set an atmosphere in the classroom that sees mistakes as a means for increased knowledge, as stepping-stones to better understanding, rather than something of which to feel ashamed.

☼ JULY 31   Read Exodus 19:4.

In his latest book, *Along the Edge of America,* Peter Jenkins speaks of a man he met on his journey as one who had a "soaring spirit." What a lovely description. Wouldn't it be grand to be a person of a soaring spirit? One who is always uplifting, a joy to be around. One who is always seeking higher plains, looking for the bright side of life, seeking and finding ways to bring joy to others. Oh how I would love to have my epitaph read, "She was a person with a soaring spirit."

In today's newspaper I read an article about a thirteen-year-old boy who must be such a person. He was born with no hands, but loves to play baseball and is successful at it. He wears a glove on one handless arm, catches the ball in that glove, drops it to his foot, and kicks it to a teammate. At the plate, he holds the bat between his chest and arm and twists his body to get force behind his swing. His mother says he has never complained about his handicap. She says he is an inspiration to their whole family.

I have known some other folks with soaring spirits. I think of Alice, who was a member of our church. She seemed old, already bent over with osteoporosis, when I first met her thirty years ago. She always had a smile and a happy word for adults and children, though she had to peer up from her stooped position to see them. She kept up with social justice events and fought for justice for all. She constantly brought issues of social concern before the congregation. She had a keen interest in the children and youth of the church, keeping track of their accomplishments, attending all of their special events, contributing money to their fund-raisers, and helping with their mission projects. Never did the name of a child, youth, or adult in our large church reach the daily newspaper that Alice did not clip the article and send it with a line of congratulation to that person, a practice she continued until shortly before her death a couple of years ago.

Who are the people you know with soaring spirits? Perhaps some of them are students or fellow teachers. What can you learn from their example?

Lord, help me to become a person of a "soaring spirit."

August

Influencing Young Lives

Ellamarie Parkison

AUGUST 1   **Read James 3:14.**

he writer of James understood the influence teachers have on the lives of students when he said, "Not many of
you should become teachers, my brothers and sisters, for you
know that we who teach will be judged with greater strictness" (James 3:1).

Tender young minds *are* in our care. I remember when my
children were in school. We would have nightly reviews of
teachers at the dinner table as each child related what each
teacher had said or done that day. Often the sessions had us
regaling in laughter; sometimes we were indignant at a
teacher's seeming unfairness. Of course, we were hearing
only one side of the discourse—and probably not always a
completely accurate reporting of proceedings. The fact
remains, however, that our children were profoundly
affected by the day's happenings and their teachers were
directly responsible for the excitement and happiness or the
boredom and indignation being expressed.

In deciding to become teachers, we have accepted responsibility that reaches far beyond that of most other profes-

sions. Our every word and action are subject to interpretation. A poor attitude is contagious and almost certainly will be caught by our students. Impatience is lethal to the learning we hope to impart. Lack of creativity results in bored students and discipline problems. Those who work with paper or machines may make mistakes that are more easily corrected than mistakes affecting the human psyche. And so, as teachers, we are judged with greater strictness—not only by our students and their parents, but also by our Creator.

Lord, keep me aware that my every word, innuendo, and action affect the students with whom I work. Keep me pure of heart and keen of mind that my words and actions will be uplifting and renewing to my students.

☼ AUGUST 2   Read Titus 2:6-8a.

In a few short weeks the new school year will begin, and again I will greet returning students and meet new faces. Once again I am struck with the unlimited possibilities that lie ahead. These children are entrusted to our care for six and a half hours of every weekday. A former principal used to tell us at the beginning of each year, "Remember, this may be the nicest and only secure place many of these children know." It is an enormous responsibility as well as an opportunity.

I heard a story yesterday of a now retired teacher who taught in an inner-city school much like ours. She taught several children from one family and grew to know all of them well. One evening after her retirement from the system, she saw on the TV news that one of those former students, I'll call him John, was poised on a city bridge threatening to jump. Police and family members were trying to cajole him from his perch. The teacher thought, *I think John would come off that bridge if I asked him to.* She called the police and was told to come at once. Just as she had thought, John came down from the bridge when she spoke to him. The hope and belief in himself she had instilled as his teacher returned when he heard her voice.

What monumental opportunities are ours as we work with these young lives!

Lord, thank you for the opportunity that is mine to influence young lives. Let me be ever aware of the responsibility I have to be a role model, to sow seeds of kindness, self-respect, hope, and belief in oneself as well as eagerness to learn.

☼ AUGUST 3   Read Proverbs 4:20-24.

I suppose any of us who work with children have wished that they would be more attentive and take heed of the wise words we offer them. Yet a recent incident helped me realize how important it is that we choose our words *carefully,* even when we are not speaking directly to children but are within their hearing.

Two Sunday school teachers in our church prepare great lessons for their children: beautiful crafts, interesting Bible stories, lively singing. And they love the children. While the children are engaged in craft activities, the teachers talk to each other. One morning they were engaged in some rather bitter conversation about the minister. One child who was visiting returned home extremely upset. The relative who had brought her was unhappy and decided never to bring her back. The child came from a home in which much bickering had led to a recent divorce. To hear such discourse at church was devastating to her and completely negated the positive message intended by the lesson.

Do care and concern permeate our beings enough that we always speak with loving and compassionate words? Are we always aware of how impressionable young minds are? Do we speak one way to our children and another way to each other while we are still within their hearing?

Sometimes we forget that our words, too, can build *and destroy.* Today and every day may we be aware of the power of our words.

Lord, guide us in using our words to the glory of God and to the betterment of our world. Keep us sensitive to young and impressionable minds who may be within earshot of our words.

The woodwork in our home is very dark. A friend suggested I wash it with Ivory soap to lighten it easily and without harming the wood. Her advice was good. Our French doors look lovely after an Ivory cleaning.

When I was a young girl, Ivory soap was advertised as being 99.44 percent pure. I don't know what the other .56 percent might have been, and I don't know if the percentages still hold true today or not. At any rate, I am reminded of Paul's words to Timothy about how our charge as Christians is to share love that "comes from a pure heart, a good conscience, and sincere faith" (I Timothy 1:5).

Those of us who teach or work with children in some way are particularly charged to become pure of heart. A pure heart, though not tangible, is discernible to all with whom we come in contact—especially children, who are quick to spot hypocrisy. They, most of all, are influenced by the words and actions that shine so clearly through a pure heart.

To be 100 percent pure in heart is impossible, even with God's help and support, for there will always be lapses and backsliding. But perhaps it is possible that we, like Ivory soap, could be 99.44 percent pure.

Lord, I know that not only my words but also all of my actions reflect my sincerity and pureness of heart—or my lack of those qualities. Uphold me as I struggle to grow more pure in my faith and in love that comes from a pure heart.

We teachers have a bad habit of gathering in the teachers' lounge and discussing students. No matter how hard we try to steer the conversation in another direction, somehow, talk always drifts around to who isn't learning, or who is making whose life miserable today. In the book *Each Day a New Beginning,* Jennie Jerome Churchill says that we should treat our friends as we treat our pictures—by putting them in the best light. What good advice not only for friends but also for family and students. I have a feeling that if we always put our students in their best light, looking for and highlighting their talents and attributes, we might see their good traits multiply. If we were to squelch all negative remarks about students and make a contest of finding positive comments to offer about our most incorrigibles, would it make a difference? It surely couldn't hurt!

Much of our talk isn't meant to be negative. Often it is offered in the vein of "What can we do about Johnny?" in an honest search for a solution. Almost without fail, however, stories are added to stories and the net result is not good for Johnny, for everyone leaves agreeing that he is an enormous problem. What if, instead, everyone shared something positive about Johnny? He has an engaging smile, a tender heart, a lovely singing voice, a talent for kickball, a love for his little sister, and a willingness to help carry anything anywhere. Would Johnny then receive more smiles, more kind words, more opportunities to help from the other teachers? Would he in turn be happier and easier to teach? In fact, would we teachers enjoy our conversations more?

Lord, fill me with the courage and perseverance necessary to refrain from joining in talk that places students in dimness. Fill my mind with loving thoughts and lead me to make positive comments. Help me, Lord, to do my part in putting my students in their best light.

☼ **AUGUST 6**   **Read Matthew 6:19-21.**

The classified ad I answered from the daily newspaper proved to be a bit misleading. The bedroom set advertised as eight pieces turned out to be four; the bed was counted as four pieces—headboard, footboard, and two side rails. The woman who had placed the ad in the paper had several other bedroom sets for sale. As we looked at what she had, she extolled the qualities of each piece and followed with what I would call a "hard sell."

I began to feel dislike for her—or at least for her tactics. She cared not what my needs were, only that I purchase a set of furniture from her before I left. She also mentioned that she would accept only cash, no checks. Somehow, the more she talked, the more convinced I became that there might be something shady about the operation. Where did she get all of this "new" furniture? Why did she refuse checks? I wondered if she might be trying to cheat the IRS out of paying tax on the sale. I felt uncomfortable; I wasn't sure I could trust this woman.

As we were making definite moves to leave, she began to talk about her teenage daughters and how much trouble she was having with them. She described them as disrespectful, lazy, greedy, and sometimes sneaky. She had mentioned church several times in the course of our visit. Obviously she thought of herself as a good person and a Christian. Yet the acquisition of goods and money was clearly the pervasive goal in her life. She was blind to the fact that her own attitude toward material possessions was being mimicked by her daughters.

The experience reminded me how important we are as role models for our children—those we parent and those we teach. Their eyes are watching. What example will they see in us?

Lord, make me ever aware that my actions are being watched by the children in my life. Keep my thought and goals on a higher plane, so that my deeds may follow. Help me to resist giving my allegiance to the gathering of things and remind me that true happiness is realized only in the giving of myself for the well-being of others.

☼ AUGUST 7   Read II Corinthians 3:12-18.

Our new bedroom set was delivered yesterday. The thing I like best about it is the lovely carving around the beveled glass mirror. As I admired the handiwork and looked into the mirror, I remembered the words of Paul in the third chapter of his second letter to the people at Corinth about how we can become more like God: "And all of us . . . seeing the glory of the Lord as though reflected in a mirror, are being transformed into the same image from one degree of glory to another" (v. 18). My next thought as I looked at my reflection in this beautiful new mirror was, *Well, it will take a lot of changing for me!*

We are mirrors not only for the children in our lives but also for everyone we meet. The choice is ours: We can mirror the Lord's character and Spirit or the more popular values of materialism and power to which our society ascribes. We have the opportunity to mirror love of justice, understanding, and acceptance. That, it seems to me, is our calling as Christians.

When someone looks at me, what is reflected to them? Is it indifference or interest? Is it anger or compassion? Is it harshness or kindness? Is it arrogance or humility? Is it drudgery or love of life? LIke it or not, we are reflectors of our attitudes and beliefs. I hope that I can become a reflector of the Spirit of the Lord.

Lord, the glory of God is too great for me to understand, but help my growth to be in the direction of that glory. May I begin to mirror more of God's character as I go about my daily tasks.

☼ AUGUST 8   Read I John 3:11-18.

Some time ago I read in the paper that Jackson, a student in my first sixth-grade class, had been arrested for selling drugs. He was a tall, good-looking, well-dressed, and well-mannered boy, but also an angry young lad. His mother wanted him to do well, and it was she who was responsible for his good manners. Somehow, though, Jackson always thought that the world was not fair to him. He responded with defiance to ordinary demands such as turning in assignments—a passive, well-mannered defiance, but very recognizable. He had a chip on his shoulder and, as his teacher, I had no success in chipping it away.

Another student, Andrew, was in my class only a few weeks before transferring to another school. Recently he has been in the newspapers almost daily—accused of killing a truck driver. He is only thirteen.

Rhonda was a pretty little blonde girl in the sixth grade. She was a cooperative, somewhat quiet student and a friendly, seemingly happy child. In seventh grade, the year after leaving my class, she experimented with glue-sniffing, which turned out to be a fatal mistake.

It is with sadness that I recall these and other students whose lives have turned sour. Is there something more I could have done to help them? Could I have approached them in a different way? Did I miss an opportunity to turn their lives around?

The questions remind me of the significant responsibility and opportunity we teachers have to influence young lives.

Lord, these children are so fragile. There are so many forces pulling them in all directions. Help me to recognize their goodness and their abilities so that I may help them develop their strengths and resist some of the temptations to which they are subjected.

☼ **AUGUST 9**   **Read James 5:7-11.**

A speaker I once heard spoke of the need to "close the distance" for inner-city kids. He said Jesus closed the distance when he said, "Let the children come to me."

That "distance" these children experience has been reinforced for me this summer as I have associated with privileged children—children privileged not by having great wealth, but by having loving parents who are devoted to nurturing their spirits; children whose parents invest time in conversing with them, reading to them, and playing with them; children whose parents take them to museums, libraries, zoos, state parks, and water parks.

This summer I met an eight-year-old and his mother on a hiking trail. With great detail and excitement, he described the "huge and disgusting" catfish he had seen in an aquarium. I talked with a ten-year-old who could discuss philosophical concepts with clarity. As I watched a six-year-old add and multiply numbers to project a date in the future, I thought of how many of my fifth-grade inner-city students use their fingers and ponder to add 8 + 2. Yes, there *is* a distance, and my job as a teacher is to narrow that distance.

The majority of my students don't value the spoken word, because no one *really* talks to them. The "language distance" is huge. They may learn to read words, but they have no experience to provide understanding. These children don't see options. They have little understanding that life can be different for them. My job is to provide experiences that will help them see options, to talk with them and encourage them to express their ideas and feelings, to build their spirits and help them have faith in their own abilities.

Right now, after a summer of renewal, I'm ready for that challenge.

Lord, keep me ready to close the distance for my students. Bolster me when I bog down. When I get tired and disgusted, remind me that the distance closed for even one child is worth the effort.

☼ **AUGUST 10**   **Read Psalm 27:13-14.**

Yesterday our community sponsored a junior fishing rodeo for children—a great event in which the little pond in the park was stocked with fish and children received free hot dogs, soft drinks, and prizes. One of the extra events for kids was face painting, an event I had always perceived to be for the pleasure of children—until yesterday.

As my six-year-old grandson was gleefully having a baseball painted on his cheek, a woman came to the painter next to us with a young child about a year old. The baby screamed when the face painter approached her with the brush, and no amount of coaxing or reassuring could comfort her. She was terrified. The mother, determined that the child would participate in this activity, held her in a hammerlock—the child screaming, kicking, and trying to wrench away—while the face painter valiantly tried to put a flower on her cheek. I watched in horrified silence, wondering how to stop the proceedings, but said or did nothing.

As I have reflected on this scene, I've had several thoughts. *Should I have spoken up? Was it any of my business?*

What is my responsibility as a Christian in such a situation?

With the new school year ahead of me, I wonder how often I insist that students participate in an event or perform in a certain way because it would please me or make me look good. What a temptation we have as teachers and parents to push, coerce, and insist on behaviors from our children that are unnecessary except for our own egos.

Lord, heighten my awareness of the interests and feelings of my students this year. Instill within me the wisdom to distinguish between those behaviors and expectations that make a real difference in the advancement of wisdom and character and those that are of little importance.

☼ **AUGUST 11**   **Read II Timothy 2:24-35.**

When I started my first teaching assignment, the principal spoke to us about dealing with parents, saying, "Be gentle. No parent can be objective about his or her own child." Well, I was twenty-one and very wise. *How ridiculous,* I thought. *When I have children, I will be objective about them.*

Now I have four grown children and four wonderful grandchildren. I may recognize their weaknesses, but I surely don't want anyone else to notice them. And if they do notice them, they had better not tell me about it!

Of course, I exaggerate. When my children were in school, I wanted to be told if a teacher recognized a need in my child; and I wanted that teacher to help me find the best possible way to work with my child. I also wanted that teacher to convey to me that she or he loved my child and was concerned that my child receive the very best nurturing possible. I wanted that teacher to approach weaknesses in my child with gentleness—gentleness toward my child and gentleness toward me, because it's not easy to hear of weaknesses or problems of someone I love and on whose behalf I have invested years of care and concern. I want the same for my grandchildren, too.

Recently I picked up my granddaughter from preschool, and there was a note in her lunchbox that read, "Hailee had a good day. She's a great kid." My granddaughter *is* a great kid. I knew that, but then I knew her teacher agreed. How proud and pleased I felt.

I want the parents of my students to experience that warm, proud feeling, too. So as the new school year approaches, I am making a commitment not only to treat parents gently, but also to send "good news" to them often.

Lord, thank you for loving parents and grandparents. May I remember to treat them with gentleness and caring. Let me be always aware of the deep emotion these caretakers feel for their children and grandchildren.

☼ AUGUST 12   Read Deuteronomy 31:6-8.

Courage is often elusive at the time we need it most. The Bible has numerous references to our need for courage. In Deuteronomy, we read how Moses told the people of Israel to be strong and of good courage, saying, "[The Lord] will not fail you or forsake you" (31:8).

A friend told me a story of a time in her early teaching years when she took a courageous stand in which she believes she was supported by the Lord. Her teaching assignment was in an extremely poor school district. The old school building had holes in the walls and a leaky roof. Her classroom was on an old stage, and she had to stoke a heater each morning—always concerned about the possibility of a fire. The students were poor, so she paid for subscriptions to the *Weekly Reader* for each of them in order to broaden their horizons.

One week they read about the open classrooms in a new and lovely school in another state. The students were amazed to read of such a spacious and beautiful school. As they discussed it further, she and the class decided they would write to the governor of their state. They included photos of their school and the lovely new school, and they wrote that they felt the students of their state deserved more.

The governor responded by sending a committee to meet the teacher and see the school. Later the school was given

$10,000 for supplies and equipment, in addition to new projectors, filmstrips, books, and tape recorders. In time, a new school building was erected.

It took courage for a teacher and her students to speak out. It took courage for them to approach the highest office in the state. It took courage for the people of Israel to travel to the promised land. It took courage for the early Christians to remain true to their faith in the midst of great adversity.

If we have the courage to stand for the right causes, God will not forsake us.

Lord, we know you are standing by us. Forgive us when we are weak and fearful. Bolster us so that we may be strong and of good courage.

☀ **AUGUST 13**   **Read Ephesians 4:22-23.**

One of my favorite phrases is, "You know, I was just thinking. . . ." Well, today I am thinking about *thinking*!

We teachers know and appreciate the power of the human mind. Besides enabling us to understand our world and make scientific and technological advances, our ability to think enables us to better ourselves and to enjoy life. Because we are able to think, we are able to engage in interesting conversation, to devise strategy for games, to enjoy humor, music, art, poetry, and all the many facets of life. How great it is to be able to think!

I wake in the morning, thinking about the day and what it holds in store. I think as I prepare and eat breakfast and walk my dog, Opie. I think as I talk with friends and family and work a crossword puzzle. I think as I plan lessons for my students and later engage them in the learning task. I think as I read the daily newspaper and react to programs on TV. I think as I spend my daily moments in meditation. In fact, every waking hour is filled with thinking!

How many stories I have heard of folks in desperate situations, such as prisoners of war in isolation from all human contact, who have managed to stay sane and healthy of mind by thinking of pleasant times and by reciting in their minds bits of poetry or Bible verses learned in their youth. My thoughts, too, can help me to renew my mind and my spirit.

The power of thought is a wonderful gift I have been so freely given, yet how seldom I *think* to be grateful for it.

Lord, keep me always aware of the wonderful power and privilege that is mine in being able to think—and in helping others develop this precious gift. May I use this ability in ways that are worthy of its value.

☼ AUGUST 14   Read Philippians 2:1-5.

Every day during the school year I drive the same route to work. It is almost as if the car is guided by radar. I know exactly when to change lanes for advantageous progression on the interstate, when to begin maneuvering to be in position for my exit, and how to expeditiously move from entry lane to left turn lane as soon as I exit. Most of this is accomplished automatically, with little conscious thought.

So it was with a start one morning that I realized that the scenery looked strange and I was not sure exactly where I was. Within a few seconds, I realized I had gone beyond my exit and then accessed a different interstate. I was chagrined at having to drive several miles out of my way to get back to where I had intended to be, but also somewhat frightened to realize that I could have been so totally oblivious to my surroundings. Was I losing my mind? Early Alzheimer's, perhaps?

As I pondered this further, I realized that I had let my mind carry me far away from the interstate on which I was traveling. I had been reminiscing about my trip to the rain forest of southern Mexico the previous summer. In fact, in my mind, I was *in* the rain forest, reliving some of the beauty and special times I had experienced there. Once again, I thought about the power of the mind.

The writer of Proverbs says, "Wise warriors are mightier than strong ones" (24:5). Imagine what might occur in this world if all Christians put the power of their minds to work for the carrying out of God's will. The world would be transformed. If, for us, the meaning of Christian commitment was not secondary to family, work, or pleasure; if we were not so intent on our own ambitions; if we served not just in our own way when it is convenient but with full concentration of our mind's power; if we, like Paul, were urged on by the love of Christ (II Corinthians 5:14), what a world this would be!

Lord, you have given us minds that allow us the ability to plan, to imagine, to create, to concentrate, to understand, and to think. How selfish we have been in the use of these gifts. Forgive us, Lord, and guide us toward a more generous acceptance of our responsibilities as Christians.

☼ **AUGUST 15**   **Read Romans 12:2.**

Today I continue to think about the amazing energizing power of our minds.

It is often my practice at the end of the day, when supper is over and the kitchen is cleaned up, to sit down to watch TV or read a book and promptly fall asleep. Sometimes I feel so groggy that I cannot even get myself up to climb the stairs and go to bed. However, if a good friend stops by with interesting or exciting news, if I become involved in a competitive game with family, if I read an intriguing novel, or even if I work on an exciting lesson plan for school, I can snap out of the tired feeling and stay up long after my normal bedtime without feeling exhausted at all. What is the key? If I can discover that, I will know how to keep not only myself but also my students excited about life and energized about learning.

Part of the answer lies in the fact that we have been given the capacity to think and create, and when we are using that creative talent in some way—be it in writing a story, painting, trying new skateboard routines, or figuring out a new mathematical formula—energy flows into our beings. Of one thing I am certain: To tap into this creative energy, we must be *actively involved.* For most of us, watching something someone else has created, such as a movie or TV show, does not lead to creative energy—unless we creatively identify and interact with the characters.

I believe our Creator meant for us to use our minds and gifts in a vital way. We were not endowed with all of these tremendous capabilities to be passive beings. We must be actively searching for ways to use our abilities to glorify God and to make our existence here on earth a meaningful one. What an exciting challenge for us as individuals and as teachers!

Lord, how gracious and kind you have been in endowing us with such grand possibilities, yet how often we fail to use our given abilities because we are lazy or frightened or apathetic. Forgive us, Lord, and spur us on to become more creative for your cause in this world.

☼ AUGUST 16   Read Genesis 1:26-27.

When I called my three-year-old granddaughter, Karlyn, to come in to eat, she paid no attention. Dressed in an adult-size blue formal and wearing a long red wig, she was busily carrying on a conversation with an unseen friend. I spoke to her again, in a louder tone. This time she responded, "I'm not Karlyn. I'm Ariel." Once I invited Ariel to come and eat, she responded willingly. For a major part of the day, all conversation was with Ariel rather than Karlyn. She stayed in character for hours.

God has given us the capacity, through our imaginations, to transform ourselves. When small children do this or invent imaginary playmates, we think, *How cute. How imaginative. Isn't she a creative child?* If an adult, however, were to do the same, we would think her mentally ill. Why is that? Does God withdraw imagination and creativity from us when we reach adulthood? Of course not. Rather, the pressures and expectations of society make us afraid to use these powers. If we did something different, we'd be laughed at or ridiculed. So we fall into a habit of trying not to be different, of looking and acting like everyone else; and that makes us milk-toast Christians, afraid to speak out for ethical issues we believe in, afraid to speak out against practices we know are wrong, afraid to speak to others about our Christian faith.

The disciples and early Christians were not like that. If they had been, we would have no church today. Many thought Paul was a madman and John the Baptist a wild man. Jesus was crucified for being a radical and a rebel.

If Christianity is to survive, we need to use our God-given imaginations and creativity to share the good news of the gospel in new and exciting ways. We need to get over the fear of being different. We need to risk appearing strange or ridiculous to some so that we can reach many who will hear.

Lord, what a grand gift is the ability to imagine. You are the great Creator, and you have shared a bit of that creative power with us. Thank you, Lord. Forgive us when we are too weak to use this gift for the furtherance of your work. Make us stronger, Lord.

☼ AUGUST 17   Read Joel 2:28.

"Close your eyes and visualize" is a frequently heard phrase these days as the success gurus tell us how to improve our lives. It seems that many folks, from world-class athletes to CEOs of major corporations, have discovered the power of using their minds to foresee themselves achieving great feats. We have been endowed with amazingly complex and powerful brains, the power of which we have not begun to tap to the fullest. I always tell my students that the greatest computer ever invented lies betwen their ears, and I believe that to be true.

What is seldom mentioned by the success seekers is that this marvelous capacity we have is a part of the Creator's plan. The unknown potential of our minds far exceeds anything created by mere humans. God gave us this miraculous capability so that we could live complete and satisfying lives. When we fall short in making full use of this gift, when we are lazy and content with things the way they are, when we don't bother to learn and grow and improve our minds and bodies, we are failing in our Christian commitment.

I'm going to try this much touted method. I'll see myself as the kind of person and the kind of teacher I believe the Christian gospel exhorts me to be. I will close my eyes and visualize God working through me. I expect great things to happen!

Lord, thank you for the gift of a mind capable of learning and growing. Direct me in using my mind in the most productive way for the advancement of your work here on earth.

☼ AUGUST 18   Read Proverbs 29:18.

Summer vacation is fast drawing to a close. Today I stopped by the school building to take a look at my room. The custodian led me to it, saying, "You're going to like what you see." The hardwood floor was gleaming. He was justifiably proud. The rest of the room looked like an abandoned graveyard. All of the computers covered with old sheets, the walls bare and cold looking. I searched my brain for ideas to make this an enticing place for learning this year. *They need to have a dream,* I thought. *What can I do to give them a dream? It is their spirits I need to feed. If their spirits are full, learning will follow.*

My thoughts drifted back to Rose, a fifteen-year-old still in the sixth grade. She was in the first class I taught twenty years ago. One day Rose climbed out of the rest room window on the second floor and threatened to jump. We averted a tragedy that time, but I realized then that Rose had no dream.

Every child, every person, needs a dream. We need something to work toward, something to look forward to, a purpose or a vision for our lives. Dreams and visions create hope. They make living an adventure to be pursued with vigor. If I can help my students realize a dream or a vision for their lives, I will have succeeded in my mission as a teacher.

People have always needed a dream. In Old Testament times, the prophet Joel, speaking to the people about the wondrous mercy of God, said, "Your old men shall dream dreams, and your young men shall see visions" (2:28). Our God is a god of hope and a god of vision.

Lord, inspire me to follow my dream and show me the way to guide my students in discovering and pursuing their own dreams.

☀ **AUGUST 19**   **Read I Corinthians 12:4-11; Isaiah 40:27-31.**

Richy was the smallest child in our fifth-grade class. He was also the most athletic, most academically gifted, and most likable. He was just an all-around great kid. Dismay filled us all when we learned that his small size was because of kidney malfunction and that his chances for a long and healthy life were slim. Richy took the news better than the rest of us. He refused to be sad. He tried to keep up his regular activities despite frequent trips to the hospital and eventual dialysis. Through it all he remained cheerful and optimistic.

Community effort raised money to put Richy on the kidney transplant list, and the eventual procedure was successful. Today Richy is completing college and looking forward to graduate school. All of this was made possible by the miracles of modern medicine and by Richy's exuberance for life, both undergirded by wonderful God-given gifts. These miracles of modern medicine are ours only because of the spirit of inquisitiveness and the perseverance of scientists who doggedly and painstakingly experiment to discover the secrets of the universe. And it is God who has made humans with the minds and spirits capable of such research.

The gifts and the opportunities are there for all of us to access, if we will. What gifts and opportunities will you use in the days and weeks to come?

Lord, we are grateful for the many gifts available to us. Guide us in using them wisely and well.

☀ **AUGUST 20**   **Read II Timothy 1:3-7.**

Today a friend's mom, Bebe, was telling about her mother being named Elah May, an unusual name. Bebe had never known of anyone else with that name until, as a grown woman, she met a young girl in Washington, D.C., many miles from her home in Tennessee. The girl's mother's name was also Elah May. While discussing this common bond, they disocvered that both mothers had been named after a schoolteacher in Decherd, Tennessee, who had been influential in the lives of their mothers. That teacher was more than one who imparted knowledge. She had to have been an inspirer of the mind!

What an opportunity we have and what an awesome responsibility for the tender young lives we spend so many hours with. We are hired to teach the three Rs and to raise the test scores, but far more important are our impressions on our students' minds. What an honor! What a tribute to have influenced a student so much that her most precious baby would be given your name!

Lord, endow me with that very special blend of expectation, kindness, fairness, and inspiration that will enable students to discover and use their own abilities in the most self-fulfilling way.

☼ AUGUST 21   Read John 13:12-15.

We're living in the Information Age. I heard someone say on the radio that 85 percent of the knowledge in the world today has emerged or been discovered since 1964. I wonder if that is an accurate statement. Whether the figure is correct or not, one thing is certain: The world is changing so rapidly that the only certainty is change. It is at once exciting and frightening. I bought a personal computer a little over ten years ago. At that time most folks were still using typewriters. Today typewriters are obsolete.

The changing world must affect the way we teach. Feeding facts will no longer work, for those facts may be obsolete tomorrow. Children must learn to think and problem-solve. They must learn to deal with change. Also, they must learn some values that are constant, values that must govern their lives and relationships without change. The biblical message of love and respect for others is as valid today as it was centuries ago. As a teacher in a public school, I may not be

327

allowed to mention the Source of these values, but by my actions, attitude, and planned activities I can inspire students to consider them.

Lord, living in this changing world is a challenge. Teaching children who are coping with change is a daunting task. Guide my actions. Let me be an example for them as Jesus, the great Teacher, provided an example for us.

☀ **AUGUST 22**   **Read Matthew 9:14-17.**

Today I continue to think about change. According to a Chinese proverb, insanity is a person who does the same thing over and over in the same way and expects different results. I wonder if, by Chinese standards, we teachers are insane. We so often teach the same thing in the same way day after day and even year after year, and then wonder why our students don't "get it." *Change* is the catchword of the times. With technology advancing so rapidly, a new computer is likely to be obsolete before we get it out of its carton.

As we considered yesterday, to meet the needs of our students we must change not only what we teach but also our teaching methods and techniques. The old routine of memorizing facts is no longer adequate, because many of the facts will change before the students are out of school. They need to know how to think and reason and problem-solve, and they need to know how to cope with change.

Changing our ways of doing things is difficult. I don't like to change. When I find a good way of teaching a lesson, one that works for me, I want to use it again and again. I don't want to scrap it and try another way. Yet I guess that is exactly what I must do if I am to effectively teach—and if I don't want to be considered "insane"!

Lord, take away my resistance to change. Help me to be flexible. Let me know when I need "new wineskins," and keep me aware of the approaches that are most effective with my students.

Not long ago a newspaper article bemoaned the low standardized test scores of students in our city's public schools. It seems our students' scores are lower than the state average. In the days following that article, there came a spate of letters to the editor denouncing teachers as a lazy, incompetent lot who fail to do their job as assigned. Some of the letters complained that taxpayers' money is wasted and children are cheated by being taken on field trips and picnics at the end of the year instead of continuing to drill on the three Rs.

Such criticism is disheartening and discouraging to those of us who feel there is much more to education than teaching our little ones to score well on tests. Some of us want to strike back at the critics by quitting this stressful and demanding job. Many excellent teachers have done just that. Another reaction is to become lackadaisical and not work so hard, to just put in our time and collect our pay. A few have chosen this path.

Those of us dedicated to our task must remember that it is the children to whom we are responsible and not the fault-finders who speak from afar. It is for the sake of the children that we must continue to nurture the *whole* child, providing many and varied experiences to promote social, mental, physical, and spiritual growth.

Lord, keep me constant to my task. Let me ignore the criticism of those who fail to see the whole needs of children. Show me the way to best meet those needs in all that I plan and present.

☼ **AUGUST 24**   **Read Matthew 13:10-17.**

A friend of mine taught Sunday school for a number of years with the pastor of her church. One day he offered her a compliment, saying, "You are doing a great job. You are like Jesus."

Noting her startled look, he quickly went on to explain: "Jesus was the greatest Teacher, and his method of teaching was to tell stories, parables. Through parables he was able to help everyone easily understand. I've watched you teach in a similar way. You always relate the lesson to something that has happened in your life or the lives of the students."

In the inner-city school where I teach, students have few life experiences that relate to our curriculum. They see little reason to know about history or geography, let alone grammar and geometry. Telling stories to illustrate the use of ideas and concept heightens their interest and gives them a reason for learning.

The greatest Teacher taught by example. I will try to follow his example.

Lord, thank you for providing a teaching model for us. Grant me the ability to follow that example as I attempt to make learning relevant to my students.

☼ **AUGUST 25**   **Read II Corinthians 5:16-17.**

Today I was watching some neighbor children try out their new in-line skates. Little Ashley, who is only five, took to them like a duck to water, while Stephen, three years older, had wobbly, new colt legs and kept falling and picking himself up time after time. But he never gave up. He was determined to master the skill, and in time, I am sure he will.

Watching them, I thought about T. J., a child whose goal wasn't to be first, but simply not to be last. He knew being first was beyond his ability, but one could almost hear his silent plea before every school yard contest: "Please don't let me be last this time."

There is a T. J. in every class, always chosen last, ridiculed silently and sometimes vocally by other children, suffering ego damage with every trip to the playground. Yet, every T. J. also has a strength. My goal as a teacher is to find that strength and capitalize on it—be it a sweet and forgiving nature, a mastery of numbers, a talent in art, or some other obscure gift. My reward is the joy of watching my students grow into the gifted individuals they were created to be.

Lord, thank you for making each of us a new creation. Sharpen my eyes and heighten my insight that I may highlight the specialness of each student in my care.

☼ **AUGUST 26**   **Read Psalm 139:1-6.**

Early one New Year's morning I was awakened by the ringing telephone. A tearful Tonya, one of my sixth-grade students, was on the line. "Do you want to hear something sad?" she asked. What was I to say? Of course I didn't want to hear something sad on the first day of a new year.

"Do you have something sad to tell me, Tonya?" I asked.

"My mommy was in a car accident last night and she's dead." What devastating news! This was an inner-city child, an only child of a single mother. A child in whom I had taken a special interest because she was so eager to learn. A child whose mother worked uncommonly hard to provide a good home for her daughter. How desperately alone she must have felt.

The last time I saw Tonya was at her mother's funeral. She seemed dazed and unbelieving. She was sent off to another part of town to live with relatives. Occasionally she called to tell me of happenings at her new school, saying, "They don't think I'm very smart at this school." I talked once with her new teacher, trying to help her understand the specialness of this child, despite her meager background. She hadn't had the cultural advantages of many children, but if encouraged, she would make up for that with sheer perseverance and determination. I hope it helped.

Not all of our students have had such traumatic life experiences, but all have had unique experiences that affect their ability to absorb knowledge, to respond socially, and to concentrate. How important it is for us to be aware and to adjust our teaching to meet each unique condition.

Lord, it is so much easier to have the same expectations for all. Teach me to "search and know" each child's unique place in life and to respond in the most helpful way for that child's growth.

I believe that as teachers we are not only to have com-passion for all our children and to love them, but also to believe in them.

A friend of mine who began her teaching career as a resource teacher told me of a student she taught in her very first year of teaching. His name was William, but he was known to all as Bo. He was big for his fourteen years of age and had a vacant look in his eyes. He had been kicked by a horse when he was young. The imprint of the horse's hoof was still visible on his forehead.

Bo seemed unable to learn, but this young teacher was diligent in her efforts. In six months, he had learned to write "Bo." He also got to the point where he could copy the alphabet from the blackboard. Bo was content copying from the board and made no trouble in class. The teacher, realiz-ing he would never grasp any ideas requiring thought, began routinely giving him copy work and turned her ener-gies to those children who were able to learn.

The rest of the class was studying the mathematical con-cepts of "more than," "less than," and "equal to." Bo con-tinued to copy from the board. One day on a nature hike, the teacher was kneeling down with a magnifying glass, helping the students study a centipede, when Bo com-mented, "Look! Mrs. Greene has freckles on her leg—*more than two.*" Sure enough, she had three large freckles on her leg. Tears rolled down her cheeks as she realized that Bo had been listening and had grasped the concept of "more than."

My friend is still teaching today, and she ardently believes that there is no child who cannot learn.

Lord, it is tempting to just give up on a child who has difficulty learn-ing. There are so many others who need our attention. Help us, Lord, to hang in there and not give up on those who may need us most.

☼ AUGUST 28   Read II Timothy 4:1-8.

I'm thinking today about Jason. A handsome little kid. One my grandmother might have described as "bright-eyed and bushy-tailed." When I first met him several years ago, he was full of energy and eager to learn.

Jason has always been a bright boy with a knack for math, able to perform all sorts of number tricks in his head. Unfortunately, an undiagnosed learning disability has taken its toll over the years. Despite his proficiency in math, reading has continued to be a difficult chore for Jason. And in our schools, reading is crucial to success in all subjects, including math.

So last year, in my fifth-grade class, Jason feigned indifference. His shoulders slumped and he lounged lazily in his chair, uttering statements such as, "This is boring," and "I don't feel like doing this," and "This is stupid."

Since my job is teaching reading and math via computer, I tried to help build Jason's self-esteem by walking by his computer when he was working on math and casually reading the problems and instructions as if I were just discovering them myself. As soon as I would do that, he would say something like, "Oh, this is simple," and quickly click in the answer; and I would catch a glimpse of the eagerness he used to exhibit.

Yet I still felt helpless in regard to Jason. I sat by his side, helping him to sound out words and use context clues and listening to him struggle through reading passages. He showed no signs of improving. I knew that neither I nor anyone else would be able to hold his hand through life, and no testing or special programs had been able to pinpoint what was keeping him from being a proficient reader. He was "slipping through the cracks," and I did not know how to help him.

Teaching can be so frustrating at times, particularly when our efforts seem futile. Yet God calls us to persevere. Though we may not be able to see the fruit of all our labor, we know that the harvest cannot come until the seed has been sown and nurtured.

Lord, give me the perseverance and tenaciousness to continue looking for solutions. Keep me constantly aware of the preciousness of each life I encounter.

Today was an in-service day in which an outside facilitator endeavored to guide us in the fashioning of a vision for our school. It was one of those affairs where we had to begin by describing ourselves in one word and then draw our visions without words for others to interpret. Most of us felt totally inadequate and somewhat threatened as soon as she said, "Draw" and "No words." Only the art teacher had a smile on her face. The rest of us were feeling inhibited and embarrassed by our lack of artistic ability and our lack of ability to project our thoughts through such a medium. She might as well have said, "Jump in and swim the English Channel."

When it became apparent we had no choice, each of us scrawled something on our large sheet of paper and taped it to the wall for others to interpret. Oddly enough, the interpretations were surprisingly accurate.

Why did we feel so lost when asked to create a picture? Could it be that we had teachers who criticized our efforts when we were young? Did someone say to us, "Bananas are not purple" or "You must color within the lines" or "That doesn't look like an elephant to me" or some other inhibiting comment? Was our creativity stifled by being unable to create something pleasing to a person important in our life? Do I ever do that to the children I teach?

It is so easy, by gesture or tone, to condemn an artistic attempt. I hope that this school year, I will be able to encourage all creative attempts be it in drawing, painting, speaking, writing, making music, thinking of a new way to play a game or even an intelligent shortcut to completing an assignment.

Lord, help me appreciate creativity. Keep me aware of the tender egos associated with ideas and creations of all persons. Teach me to offer suggestions in a gentle and positive way, and remind me that my ideas are not always the best.

☼ **AUGUST 30**   **Read Romans 15:1-6.**

Sometimes children seem so ungrateful. Time and effort I've given to a special class art project bring responses of

"This is dumb" from some, and a small gift is greeted with "Is this all?" At those times, I wonder why I am a teacher. *Why do I try?* I ask myself. *Is it worth the effort?* Then the next time the responses are "This is fun!" and "Oh, thank you! I love it!" And later I find a drawing on my desk with this message: "You are the best teacher in the whole world." Yes, it is worth the effort.

A retired friend of mine used to teach high school. One year she had two seniors in her class who were very much in love. One day the girl discovered she was pregnant. They were bright kids who wanted to make something of their lives, but they had no family support. Scared and unsure of what to do, they turned to this teacher for counsel. She helped them look at options, and the end result was a wedding in her living room. They named their little girl Andrea Lee after their teacher. Years later, my friend had the privilege of teaching Andrea Lee, a well-adjusted girl who had been raised by two loving parents.

Though my students are younger and their challenges and needs may seem less dramatic, the opportunities I have to touch their lives in significant ways are no less important. Yes, it *is* worth the effort!

Lord, thank you for the privilege of being a teacher. Direct both my thoughts and actions in exercising that privilege with the greatest of care. Forgive me when my thoughts are on receiving recognition and praise rather than on guiding and influencing young lives on the path to fulfillment.

☼ **AUGUST 31**   **Read Matthew 5:17-20.**

My summer holiday is over. It has been a good summer—filled with many pleasures. I have had time to travel, reflect, spend leisurely time with family and friends, take long walks in the beauty of nature, enjoy good food, read, write, attend workshops, and explore new ways of using technology. How blessed I am! I am ready to begin the school year.

It is both challenging and frightening to begin working with new groups of students: challenging to figure out ways to meet the needs of each child, for one method will never appeal to all; frightening to realize that my every action and word may be influential in some young life and that, unless I am ever mindful of what I say and do, I might miss an opportunity to teach or inspire.

It is interesting for me to note which students come back to visit or continue to keep in touch after leaving our school. Sometimes it is one whom I thought had not responded to my efforts at all. This past week I received a letter from a girl who was in my class two years ago. She often appeared disinterested, was quick to distract with silliness or inappropriate behavior, and disliked academic pursuits. She wrote of being on the honor roll in eighth grade and thanked me for being the "best teacher she had ever had." What a surprise and what an inspiration for me as I prepare for a new school year!

I am going to place that letter in my plan book where I will see it each day. It will remind me that I must never give up on any student, that I am setting an example in all I do, and that I am to be genuine, to "walk my talk," for young folks are watching and are quick to mimic what they see.

Lord, as the new school year begins, stay by my side and hold my hand. The most precious of lives are in my care. Let me teach by my example, let me inspire these young children to know the joy of learning, and let me help them to believe in themselves.